The Besterman World Bibliographies

The Besterman World Bibliographies

Literature

English & American

A BIBLIOGRAPHY OF
BIBLIOGRAPHIES

By Theodore Besterman

TOTOWA, N. J.
Rowman and Littlefield
1971

Published by
Rowman and Littlefield
A Division of
Littlefield, Adams & Co.
81 Adams Drive
Totowa, N. J. 07512

★

★

Typography by George Hornby
and Theodore Besterman

ISBN 0-87471-052-9

Contents

Preface

I have explained in the Introduction to the successive editions of *A World bibliography of bibliographies* why I decided to arrange it alphabetically by specific subjects. Since that decision was taken, and after prolonged experience of the book in use, I have had no reason to regret it, nor among the many letters I have received from librarians has there been a single one complaining of the alphabetical form of the *World bibliography.*

The *World bibliography of bibliographies* covers all subjects and all languages, and is intended to serve reference and research purposes of the most specific and specialised kind. Yet contained in it are broad and detailed surveys which, if relevant entries throughout the volumes are added to them, can serve also the widest reference inquiries, and be useful to those who seek primary signposts to information in varied fields of inquiry.

Therefore I can only thank Rowman and Littlefield for having gathered together all the titles in some of the major fields found throughout the 6664 columns of the fourth edition (1965-1966) of *A World bibliography of bibliographies.*

Preface

These fields are:

1. Bibliography
2. Printing
3. Periodical Publications
4. Academic Writings
5. Art and Architecture
6. Music and Drama
7. Education
8. Agriculture
9. Medicine
10. Law
11. English and American Literature
12. Technology
13. Physical Sciences
14. Biological Sciences
15. Family History
16. Commerce, Manufactures, Labour
17. History
18. Geography

Of course these categories by no means exhaust the 117,000 separately collated volumes set out in the *World bibliography*, and the above titles will be added to if librarians wish for it.

Th. B.

Notes on the Arrangement

An Alternative to critical annotation

Consider what it is we look for in a normal bibliography of a special subject. Reflection will show, I think, that we look, above all, for completeness, just as we do in a bibliography of bibliographies. We desire completeness even more than accuracy (painfully uncongenial though it is for me to make such a statement); for in most cases a bibliography is intended to give us particulars of publications to which we wish to refer; thus we can always judge for ourselves (waiving gross errors) whether the bibliographer has correctly described these publications. On the other hand, anything that is omitted is lost until rediscovered.

The question is, therefore, whether it is possible to give some indication of the degree of completeness of a bibliography without indulging in the annotation which is impossible in a work of the present scope and scale. It seemed to me that this could be achieved, to a considerable extent, by recording the approximate number of entries set out in it. This method is, of course, a rough-and-ready one, but experience shows that it is remarkably effective: and I hope that its novelty will not tell against it.

The recording of the number of works set out in a bibliography has another advantage in the case of serial publications: it displays in statistical form the development of the subject from year to year—often in a highly significant manner.

This procedure, then, is that which I have adopted, the number of items in each bibliography being shown in square brackets at the end of the entry. This, I may add, is by no means an easy or mechanical task, as can be judged from the fact that this process, on the average, just about doubles the time taken in entering each bibliography.

Supplementary information in footnotes

I have said that this method of indicating the number of entries is intended to replace critical treatment; but it is not possible to exclude annotation altogether, for a certain minimum of added information is indispensable. Consequently many of my entries will be seen to have footnotes, in which the following types of information are recorded: a few words of explanation where the title is inaccurate, misleading, obscure, or insufficiently informative; a statement to that effect where a work is in progress, where intermediate volumes in a series have not been published, or where no more have been published; an attempt to clarify complicated series; a note that a book was privately printed or in a limited number of copies, where this does not exceed 500, or in some abnormal manner, as on one side of the leaf, on coloured paper, or in a reproduction of handwriting, or with erratic pagination; when I have come across copies containing manuscript or other added matter, I have recorded the fact; substantial corrections and additions to bibliographies are sometimes published in periodicals, and I have noted a good many of these—but without aiming at anything even remotely approaching completeness, the attainment of which would be impossible. Various minor types of information are also occasionally to be found in the footnotes.

Owing to the great increase in the number of bibliographies reproduced directly from typewritten copy, such publications are designated by an asterisk at the end of the entry; this device saves a good deal of space.

Place of publication

The place of publication is not shown when it is London in the case of an english book and

Paris in the case of a french one. In the case of a series or sequence of entries, however, the absence of a place of publication means that it is the same as the place last shown in the series. The same applies to the names of editors and compilers. The place of publication is given as it appears on the titlepage, but prepositions are omitted even if violence is done to grammatical construction.

The Order of entries

Under each heading the order of the entries is chronological by date of publication; in the case of works in successive volumes or editions the chronological order applies to the first volume or edition. In suitable long headings an additional chronological order by period covered has been created; see, for instance, France: History, or Drama: Great Britain.

Method of collating

An effort has been made, so far as space allows, to give detailed and accurate information of the kind more usually found in small bibliographies. For instance, I have paid special attention to the collation of bibliographies in several (or even numerous) parts or volumes. It is, in fact, difficult to understand why it is usually considered necessary to give collations of works in a single volume, where difficulties seldom occur (from the point of view of systematic bibliography), but not of a work in several volumes, where confusion much more frequently arises. An occasional gap in the collations of such publications will be noticed. This is because, naturally enough, I have not been able in every case to see perfect sets; and I have thought it better to leave a very small number of such blanks rather than to hold up the bibliography indefinitely.

Serial publications

Where successive issues of a serial publication are set out, the year or period shown is usually that covered by the relevant issue; in such cases no date of publication is given unless publication was abnormal or erratic in relation to the period covered.

Bibliographies in more than one edition

Where a bibliography has gone into more than one edition I have tried (though I have not always been able) to record at least the first and latest editions. Intermediate editions have also been recorded wherever it seemed useful to do so, that is, for bibliographies first published before 1800, and for those of special interest or importance; but in general intermediate editions, though examined, have not been recorded.

Notes

Transcription of titles

Titles have been set out in the shortest possible form consistent with intelligibility and an adequate indication of the scope of the bibliography; omissions have of course been indicated. The author's name, generally speaking, is given as it appears on the titlepage, amplified and interpreted within square brackets where necessary.

Anonymous bibliographies

Far too large a proportion of bibliographical work is published anonymously. This is due, in part, to the all too common practice of library committees and similar bodies of suppressing altogether or of hiding in prefaces the names of those who have compiled bibliographies and catalogues for them. I have spent a good deal of time in excavating such and other evidences of authorship, and the result may be seen in the large number of titles preceded by names enclosed within square brackets.

Th. B.

English literature.

1. *Bibliographies and history*

GUSTAV KÖRTING, Grundriss der geschichte der englischen litteratur von ihren anfängen bis zur-gegenwart. Sammlung von kompendien für das studium und die praxis (1st ser., vol.i): Münster i. W. 1887. pp.xvi.412. [7500.]

— — Fünfte ausgabe. 1910. pp.xv.443. [7500.]

TOM PEETE CROSS, A list of books and articles, chiefly bibliographical, designed to serve as an introduction to the bibliography and methods of english literary history. Chicago 1919. pp.viii.53. [450.]

— — [another edition]. A reference guide to english studies. Compiled by Donald F[rederic] Bond. 1962. pp.xii.172. [1230.]

there are numerous intermediate editions.

CLARK SUTHERLAND NORTHUP, A register of bibliographies of the english language and literature. . . . With contributions by Joseph Quincy Adams and Andrew Keogh. Cornell studies in english [vol.ix]: New Haven 1925. pp.[xi].507. [10,000.]

a facsimile was issued New York 1962.

JOHN GERARD O'LEARY, English literary history and bibliography. 1928. pp.xii.192. [1000.]

ARUNDELL ESDAILE, The sources of english literature. Cambridge 1928. pp.vii.131. [500.]

— — [second edition]. 1929. pp.vii.131. [500.]

GEORGE WATSON COLE, A survey of the bibliography of english literature, 1475–1640. With especial reference to the work of the Bibliographical society of London. Chicago 1930. pp.[iii]. 95. [45.]

150 copies printed.

THE HISTORY of english literature: a brief list of references. Library of Congress: Washington 1930. ff.3. [27.]*

J. BARTLET BREBNER and EMERY NEFF, A bibliography of english literature and history. New York 1932. pp.20. [150.]

NATHAN VAN PATTEN, An index to bibliographies and bibliographical contributions relating to the work of american and british authors 1923–1932. Stanford university: 1934. pp.vii.324. [2500.]

ENGLISH literature. An exhibition of manuscripts and of first and other early editions. National library of Scotland: Edinburgh 1962. pp.[v].33. [250.]*

2. *Periodicals*

DONNA [LORINE] GERSTENBERGER and GEORGE HENDRICK, Directory of periodicals publishing articles in english and american literature and language. Denver [1959]. pp.178. [450.]*

3. *Writings on english literature*

VERZEICHNIS der an der universität Leipzig erschienenen dissertationen und fakultätsschriften auf englischem gebiet. [Leipzig 1900]. pp.7. [150.]

covers works published during the period 1875–1900.

A SHORT list of books on english literature from the beginning to 1832 for the use of teachers. English association: Leaflet (no.3): Bromley [printed] [1907]. pp.8. [100.]

A REFERENCE library: English language & literature. English association: Pamphlet (no.46): 1920. pp.34. [1000.]

— Third edition. Revised by V[ivian] de S[ola] Pinto. 1962. pp.44. [2000.]

THE YEAR'S work in english studies. The English association.

[i]. 1919–1920. Edited by sir Sidney Lee. 1921. pp.140. [300.]

[ii]. 1920–1921. Edited by sir Sidney Lee and F[rederick] S[amuel] Boas. 1922. pp.192. [400.]

[iii]. 1922. 1923. pp.220. [400.]

iv. 1923. 1924. pp.269. [418.]

v. 1924. Edited by F. S. Boas and C[harles] H[erford] Herford. 1926. pp.318. [488.]
vi. 1925. 1927. pp.346. [626.]
vii. 1926. 1928. pp.322. [661.]
viii. 1927. 1929. pp.386. [706.]
ix. 1928. 1930. pp.390. [866.]
x. 1929. Edited . . . by F. S. Boas. 1931. pp.148. [839.]
xi. 1930. 1932. pp.400. [870.]
xii. 1931. Edited . . . by F. S. Boas and Mary S. Serjeantson. 1933. pp.342. [812.]
xiii. 1932. 1934. pp.348. [898.]
xiv. 1933. 1935. pp.388. [1097.]
xv. 1934. 1936. pp.372. [1018.]
xvi. 1935. 1937. pp.380. [1056.]
xvii. 1936. 1938. pp.311. [910.]
xviii. 1937. 1939. pp.290. [781.]
xix. 1938. 1940. pp.275. [860.]
xx. 1939. 1941. pp.214. [750.]
xxi. 1940. 1942. pp.267. [750.]
xxii. 1941. 1944. pp.245. [750.]
xxiii. 1942. 1944. pp.246. [750.]
xxiv. 1943. 1945. pp.245. [500.]
xxv. 1944. Edited by F. S. Boas. 1946. pp.233. [500.]
xxvi. 1945. 1947. pp.251. [500.]
xxvii. 1946. 1948. pp.278. [500.]

xxviii. 1947. 1949. pp.290. [500.]
xxix. 1948. 1950. pp.296. [500.]
xxx. 1949. 1951. pp.256. [500.]
xxxi. 1950. Edited by F. S. Boas and Beatrice White. 1952. pp.288. [500.]
xxxii. 1951. 1953. pp.311. [750.]
xxxiii. 1952. 1954. pp.308. [750.]
xxxiv. 1953. 1955. pp.338. [800.]
xxxv. 1954. 1956. pp.267. [1000.]
xxxvi. 1955. 1957. pp.255. [1000.]
xxxvii. 1956. 1958. pp.268. [1000.]
xxxviii. 1957. Edited by B. White and T. S. Dorsch. 1960. pp.275. [1000.]
xxxix. 1958. 1960. pp.320. [1200.]
xl. 1959. 1961. pp.312. [1200.]
xli. 1960. 1963. pp.321. [1300.]

in progress.

BIBLIOGRAPHY [*afterwards:* Annual bibliography] of english language and literature. 1920 [&c.]. Modern humanities research association: Cambridge 1921 &c.

details of this series are set out under English language, above.

ORIGINAL manuscripts and drawings of english authors from the Pierpont Morgan library, on exhibition at the New York public library. [New

York 1924]. pp.[i].55. [400.]
privately printed.

A. H. SMITH and A. T. HATTO, A list of english, scandinavian and german theses in the university of London. London mediæval studies: Monograph (no.2): 1939. pp.viii.40. [english: 332.]

READERS' guide to books on literature. Library association: County libraries section [no.21]: 1939. pp.[iii].57. [1250.]
on the cover the title appears as Readers' guide to books on english literature.

JOHN WEBSTER SPARGO, A bibliographical manual for students of the language and literature of England and the United States. Chicago 1939. pp.xii.191. [1108.]
printed on one side of the leaf.

—— Third edition. New York 1956. pp.x.285. [1352.]

ARTHUR G[ARFIELD] KENNEDY, A concise bibliography for students of english.... Second edition. Stanford 1945. pp.vii.161. [1844.]
the first edition was published in the Papers of the Bibliographical society of America *(1931), xxv. 129–180.*

— — Fourth edition. By A. G. Kennedy, Donald B. Sands. 1960. pp.xi.467. [5438.]

ENGLISH literature, 1660–1800. A bibliography of modern studies compiled for Philological quarterly. Princeton.

i. 1926–1938. By Ronald S[almon] Crane [*and others*]. 1950. pp.[v].575. [5000.]

ii. 1939–1950. 1952. pp.[iv].577–1292. [5000.]

THE YEAR's work in literature. British council.

1949. Edited by John Lehmann. pp.72. [250.]

1950. pp.90. [250.]

no more published; limited to english literature.

THOMAS R. BROWN, *ed.* A selected list of books on english literature. Public libraries: Glasgow [1954]. pp.16. [250.]

ABSTRACTS of english studies. An official organ of the National council of teachers of english. Boulder, Cal.

i. 1958. pp.420. [1900.]*

ii. 1959. pp.494. [1967.]

iii. 1960. pp.610. [2785.]

iv. 1961. pp.609. [2791.]

v. 1962. pp.612. [2826.]

vi. 1963. pp.609. [2831.]

in progress.

RICHARD D[ANIEL] ALTICK and ANDREW [H.] WRIGHT, Selective bibliography for the study of english and american literature. New York [1960]. pp.xii.138. [996.]

largely printed on one side of the leaf.

— — Second edition. [1963]. pp.x.149. [1000.]

A. FREDERICK DEVERELL, Canadian bibliography of reading and literature instruction (english) 1760 to 1959. Vancouver &c. [1963]. pp.viii.241. [4500.]

PHILIP H. VITALE, Basic tools of research. An annotated guide for students of english. Great Neck, N.Y. [1963]. pp.[iv].173. [3500.]

4. *Manuscripts*

GASTON RAYNAUD, Catalogue des manuscrits anglais de la Bibliothèque nationale. 1884. pp.30. [1000.]

MOSES TYSON, Hand-list of the collection of english manuscripts in the John Rylands library. Manchester 1929. pp.70. [1000.]

— — Hand-list of additions . . . 1928–35. 1935. pp.74. [500.]

— — Hand-list of additions . . . 1937–1951. By F. Taylor. 1951. pp.50. [250.]

AN EXHIBITION of fifteenth century manuscripts and books in honor of the six hundredth anniversary of the birth of Geoffrey Chaucer. Rosenbach company: [New York 1940]. pp.16. [15.]

N[EIL] R[IPLEY] KER, Catalogue of manuscripts containing anglo-saxon. Oxford 1957. pp.lxiv. 567. [451.]

ENGLISH literature. An exhibition of manuscripts and of first and other early editions. National library of Scotland: Edinburgh 1962. pp.[v].33. [250.]*

5. *General*

JOHN BALE, Illvstrivm Maioris Britanniae scriptorvm, hoc est, Angliae, Cambriae, ac Scotiæ summariū, in quasdam centurias diuisum, cum diuersitate doctrinarū atq; annorū recta supputatione per omnes ætates a Iapheto sanctissimi Noah filio, ad annum domini M. D. XLVIII. Gippeswici 1548. ff.[xii].255. [4000.]

this book was reissued with the additional imprint Wesaliæ 1549; both imprints are fictitious.

— — [second edition]. Scriptorvm illustriū maioris Brytannię, quam nunc Angliam & Scotiam uocant: catalogus. Basileæ 1557–1559. pp.[xxviii].744+[xx].250.[lxxxvi]. [10,000.]

there are at least three issues of this edition; Bale's

own copy, with annotations in his hand, is in the British museum.

— — Index Britanniae scriptorum quos ex variis bibliothecis non parvo labore collegit Ioannes Balęus, cum aliis. . . . Edited by Reginald Lane Poole . . . with the help of Mary Bateson. Anecdota oxoniensia [: Mediaeval and modern series (part ix):] Oxford 1902. pp.xxxvi.580. [3500.]

JOANNES PITSEUS [JOHN PITS], Relationvm historicarvm de rebus anglicis tomvs primvs. [Edited by William Bishop]. Parisiis 1619. pp.16.990. [10,000.]

no more published; in the colophon the author's name is written 'Pitsius'; the running title throughout nearly the whole of the book is 'De illustribus Britanniæ [afterwards: *Angliæ*] *scriptoribus'; there is another issue in which the titlepage is from a different setting.*

THOMAS TANNER, Bibliotheca britannico-hibernica: sive, de scriptoribus, qui in Anglia, Scotia, et Hibernia ad saeculi XVII initium floruerunt . . . commentarius. [Edited by David Wilkins]. Londini 1748. pp.[ii].xlviii.788. [20,000.]

[*THE BENT, BRITISH, COMPLETE, ENGLISH, GENERAL, HODGSON, LONDON, LOW, MODERN LONDON, NEW LONDON CATALOGUES. The series known by these names overlap and interconnect to such an extent that it has been thought most useful to set them out, until their final consolidation in the English catalogue, in a single chronological sequence of the termini a quibus; the publisher's name is given where it appears in the original; the make-up of some of the later volumes varies from copy to copy.*]

1700–1766. A complete catalogue of modern books published from the beginning of this century, to the present time. 1766. pp.[iii].92. [5750.]

a copy in the Bodleian library contains numerous additions in ms.

1700–1767. A new and correct catalogue of all the english books which have been printed from the year 1700, to the present time. 1767. pp.[iii]. 108. [6500.]

1700–1773. The London catalogue of books . . . that have been printed in Great Britain, since the year M.DCC. [By William Bent]. 1773. pp.viii.144. [8500.]

1700–1779. A general catalogue of books . . . that have been printed in Great Britain, and published in London, since the year M.DCC. to the present time. [By William Bent]. 1779. pp.[iv] 152. [9000.]

1700–1785. A general catalogue of books . . . printed in Great Britain, and published in London, from the year MDCC to the present time. [By William Bent]. W. Bent: 1785. pp.164. [10,000.]

1700–1786. A general catalogue of books . . . printed in Great Britain, and published in London, from the year MDCC to MDCCLXXXVI. [By William Bent]. W. Bent: 1786. pp.168. [10,000.]

1700–1791. The London catalogue of books, selected from the General catalogue published in MDCCLXXXVI, and including the additions . . . to September MDCCXCI. [By William Bent]. W. Bent: 1791. pp.160. [9500.]

[1700–]1799. The London catalogue of books. . . . Corrected to September MDCCXCIX. [By William Bent]. W. Bent: 1799. pp.166. [10,000.]

[1700–]1811. The London catalogue of books. . . . Corrected to August MDCCCXI. [By William Bent]. W. Bent: 1811. pp.239. [15,000.]

[1700–]1814. The London catalogue of books. [By William Bent]. W. Bent: 1814. pp.260. [16,500.]

1779–1780. An appendix to the General catalogue of books printed in the year MDCCLXXIX: containing . . . the books published in London since that time, to the end of the year MDCCLXXX. 1781. [By William Bent]. pp.[ii].10. [500.]

1785–1788. A modern catalogue of books printed in Great Britain and published in London, since the year MCCLXXXV [*sic*] to the present time. [By William Bent]. W. Bent: 1788. pp.[iv].160. [9750.]

1791–1792. Supplement, 1792, to the London catalogue. [By William Bent]. pp.8. [500.]

1791–1797. A modern catalogue of books, containing the new publications since the London catalogue of 1791 to the present time. [By William Bent]. W. Bent: 1797. pp.48. [2500.[

1792–1803. The modern catalogue of books . . . containing the books which have been published in London since the year 1792, and such as have been altered in size or price since the London catalogue of 1800. [By William Bent]. W. Bent: 1803. pp.88. [5500.]

1793. Supplement, 1793, to the London catalogue. [By William Bent]. pp.7. [450.]

1799–1800. An appendix to the London catalogue of books: containing the new publications . . . since August 1799 to the end of the year 1800. [By William Bent]. [1801]. pp.167–182. [1000.]

1801–1805. The new London catalogue of books. . . . Containing the books which have been published . . . since the London catalogue of 1800. [By William Bent]. W. Bent: 1805. pp.76. [4500.]

1801–1807. The new London catalogue of books. . . . Containing the books which have been published . . . since the London catalogue of books to the end of the year 1800. [By William Bent]. W. Bent: 1807. pp.94. [6000.]

[1801–]1811. The London catalogue of books. [By William Bent]. W. Bent: 1811. pp.239. [16,000.]

[1801–]1814. The London catalogue of books. [By William Bent]. W. Bent: 1814. pp.260. [17,500.]

1801–1818. The modern London catalogue of books. . . . Containing the books published in London . . . since the year 1800 to October 1818. [By William Bent]. William Bent: 1818. pp. [iv].200. [12,500.]

1801-1822. The London catalogue of books. Containing the books published in London . . . since the year 1800 to October 1822. [By William Bent]. William Bent: 1822. pp.[iv].240. [15,000.]

1801–1827. The London catalogue of books. . . . Containing the books published in London . . . since the year 1800 to March 1827. [By Robert Bent]. For the executor of the late W. Bent: 1827. pp.[iv].310. [20,000.]

1801–1836. The english catalogue of books (including the original 'London' catalogue) . . . issued in the United Kingdom . . . 1801–1836. . . . Compiled by Robert Alexander Peddie . . . and Quintin

Waddington. Publishers' circular: 1914. pp.[vi]. 655. [30,000.]

1811–1812. A modern catalogue of books . . . containing the books that have been published in London . . . since the publication of the London catalogue of books, 1811, to the present time, or from August 1811 to September 1812. [By William Bent]. W. Bent: 1812. pp.[ii].24. [1500.]

1811–1831. The London catalogue of books. . . . Containing the books published in London . . . since the year 1810 to February 1831. [By Robert Bent]. Robert Bent (executor of the late W. Bent): 1831. pp.[iv].336. [22,500.]

1814–1816. A catalogue of books . . . containing the books that have been published . . . since the London catalogue of books, 1814, to September 1816. [By William Bent]. W. Bent: 1816. pp.[ii]. 36. [2250.]

1814–1834. London catalogue of books. . . . Containing the books published in London . . . since the year 1814 to December 1834. [By Robert Bent]. Robert Bent: 1835. pp.[iv].350. [22,750.]

1814–1839. The London catalogue of books. . . . Containing the books published in London . . . since the year MDCCCXIV to MDCCCXXXIX. [By Robert Bent]. Robert Bent: 1839. pp.iv.415. [27,500.]

1814–1846. The London catalogue of books published in Great Britain . . . from 1814 to 1846. [By Thomas Hodgson]. Thomas Hodgson: 1846. pp.viii.542. [35,000.]

— Bibliotheca londinensis: a classified index to the literature of Great Britain during thirty years. Arranged from and serving as a key to the London catalogue of books, 1814–46. [By Thomas Hodgson]. Thomas Hodgson: 1848. pp.viii.284.

1816–1851. The London catalogue of books published in Great Britain . . . 1816 to 1851. Thomas Hodgson: 1851. pp.[iii].644. [45,000.]

— The classified index to the London catalogue of books . . . 1816 to 1851. Thomas Hodgson: 1853. pp.xiv.286.

1818–1820. A catalogue of books. . . . Containing the books published in London . . . since the London catalogue of books 1818, or from October 1818 to October 1820. [By William Bent]. William Bent: 1820. pp.[iv].32. [2000.]

1822–1824. A catalogue of books. . . . Containing the works published in London . . . since the London catalogue of 1822, or from October 1822 to October 1824. [By Robert Bent]. For the executor of the late William Bent: 1824. pp.[ii].44. [2750.]

1827–1829. A supplement to the London catalogue of books, published in March 1827, containing all the new works and new editions published in London, from that period to June 1829. [By Robert Bent]. For the executor of the late W. Bent: 1829. pp.[ii].47. [3000.]

1831–1832. A supplement to the London catalogue of books published in February 1831; containing all the new works published in London, from that period to December 1832, inclusive. [By Robert Bent]. Robert Bent: 1833. pp.[ii].43. [2750.]

1831–1855. The London catalogue of books published in Great Britain . . . 1831 to 1855. Thomas Hodgson: 1855. pp.vi.583. [40,000.]

1834–1836. Supplement to the London catalogue of books . . . containing the books published in London, from December 1834 to December 1836. [By Robert Bent]. Robert Bent: 1837. pp. [ii].48. [3000.]

1835–1863. The english catalogue of books published from January, 1835, to January, 1863, comprising the contents of the 'London' and the 'British' catalogues. . . . Compiled by Sampson Low. Sampson Low, son, and Marston: 1864. pp.vii.910. [67,500.]

— Memorandum of corrections and omissions.

[1865]. pp.[4]. [250.]

1837–1852. The British catalogue of books published from October 1837 to December 1852. . . Compiled by Sampson Low. Vol.1. — General alphabet. Sampson Low and Son: 1853. pp.[vii]. 408.50.58.62.[14]. [40,000.]

no more published.

1837–1857. Index to the British catalogue of books published during the years 1837 to 1857 inclusive. Compiled by Sampson Low. Sampson Low and Co.: 1858. pp.[iii].292.xxx.xlviii.297–341.[3]. [72,500.]

1839. Hodgson's annual catalogue of books and engravings published during 1839. [By Thomas Hodgson]. Thomas Hodgson: 1840. pp.40. [2500.]

1839–1840. Bent's first appendix to the London catalogue of books, 1814–1839. Containing the new works . . . since the publication of the catalogue dated 1839. [By Robert Bent]. Robert Bent: 1840. pp.[ii].28. [1750.]

1839–1844. Supplement to the London catalogue of books, edition dated 1839. Containing the new works and new editions published in London from January 1839 to January 1844. [By Thomas Hodgson]. Thomas Hodgson: 1844. pp. vii.156. [8500.]

1846–1849. Supplement to the London catalogue of books published in Great Britain . . . from 1846 to 1849. [By Thomas Hodgson]. Thomas Hodgson: 1849. pp.[iii].125.56. [8000.]

— A catalogue of books published in London [1845–9: in the United Kingdom]. [Publishers' circular: Supplement]. London [ciii–   : Beckenham].

[i]. Sept. 1837–Dec. 1838. pp.70. [2500.]
[ii]. 1839. pp.38. [2000.]
[iii]. 1840. pp.48. [2000.]
[iv]. 1841. pp.40. [2000.]
[v]. 1842. pp.42. [2000.]
[vi]. 1843. pp.40. [3000.]
[vii]. 1844. pp.34. [3000.]
[viii]. 1845. pp.40. [3000.]
[ix]. 1846. pp.35. [3250.]
[x]. 1847. pp.37. [3500.]
[xi]. 1848. pp.40. [3750.]
[xii]. 1849. pp.42. [4000.]

[*continued as:*]

Sampson Low's catalogue of books published in the United Kingdom.

[xiii]. 1850. pp.58. [4000.]
[xiv]. 1851. pp.64. [4000.]
[xv]. 1852. pp.62. [4000.]
[xvi]. 1853. pp.64. [4000.]

[xvii]. 1854. pp.96. [4000.]
[xviii]. 1855. pp.54.xxxiv. [3750.]
[xix]. 1856. pp.48.xxx. [3250.]

[*continued as:*]

The British catalogue of books published during the year.

[xx]. 1857. pp.[v].xlviii.90. [5184.]
[xxi]. 1858. pp.[iii].lii.116. [4458.]
[xxii]. 1859. pp.[ii].104. [4544.]
[xxiii]. 1860. pp.[ii].48. [5059.]

[*continued as:*]

The English catalogue of books. . . . A supplement to the London catalogue, and the British catalogue.

[xxiv]. 1860. pp.[iii].68. [3000.]
[xxv]. 1861. pp.[iii].68. [3000.]
[xxvi]. 1862. pp.[iii].52. [4000.]
[xxvii]. 1863. pp.[ii].54. [4000.]
[xxviii]. 1864. pp.60. [4500.]
[xxix]. 1865. pp.[ii].61. [4500.]
[xxx]. 1866. pp.74. [5000.]
[xxxi]. 1867. pp.84. [5500.]
[xxxii]. 1868. pp.88. [5500.]
[xxxiii]. 1869. pp.88. [5500.]
[xxxiv]. 1870. pp.90. [5500.]
[xxxv]. 1871. pp.94. [5500.]
[xxxvi]. 1872. pp.88. [5500.]

[xxxvii]. 1873. pp.94. [5500.]
[xxxviii]. 1874. pp.88. [5000.]
[xxxix]. 1875. pp.96. [6000.]
[xl]. 1876. pp.96. [6000.]
[xli]. 1877. pp.108. [6500.]
[xlii]. 1878. pp.112. [7000.]
[xliii]. 1879. pp.120. [7500.]
[xliv]. 1880. pp.114. [7500.]
[xlv]. 1881. pp.108. [7500.]
[xlvi]. 1882. pp.112. [7500.]
[xlvii]. 1883. pp.127. [8500.]
[xlviii]. 1884. pp.130. [8500.]
[xlix]. 1885. pp.120. [8000.]
[l]. 1886. pp.114. [7500.]
[li]. 1887. pp.124. [8000.]
[lii]. 1888. pp.136. [9000.]
[liii]. 1889. pp.128. [8500.]
[liv]. 1890. pp.120. [8000.]
[lv]. 1891. pp.130. [7000.]
[lvi]. 1892. pp.146. [7500.]
[lvii]. 1893. pp.148. [7500.]
[lviii]. 1894. pp.148. [7500.]
[lix]. 1895. pp.154. [7500.]
lx. 1896. pp.224. [6500.]
lxi. 1897. pp.236. [7000.]
lxii. 1898. pp.256. [7500.]
lxiii. 1899. pp.248. [7567.]

lxiv. 1900. pp.266. [7149.]
lxv. 1901. [6044.]
lxvi. 1902. [7381.]
lxvii. 1903. [8381.]
lxviii. 1904. [8334.]
lxix. 1905. [8252.]
lxx. 1906. pp.312. [8603.]
lxxi. 1907. pp.334. [9914.]
lxxii. 1908. pp.313. [9821.]
lxxiii. 1909. pp.[viii].328. [10,725.]
lxxiv. 1910. pp.[viii].328. [10,804.]
lxxv. 1911. pp.[viii].328. [10,914.]
lxxvi. 1912. pp.[viii].355. [12,067.]
lxxvii. 1913. pp.[vi].359. [12,379.]
lxxviii. 1914. pp.[vi].331. [11,537.]
lxxix. 1915. pp.[vi].333. [10,665.]
lxxx. 1916. pp.[vi].284. [9149.]
lxxxi. 1917. pp.[vi].275. [8131.]
lxxxii. 1918. pp.[v].274. [7716.]
lxxxiii. 1919. pp.[v].290. [8622.]
lxxxiv. 1920. pp.[v].339. [11,004.]
lxxxv. 1921. pp.[vi].324. [11,026.]
lxxxvi. 1922. pp.[vi].337. [10,842.]
lxxxvii. 1923. pp.[vi].414. [12,274.]
lxxxviii. 1924. pp.[vi].416. [12,706.]
lxxxix. 1925. pp.[vi].406. [13,202.]
xc. 1926. pp.[vi].350. [12,799.]

xci. 1927. Edited by James D[ouglas] Stewart. pp.[vi].386. [13,810.]

xcii. 1928. pp.[vi].410. [14,399.]

xciii. 1929. pp.[vi].385. [14,086.]

xciv. 1930. pp.[viii].411. [15,393.]

xcv. 1931. pp.[viii].395. [14,688.]

xcvi. 1932. pp.[viii].394. [14,834.]

xcvii. 1933. pp.[viii].419. [15,022.]

xcviii. 1934. pp.[viii].442. [15,628.]

xcix. 1935. pp.[viii].456. [16,110.]

c. 1936. pp.[viii].448. [16,572.]

ci. 1937. pp.[viii].456. [17,286.]

cii. 1938. pp.[viii].423. [16,091.]

ciii. 1939. pp.[viii].391. [14,913.]

civ. 1940. Edited by J. D. Stewart and Percy Clare. pp.[viii].269. [10,732.]

cv. 1941. pp.[vii].126. [5092.]

cvi. 1942. pp.[iv].81. [4311.]

cvii. 1943. pp.[iv].115. [4500.]

cviii. 1944. pp.[iii].110. [5000.]

cix. 1945. pp.[iii].115. [5000.]

cx. 1946. pp.[iii].135. [6000.]

cxi. 1947. pp.[iii].191. [10,000.]

cxii. 1948. pp.[iii].222. [12,000.]

cxiii. 1949. pp.[iii].227. [12,000.]

cxiv. 1950. pp.[iii].252. [14,000.]

cxv. 1951. pp.[iii].275. [15,000.]

cxvi. 1952. pp.[iii].281. [15,000.]
cxvii. 1953. pp.[iii].249. [14,000.]
cxviii. 1954. pp.[iii].292. [15,000.]
cxix. 1955. pp.[iii].355. [17,000.]
cxx. 1956. pp.[iii].340. [17,000.]
cxxi. 1957. pp.[iii].366. [17,000.]
cxxii. 1958. pp.[iii].348. [16,000.]
cxxiii. 1959. pp.[iii].332. [16,000.]
cxxiv. 1960. pp.[iii].368. [17,000.]
cxxv. 1961. pp.[iii].401. [18,000.]
cxxvi. 1962. pp.[iii].363. [17,000.]

in progress; the subtitle varies; the issues for 1854–6 include an index entitled 'British catalogue'; there are two issues for 1860, as shown; no editor's name appears after vol.cv.

— — [cumulative edition]. The english catalogue of books . . . comprising the contents of the 'London' and the 'British' catalogues.

[i]. 1835–1863. [*see above*].
ii. 1863–1872. Compiled by Sampson Low. pp.[iii].452. [30,000.]
iii. 1872–1880. 1882. pp.[iii].562. [40,000.]
iv. 1881–1889. 1891. pp.vi.710. [50,000.]
v. 1890–1897. 1898. pp.1180. [35,000.]
vi. 1898–1900. 1901. pp.[iii].782. [25,000.]
vii. 1901–1905. 1906. pp.[iii].1328. [45,000.]
viii. 1906–1910. [Edited by James Douglas

Stewart]. 1911. pp.[iii].1495. [50,000.]
ix. 1911–1915. 1916. pp.[iv].1581. [57,500.]
x. 1916–1920. 1921. pp.[iv].1328. [45,000.]

xi. 1921–1925. 1926. pp.[v].1758. [60,000.]
xii. 1926–1930. 1931. pp.[viii].1780. [70,000.]
xiii. 1931–1935. 1936. pp.[viii].1984. [76,000.]
xiv. 1936–1941. 1945. pp.[viii].1880. [80,686.]
xv. 1942–1947. 1949. pp.[vii].674. [46,000.]
xvi. 1948–1951. 1952. pp.[vii].888. [72,000.]
xvii. 1952–1955. 1956. pp.[vii].1112. [65,000.]
xviii. 1956–1959. 1960. pp.[vii].1343. [75,000.]

in progress; the title varies; also published monthly in 1897–1900.

— Index.

[i]. 1837–1857. [*see above*].
ii. 1856–1876. 1876. pp.[iv].408.
iii. 1877–1880. 1884. pp.[iv].175.
iv. 1881–1889. 1893. pp.[iii].253.

no more published, the subsequent indexes forming one alphabet with the main work.

S[AMUEL] AUSTIN ALLIBONE, A critical dictionary of english literature, and british and american authors, . . . from the earliest accounts to the middle of the nineteenth century. 1859–1871.

pp.[iv].1005 + [iii].1005–2326 + [v].2327–3140. [250,000.]

actually extends to 1850–1870; reissued Philadelphia 1871–1872, 1877 and 1880.

— — A supplement. . . . By John Foster Kirk. Philadelphia 1891. pp.[ii].x.734+[iv].735–1562. [93,000.]

[MARIE E. DE MEESTER], Catalogus der afdeeling engelsche taal- en letterkunde. Rijksuniversiteit: Bibliotheek: Groningen 1917. pp.x.227. [2489.]

THE CAMBRIDGE bibliography of english literature. Cambridge.

i. 600–1660. Edited by F[rederick Noel] W[ilse] Bateson. 1940. pp.xl.912. [30,000.]
ii. 1660–1800. 1940. pp.xx.1003. [45,000.]
iii. 1800–1900. 1940. pp.xxi.1098. [50,000.]
iv. Index. 1940. pp.[iv].288.
v. Supplement. Edited by George [Grimes] Watson. 1957. pp.xiv.710. [27,500.]

— The concise Cambridge [&c.]. Edited by G. Watson. 1958. pp.xi.272. [5000.]

STANLEY J[ASSPON] KUNITZ and HOWARD HAYCRAFT, British authors before 1800. A biographical dictionary. New York 1952. pp.vii.584. [8000.]

6. *Select*

JOHN LELAND, Commentarii de scriptoribus britannicis. . . . Ex autographo lelandino nunc primus edidit Antonius Hall. Oxonii 1709. pp. [xvi].255+[ii].257–486.[xxviii]. [2000.]

one of the British museum copies contains numerous ms. additions, and a copy with ms. annotations is in the Bodleian library.

JOHN BOSWELL, A method of study: or, an useful library. In two parts. Part I. Containing short directions and a catalogue of books for the study of several parts of learning. 1738. pp.xiii. 399. [1000.]

the second part is entered under Theology, below.

JOHN BERKENHOUT, Biographia literaria; or a biographical history of literature: containing the lives of english, scotish [*sic*], and irish authors. . . . Volume I. From the beginning of the fifth to the end of the sixteenth century. 1777. pp.[iii].xxxiv. 537.[iv]. [2000.]

no more published.

[F. WRANGHAM], The english portion of the library of the ven. Francis Wrangham. Malton [printed] 1826. pp.x.646. [12,500.]

70 copies privately printed.

WILLIAM GOODHUGH, The english gentleman's library manual; or a guide to the formation of a library of select literature. 1827. pp.x.392. [2000.]

THE BOOK-COLLECTOR's hand-book: a modern library companion. 1845. pp.[iii].76. [750.]

HENRY STEVENS, Catalogue of my english library. 1853. pp.xi.108. [2000.]

privately printed; one of the British museum copies contains ms. notes apparently by the author.

CATÁLOGO de las obras en inglés existentes en la Biblioteca nacional. Bogotá 1856. pp.22. [500.]

A GENERAL catalogue of books in every department of literature, for public school libraries in Upper Canada. Toronto 1857. pp.263. [3500.]

CATALOGUE of english books in the Public library of Malta. Valetta 1857. pp.63. [1000.]

CATALOGUE of books, tracts, & school-materials. S. Anselm's society for the diffusion of good books: [*c.*1860]. pp.40. [1500.]

THE LIBRARY; or some hints about what books

to read. . . . By an old bookseller. Philadelphia 1870. pp.64. [1250.]

HENRY MORLEY, Tables of english literature. 1870. pp.iii–vii+20 plates. [4000.]

— — Second edition. 1870. p.iii–vii.viii + 20 plates. [4000.]

FREE public libraries . . . with a selected list of books. Revised edition. American social science association: New York 1871. pp.74. [1500.]

[FREDERIC BEECHER PERKINS], The best reading. New York 1872. pp.255. [5000.]

— — Fourth . . . edition. 1876. pp.x.343. [12,500.]

— — Second series . . . for the five years ending Dec. 31, 1881. Edited by Lynds E. Jones. 1885. pp.iv.119. [5000.]

— — Third series . . . for the five years ending Dec. 1, 1886. 1888. pp.[iii].108. [4000.]

— — Fourth series . . . for the five years ending Dec. 1, 1891. 1893. pp.[iv].126. [5000.]

W[ILLIAM] DAVENPORT ADAMS, Dictionary of english literature, being a comprehensive guide to english authors and their works. [1877]. pp.iv.708. [15,000.]

— — New . . . edition. [1880]. pp.iv.708. [15,000.]

GENERAL english book catalogue for the retail trade, comprising a selection of works in the various departments of literature. Berlin 1880. pp.xii.107. [2500.]

JAMES BALDWIN, The book-lover. A guide to the best reading. Chicago 1885. pp.201. [2000.]

— — Fourteenth edition. [1904]. pp.[ii].293. [2500.]

J. S. BANKS, A preacher's general reading. 1886. pp.31. [300.]

— — New edition. A preacher's library. 1902. pp.48. [250.]

BRITISH literary classics and miscellanies. Public libraries: Class list (no.9): Nottingham 1887. pp. 44. [1250.]

M. E. TOWNSEND, What shall I read? A specimen catalogue compiled for the department for G.F.S. [Girls' friendly society] members in professions and business. 1887. pp.vii.111. [2500.]

ALEXANDER IRELAND, Books for general readers. Manchester &c. 1887. pp.36. [500.]

CHARLOTTE M[ARY] YONGE, What books to lend and what to give. [1887]. pp.126. [955.]

E[DMOND] B[EALE] SARGANT and BERNARD WHISHAW, A guide book to books. 1891. pp.xvi. 344. [100,000.]

ARTHUR H. D. ACLAND, A guide to the choice of books for students & general readers. 1891. pp. xvi.128. [3500.]

J[OHN] HERBERT SLATER, The library manual: a guide to the formation of a library. . . . Third edition. 1892. pp.xii.424. [5000.]

THOMAS GREENWOOD, Sunday-school and village libraries, with a list of suitable books. 1892. pp.viii.95. [1500.]

ROBERT JOHN LISTER, A catalogue of a portion of the library of Edmund Gosse. 1893. pp.[ii].xxi.196. [1000.]

65 copies privately printed.

CATALOG of 'A.L.A.' library: 5000 volumes for a popular library, selected by the American library association and shown at the world's columbian exposition. Bureau of education (no.200): Washington 1893. pp.xx.592. [5230.]

— [second edition]. Melvil Dewey. A.L.A.

catalog. 8,000 volumes for a popular library. Library of Congress: Washington 1904. pp.404. 484. [8000.]

— — [first supplement]. Elva L[ucile] Bascom, A.L.A. catalog, 1904–1911. American library association: Chicago 1912. pp.350. [3000.]

— — [second supplement]. [May Massee], A.L.A. catalog, 1912–1921. 1923. pp.xiv.409. [4000.]

— [third edition]. Isabella M. Cooper, A.L.A. catalog. An annotated basic list of 10,000 books. 1926. pp.1296. [10,295.]

— — [first supplement]. Marion Horton, A.L.A. catalog, 1926–1931. 1933. pp.340. [3000.]

— — [second supplement]. M. Horton, A.L.A. catalog, 1932–1936. 1938. pp.365. [4000.]

— — [third supplement]. M. Horton, A.L.A. catalog, 1937–1941. 1943. pp.306. [4000.]

FRANK J. BURGOYNE and JOHN BALLINGER, Books for village libraries. Library association series (no.6): 1895. pp.vi.42. [1000.]

NEW books worth reading. Edited by Neville Beeman. No.1[–5]. 1896–1897. pp.[52]. [350.]
no more published.

R[OBERT] FARQUHARSON SHARP, A dictionary of

english authors, biographical and bibliographical, being a compendious account of the lives and writings of 200 british writers from the year 1400 to the present time. 1897. pp.vi.310.2. [15,000.]

— — New edition. 1904. pp.[v].363. [20,000.]

HENRY MATSON, References for literary workers. Third edition. Chicago 1897. pp.582. [10,000.]

MATTIE ANSTICE HARRIS, Two hundred works suggested as a nucleus for the library of the english student. [*s.l.* 1902]. pp.8. [200.]

SUGGESTIVE list of books for a small library recommended by the state library commissions of Wisconsin, Iowa, Minnesota, Nebraska, Idaho, and Delaware. Wisconsin free library commission: Madison [1902]. pp.43. [1500.]

— Supplement. [1903]. pp.22. [500.]

[SIR] W[ALTER] W[ILSON] GREG, Catalogue of the books presented by Edward Capell to the library of Trinity college. Cambridge 1903. pp.ix.172. [400.]

the half-title reads 'Capell's Shakespeariana'; 12 sets of plates were privately printed for this book.

HENRY W. KENT, Bibliographical notes on one hundred books famous in english literature. Grolier club: New York 1903. pp.xii.228. [100.]

308 copies printed.

W. HATFIELD, Our noble literature: British authors, and their works. 'Register' series: Manchester [1904]. pp.96. [1000.]

CAROLYN SHIPMAN, A catalogue of books in english later than 1700 forming a portion of the library of Robert Hoe. New York 1905. pp.[vii]. 341+[vii].329+[vii].222. [4000.]

100 copies privately printed.

CLASS list of best books, 1905–1906. Library association: 1906. pp.[iv].70. [1500.]

— 1906–1907. 1907. pp.x.80. [1750.]

— 1907–1908. 1908. pp.vi.114. [2500.]

M. MCCROBEN, A dictionary of english literature. Miniature reference library: [1906]. pp.[viii].215. [6000.]

— — [reissue]. A reader's manual, comprising (1) a biographical and bibliographical dictionary of english literature, and (2) an alphabetical list of literary terms. [1909]. pp.[iii].214.[ii].200.

A. CAPEL SHAW, What shall I read? Free libraries: Birmingham 1909. pp.39. [400.]

JOHN W. COUSIN, A short biographical dictionary of english literature. Everyman's library: [1910]. pp.viii.453. [5000.]

ZAIDEE BROWN, Buying list of books for small libraries. New York state education department: Albany 1910. pp.40. [1000.]

— — Eighth edition . . . by Orrilla Thompson Blackshear. American library association: Chicago 1954. pp.ix.198. [1742.]*

C[ALEB] T[HOMAS] WINCHESTER, Five short courses of reading in english literature, with biographical and critical references. . . . Third revised edition. Boston &c. 1911. pp.v.150. [2000.]

A STUDENT's library. 1911. pp.297. [1000.]

ENGLISH literature in schools. A list of authors and works for successive stages of study. English association: Leaflet (no.21): 1912. pp.20. [1000.]

LOUIS N. WILSON, Suggestions for a model private library at Clark college. Clark university: Library: Publications (vol.iii, no.2): Worcester, Mass. 1912. pp.[ii].13. [200.]

— — Further suggestions [&c.]. . . . (vol.iii, no.4): 1913. pp.30. [400.]

W[ILLIAM] FORBES GRAY, Books that count. A dictionary of standard books. 1912. pp.xx.coll. 630.pp.lviii. [5000.]

— — Second edition. Black's books of reference: 1923. pp.xx.coll.500.pp.xl. [4000.]

ARTHUR JOHN HAWKES, Best books of 1914 (first half-year). 1915. ff.3–76.pp.77–88. [600.]

[*continued as:*]

Best books. . . . New series. Gravesend.

i. 1929. pp.159. [4000.]
ii. 1930. pp.123. [2500.]
iii. 1931. General editor: Alex J. Philip. pp. 131. [3000.]
iv. 1932. pp.131. [3000.]
v. 1933. pp.127. [3000.]
vi. 1934. pp.115. [2500.]
vii. 1935. pp.132. [3000.]
viii. 1936. pp.106. [2500.]
ix. 1937. pp.123. [2500.]
x. 1938. pp.112. [2500.]
xi–xii. [*not published*].
xiii. 1941. pp.64. [1500.]
xiv. 1942. pp.72. [2500.]
xv. 1943. pp.84. [2750.]
xvi. 1944. pp.80. [2500.]
xvii. 1945. pp.81. [2500.]
xviii. 1946. pp.94. [3000.]

not published for 1915–1928.

[CHARLES E. B. RUSSELL], Libraries for reformatory and industrial schools. His majesty's stationery office: 1916. pp.25. [700.]

JOHN COWPER POWYS, One hundred best books. New York 1916. pp.73. [100.]

— — [another edition]. 1922. pp.63. [100.]

BOOKS to grow on. Reading for pleasure and profit. Public library: Buffalo 1916. pp.24. [1000.]

— [second edition]. 1923. pp.52. [1500.]

HENRI DE VOCHT, La langue, la littérature et les écrivains anglais. [Répertoire des ouvrages à consulter:] Bruxelles 1917. pp.[ix].58.[vii]. [466.]

MARTHA WILSON, Library books for high schools. Bureau of education: Bulletin (1917, no.41): Washington 1918. pp.175. [2165.]

CATALOGUE of books recommended by the Ontario Department of education for libraries of collegiate institutes, high schools, and continuation schools. Toronto 1918. pp.vii.91. [2250.]

CATALOGUS van de engelsche, duitsche en fransche handbibliotheken (Seminarium-verzamelingen). Universiteit: Bibliotheek: Amserdam 1918. pp.[iv].121. [English: 750.]

STANDARD catalog for public libraries. Minneapolis 1918. pp.99. [1000.]

— Fourth edition. Compiled by Dorothy Herbert West, Estelle A. Fidell. 1959. pp.1349. [7610.]

published in various forms, editions and supplements.

REGINALD R. BUCKLEY, How and what to read. Suggestions towards a home library. 1919. pp.176. [500.]

HAROLD B[RENT] WRENN, A catalogue of the library of the late John Henry Wrenn. . . . Edited by Thomas J[ames] Wise. University of Texas: Austin 1920. pp.xii.315+[v].293+[v].307+[v].280+[v].187.xviii. [6000.]

120 copies printed; the collection now forms part of the university of Texas library.

BESSIE GRAHAM, The bookman's manual. A guide to literature. New York 1921. pp.x.434. [6000.]

— — 9th edition . . . by Hester R[osalyn Jacoby] Hoffman. 1960. pp.xix.1116. [15,000.]

[W. E. HARRISON], 100 Books to read and enjoy. Ipswich [1922]. pp.[19]. [100.]

WHAT to read. A guide for worker students. Plebs league: 1923. pp.[vi].61. [750.]

THE BOOK-SELECTOR. A guide to current books and an essay in co-operative cataloguing. No.1 [-12]. 1923–1924. ff.176. [1250.]

no more published.

MAY LAMBERTON BECKER, A reader's guide book. New York 1924. pp.x.374. [1500.]

GUY BOAS, Short guide to the reading of english literature. 1924. pp.32. [400.]

ASA DON DICKINSON, One thousand best books. Garden City, N.Y. 1924. pp.416. [1000.]

SMITH college alumnae directed reading. Northampton, Mass. 1924 &c.

HELEN REX KELLER, The reader's digest of books. New York 1924. pp.[iv].941. [2000.]
— — New . . . edition. 1929. pp.[v].1447. [2500.]
first published in 1896.

STANDARD catalog for high school libraries. Edited by Zaidee Brown. New York 1926–1928.
— Seventh edition. Edited by Dorothy Herbert West, Marion L. McCormell. 1952. pp.xii.948. [3585.]
— Abridged high school catalog. . . . Edited by Zaidee Brown [*and others*]. 1935. pp.xii.301. [1200.]

JACK R[ANDALL] CRAWFORD, What to read in english literature. New York &c. 1928. pp.xxi. 388. [2500.]

JOHN L. YOUNG, English from Piers Plowman

to the Forsyte saga: a chronological record . . . and a list of available editions. 1928. pp.74.xxii. [1000.]

FOUR thousand books recommended to the general reader. Public libraries: [Dagenham] 1931. pp.119. [4000.]

— Third edition. 1956. pp.126. [4000.]

ESSAY and general literature index. . . . An index to . . . essays and articles in . . . volumes of collections of essays and miscellaneous works. New York.

i. [1911–1928]. Edited by Minnie Earl Sears and Marian Shaw. 1931. pp.xviii.423. [6350.]

ii. [1926–1931]. 1931. pp.iii–xviii.377. [7742.]

iii. [1922–1925, 1930–1931]. 1932. pp.iii–xvi. 272. [4853.]

iv. [1911–1922, 1930–1932]. 1932. pp.iii–xviii.296. [5970.]

v. [1911–1932]. 1933. pp.xvi.279. [5410.]

vi. [1900–1933]. 1933. pp.iii–xvi.290. [6384.]

— [revised series].

1900–1933. 1934. pp.iii–xviii.1952. [40,000.]

1934–1940. Edited by Marian Shaw. 1941. pp.x.1362. [23,090.]

1941–1947. Edited by Dorothy Herbert West, Estelle A. Fidelle. pp.xii.1908.

[32,226.]

1948–1950. Edited by D. H. West, Margaret B. Dirk. pp.[iv].1122. [16,603.]

1951–1954.

1955–1959. pp.[viii].1421. [20,091.]

1960. pp.[vi].370. [4698.]

1961. pp.[vi].321. [4105.]

1962. pp.[vi].382. [4538.]

1963. pp.[vi].330. [3886.]

in progress.

ANDREW BLOCK, Key books of british authors, 1600–1932. 1933. pp.384. [1150.]

C. W. EVERETT, Visual outline of english literature. Students outline series: New York 1933. pp.[iv].78. [500.]

interleaved.

ATWOOD H[ALSEY] TOWNSEND, Students' guide to good reading. [New York 1933]. pp.32. [600.]

— — [another edition]. 1960. pp.288. [1250.]

there are numerous intermediate editions.

POWELL STEWART and MICHAEL BRADSHAW, A goodly company. A guide to parallel reading. New York &c. 1934. pp.xxxv.300. [300.]

[J. C. GHOSH (JYOTIṢCHANDRA GHOSHA)], Annals of english literature, 1475–1925. The principal publications of each year. Oxford 1935. pp.vi.340. [7500.]

[—] — Second edition. [Revised by R. W. Chapman]. 1961. pp.[ii].vi.380. [12,500.]

[C. A. W.], First appearance in print of some four hundred familiar quotations. Exhibited at the Olin memorial library. Wesleyan university: Middletown, Conn. 1935. pp.iii–xv.261. [250.]

[BESSIE GRAHAM]. Famous literary prizes and their winner. New York 1935.

[—] — [third edition]. Literary prizes [&c.]. 1946. pp.vii.119. [1000.]

includes a few foreign lists.

LITERARY prizes. A list of the better known literary awards. National book council: Book list (no.144): 1935. pp.[2]. [60.]

— Third edition. 1944. pp.[4]. [125.]

A CATALOGUE of a library of living books. An anonymous selection representative of the general booksellers' stock of non-fiction and children's books which have proved their lasting or immediate worth. Sunday Times book exhibition: 1936. pp.100. [6500.]

500 copies printed.

SUGGESTED books for indian schools. Office

[Bureau] of indian affairs: Washington 1938. pp. [ii].45. [1053.]

— Sixth edition. 1953. pp.91.[xxv]. [1750.]

— — Supplement. 1956. pp.[iii].16. [200.]*

W[ILLIAM] A[RTHUR] MUNFORD, Three thousand books for a public library. 1939. pp.188. [3000.]

on the publishers' case the title appears as Books for basic stock.

CATALOGUE of books for the services. Selected by a committee appointed by the Incorporated society of authors and the National book council. 1939. pp.[ii].38. [1500.]

ERNEST RHYS, A breviary of books in wartime. Everyman pamphlets (no.1): [1941]. pp.16. [21.]

MORTIMER J. ADLER, Invitation to learning. Everyman pamphlets (no.2): [1941]. pp.16. [200.]

ERIC [HONEYWOOD] PARTRIDGE, The teaching of english in his majesty's forces. A representative library. [*s.l.*] 1941. pp.16. [100.]

the title is misleading.

FRANCIS X[AVIER] CONNOLLY and JAMES EDWARD TOBIN, To an unknown country. Discovery and exploration in english literature. A reading list. New York 1942. pp.56. [1200.]

MARY FRANK MASON, The patients' library. A guide book for volunteer hospital library service. New York 1942. pp.111. [225.]

ISABEL S[TEVENSON] MONRO, *ed.* Standard catalog for high school libraries. Fourth edition. New York 1942. pp.xii.1150. [3800.]

[KATHARINE KOSMAK], Books for the dimout. Public library: New York 1942. pp.15.

F. SEYMOUR SMITH, An english library. An annotated list of 1300 classics. National book council: 1943. pp.88. [1300.]

— — Revised . . . edition. 1963. pp.384. [1500.]

PERRIE JONES, One thousand books for hospital libraries. An annotated bibliography. Minneapolis [1944]. pp.v.58. [1000.]

HOLIDAYS at home. Suggestions for reading. [Third edition]. Public libraries: Bristol 1944. pp.40. [1500.]

[JOHN REDLINGER], Reader's guide to the public libraries. A list of the latest popular books selected in accord with the reviews of catholic magazines, with a religious bibliography, 1943. 1946. [Jacksonville, Fla. 1946]. pp.56. [1000.]

WILLIAM A[MBROSE] FITZGERALD, The family book shelf. Paterson, N.J. [1948]. pp.40. [200.]
— — Second edition. [1954]. pp.40. [200.]

LIBRARY catalog. . . . Part I. Books in english. U.S. information centers in Germany. [Office of High commissioner for Germany: Education and cultural relations division:] Information centers branch: [*s.l.*] 1950. pp.[iii].431. [12,500.]

BERNICE C. BUSH, ANITA E[LIZABETH] DUNN and MABEL E. JACKMAN, Fare for the reluctant reader. 1951. pp.[iv].43. [450.]*
— — Third . . . edition. By A. E. Dunn and M. E. Jackman. [1964]. pp.271. [2000.]

J. SHERWOOD WEBER, *ed.* Good reading. Prepared by the Committee on college reading. National council of teachers of english: Mentor book (no. MD178): New York 1956. pp.288. [1500.]

THE WORLD of books. Leisure reading for catholic youth. Catholic library association [&c.]: [Pittsburgh] 1956. pp.30. [750.]

PHILIP H. VITALE, An outline guide for english majors. Chicago [1959]. pp.246. [1250.]

[HAZEN C. CARPENTER], A selective annotated

bibliography of the major english writers, 1798–1832. Air force academy: Library: Special bibliography series (no.6): [Denver] 1959. pp.[ii].50. [200.]*

JOHN D[OZIER] GORDAN, Landmarks in english literature in first or early editions. 1490–1900. An exhibition from the Berg collection. Public library: New York 1959. pp.25. [75.]

PAPERBOUND book guide for colleges. New York 1960. pp.[iv].60. [2000.]

HELEN B. HOGAN, Treasures in paperbacks. University of North Carolina: Library: Library Study outlines (vol.i, no.2): Chapel Hill 1960. pp.55. [144.]

MARY K. EAKIN, Subject index to books for intermediate grades. Third edition. American library association: 1963. pp.vi.308. [1750.]

MARY FABIAN WARMER, Books for religious sisters. A general bibliography. Washington 1963. pp.184. [1200.]

DAVID BONNELL GREEN [*and others*], Keats, Shelley, Byron, Hunt and their circles. A bibliography July 1, 1950–June 30, 1962. Lincoln, Neb. [1964]. pp.vii.323.

English Literature

7. *Periods*

i. *Anglosaxon*

HUMPHREY WANLEY, Librorum vett. septentrionalium, qui in Angliæ bibliothecis extant, nec non multorum vett. codd. septentrionalium alibi extentium catalogus historico-criticus. Antiquæ literaturæ septentrionalis [by George Hickes] liber alter: Oxoniæ 1705. pp.[xviii].326.[xxxii]. [2000.]

FRANCISQUE [FRANÇOIS XAVIER] MICHEL, Bibliothèque anglo-saxonne. Anglo-saxonica (vol.ii): 1837. pp.viii.168. [400.]

THOMAS WRIGHT, Biographia britannica literaria. . . . Anglo-saxon period. [Royal society of literature:] 1842. pp.[vii].554. [1000.]

RICHARD [PAUL] WÜLKER, Grundriss zur geschichte der angelsächsischen litteratur. Leipzig 1885. pp.xii.532. [4000.]

PRINTING with anglo-saxon types, 1566–1715. Catalogue of a small exhibition at Corpus Christi college. Cambridge [1946]. pp.14. [16.]

WILFRID BONSER, An anglo-saxon and celtic bibliography (450–1087). Oxford 1957. pp.xxxix. 574+[v].123. [11,975.]

ii. *Medieval*

W[ILLIAM] W[ITHERLE] LAWRENCE, Selected bibliography of medieval literature in England from the beginning to the death of Chaucer. Revised edition. Columbia university: New York 1930. pp.23. [200.]

ROGER SHERMAN LOOMIS, Introduction to medieval literature, chiefly in England. Reading list and bibliography. New York 1939. pp.25. [500.]

iii. *Eleventh-fifteenth centuries*

THOMAS WRIGHT, Biographia britannica literaria. . . . Anglo-norman period. [Royal society of literature:] 1846. pp.[vii].491. [1000.]

JOHN EDWIN WELLS, A manual of the writings in middle english, 1050–1400. Connecticut academy of arts and sciences: New Haven 1916. pp.xvii.941. [5000.]

— — First supplement. 1919. pp.943–1037. [1000.]

— — Second supplement. 1923. pp.1039–1155. [1500.]

— — Third supplement. 1926. pp.1157–1247. [1500.]

— — Fourth supplement. 1929. pp.1249–1332.

[1000.]

— — Fifth supplement. 1932. pp.1333–1432. [1500.]

— — Sixth supplement. 1935. pp.1433–1549. [2000.]

— — Seventh supplement. 1938.pp. 1550–1652. [1500.]

— — Eighth supplement. 1941. With an index to pieces first treated in supplements I–VIII. pp. 1653–1763. [1500.]

— — Ninth supplement. By B[eatrice] D. Brown, Eleanor K. Heningham and F[rancis] L. Utley. 1951. pp.1765–1938. [881.]

JOHN MANNING BOOKER, A middle english bibliography. Dates, dialects and sources of the XII, XIII, and XIV century monuments and manuscripts exclusive of the works of Wyclif, Gower, and Chaucer and the documents in the London dialect. Heidelberg 1912. pp.[iii].76. [750.]

[PER] JOHAN VISING, Anglo-norman language & literature. Language & literature series: 1923. pp.112. [2000.]

JOSIAH COX RUSSELL, Dictionary of writers of thirteenth century England. Institute of historical research: Bulletin: Special supplement (no.3): 1936. pp.x.210. [1000.]

LENA LUCILE TUCKER and ALLEN ROGERS BENHAM, A bibliography of fifteenth century literature, with special reference to the history of english culture. University of Washington: Publications in language and literature (vol.ii, no.3): Seattle 1928. pp.162. [1500.]

iv. *Sixteenth-seventeenth centuries*

a. General

SIR EGERTON BRYDGES [vols.ii–iv: and JOSEPH HASLEWOOD], The british bibliographer. 1810–1814. pp.x.588 + x.664 + [iv].22.xxx.[viii].120. [iii].xxxvi.[xvi].248+[ii].xii.400.260. [1000.]

vol.iii is a collection of reprints; 150–250 copies printed.

SIR EGERTON BRYDGES, Restituta: or, titles, extracts, and characters of old books in english literature, revived. 1814–1816. pp.[ii].xi.571+[ii]. 550+vi.vii.564+iii–xviii.578. [400.]

[JOHN FRY], Bibliographical memoranda; in illustration of early english literature. Bristol 1816. pp.xx.404. [500.]

[*99 copies privately printed*].

J[OHN] PAYNE COLLIER, A catalogue, bibliographical and critical, of early english literature;

forming a portion of the library at Bridgewater house, the property of . . . lord Francis Egerton. 1837. pp.iv.366. [250.]

J[AMES] O[RCHARD] HALLIWELL [-PHILLIPPS], A hand-list of the early english literature preserved in the Douce collection in the Bodleian library. 1860. pp.[vii].151. [2250.]

51 copies privately printed.

J. O. HALLIWELL [-PHILLIPPS], A hand-list of the early english literature preserved in the Malone collection in the Bodleian library. 1860. pp.[vii]. 96. [1750.]

51 copies privately printed.

W[ILLIAM] CAREW HAZLITT, A catalogue of early english miscellanies formerly in the Harleian library. Camden society: Camden miscellany (vol.v [no.3]): 1862. pp.34. [600.]

W[ILLIAM] CAREW HAZLITT, Hand-book to the popular, poetical, and dramatic literature of Great Britain, from the invention of printing to the restoration. 1867. pp.xii.[ii].701. [8000.]

[A. BALLOCH GROSART], Hand-list of unique or extremely rare elizabethan-jacobean-carolian books . . . edited . . . by the rev. Alexander B. Grosart. Blackburn 1884–1885. pp.34. [100.]

[JAMES OSBORNE WRIGHT and CAROLYN SHIPMAN], Catalogue of books by english authors who lived before the year 1700, forming a part of the library of Robert Hoe. New York 1903–1905. pp.ix.361 + [v].399 + [v].351 + [v].303 + [v].426. [3500.]

100 copies printed.

[JOHN BUXTON and D. G. NEILL], English literature in the seventeenth century. Guide to an exhibition. Bodleian library: Oxford 1957. pp. 168. [234.]

b. Chronological

–1595

ANDREW MAUNSELL, The first[–seconde] part of the Catalogue of english printed books . . . eithef written in our owne tongue, or translated out or anie other language. 1595. pp.[iii].123+[vi].27. [2960.]

titles omitted by Maunsell, chiefly for political and religious reasons, are supplied in ms. in copies in the libraries of Trinity college, Cambridge, and the Grolier club, New York.

1554–1640

A TRANSCRIPT of the registers of the Company of stationers of London; 1554–1640 A.D.... Edited by Edward Arber. [Vol.v: Birmingham]. 1875–1894. pp.xliv.596 + viii.888 + 704 + 536 + cxii. 277. [4691.]

230 copies privately printed.

1557–1587

J[OHN] PAYNE COLLIER, Extracts from the registers of the Stationers' company of works entered for publication between the years 1557 and 1570 [–1587]. Shakespeare society: 1848–1849. pp.x.251 +xvi.252. [2500.]

1618

[WILLIAM JAGGARD], A catalogve of such english bookes, as lately have bene, and now are in printing for publication. From the ninth day of October, 1618. vntill Easter terme, next ensuing. 1618. pp.[12]. [204.]

reprinted by Oliver M. Willard in Stanford studies in language and literature *(1941), pp.160–170.*

1626–1631

A CATALOGUE of certaine bookes, which haue beene published, and (by authoritie) printed in

England, both in latine and english, since the yeare 1626, vntill November this present yeare. 1631. pp.[18]. [225.]

1640–1708

A TRANSCRIPT of the registers of the Worshipful company of stationers; from 1640–1708 A.D. [Roxburghe club:] 1913–1914. pp.iii–xi.488+[vii].512+[viii].501. [10,000.]

c.1650–1660

[WILLIAM LONDON], A catalogue of the most vendible books in England, orderly and alphabetically digested, under the heads of divinity, history, physick and chyrurgery, law . . . with hebrew, greek and latine for schools and scholars. 1657. pp.[240]. [3000.]

[—] — — A supplement of new books, come forth since August the first 1658 [*sic*, 1657] till June the first 1658. [1658]. pp.[10]. [100.]

[—] — [another edition]. A catalogue [&c.] 1658. pp.[248]. [3000.]

a copy in the Bodleian library contains ms. notes.

[—] — — A catalogue of new books, by way of supplement to the former, being such as have been printed from that time, till Easter-term, 1660. 1660. pp.[24]. [400.]

1662–1663

G[EORGE] T[OKEFIELD], A catalogue of such books as have been entered in the registers of the Company of stationers: and printed from the 25. of December, 1662. to the 25. of December, 1663. Published by G. T. clerk to the Company of stationers. 1664. pp.8. [100.]

1666–1695

ROBERT CLAVEL [CLAVELL], A catalogue of all the books printed in England since the dreadful fire of London, in 1666. . . . Together with the titles of publick acts of Parliament: the texts of single sermons, with the authors names: playes, acted at both the theatres: and an abstract of the general bills of mortality (extant since the year 1660). 1673. pp.[iii].48.32. [1500.]

W. C. Hazlitt, Third and final series of bibliographical collections *(1887), p.44, records a 'supplement of 7 leaves with the books printed to Michaelmas Term, 1674'.*

— — [second edition]. The general catalogue of books [&c.]. 1675. pp.[iii].120. [2500.]

— — [third edition]. 1680. pp.[iv].99. [3500.]
the catchword 'Cata-' on p.99 refers to Clavel's

Catalogus librorum latinorum in diversis Europæ partibus impressorum, *1681, which is paged* [*101*]-*191; in some copies a catalogue of the bookseller William Miller is inserted between pp.28 and 29.*

[—] — The fourth edition. 1696. pp.[iii].127. [8500.]

1668–1670

MERCURIUS librarius, or a catalogue of books printed and published in Michaelmass-term, 1668 [&c.].

- i. Michaelmass 1668. By John Starkey. pp.[2]. [60.]
- ii. Hilary 1668–1669. pp.[2]. [60.]
- iii. Easter 1669. By J. Starkey and Robert Clavel. pp.[2]. [50.]
- iv. Trinity 1669. pp.[2]. [50.]
- v. Michaelmas 1669. pp.[4]. [90.]
- vi. Hilary 1669–1670. pp.[2]. [50]
- vii. Easter 1670. pp.[2]. [50.]
- viii. Midsummer 1670. By J. Starkey. pp.[2]. [40.]

no more published.

1670–1711

A CATALOGUE of books printed and published at [*afterwards:* in] London in Easter-term, 1670 [&c.].

Easter 1670. By the booksellers of London. pp.[4]. [90.]
Midsummer 1670. pp.[4]. [70.]
Michaelmas 1670. By Robert Clavel. pp.[6]. [125.]
Hilary 1670. pp.[4]. [60.]
Easter 1671. pp.[6]. [90.]

[*continued as:*]

A catalogue of books continued, printed [&c.].
Trinity 1671. By Robert Clavel. pp.[4]. [70.]
Michaelmas 1671. pp.[6]. [125.]
Hilary 1671. pp.[4]. [75.]
Easter 1672. pp.[6]. [100.]
Trinity 1672. pp.[4]. [75.]
Michaelmas 1672. pp.[6]. [125.]
Hilary 1673. pp.[4]. [75.]
Easter 1673. pp.[6]. [90.]
Trinity 1673. pp.[4]. [60.]
Michaelmas 1673. pp.[10]. [175.]
Hilary 1674. pp.[4]. [100.]
Easter 1674. pp.[6]. [125.]
Trinity 1674. pp.[6]. [125.]
Michaelmas 1674. pp.[8]. [150.]
Hilary 1674. [By Robert Clavell]. pp.[6]. [125.]
Easter 1675. pp.[4]. [75.]
Trinity 1675. pp.[4]. [75.]

Michaelmas 1675. pp.[6]. [150.]
Hilary 1675. pp.[6]. [100.]
Easter 1676. pp.[6]. [150.]
Trinity 1676. pp.[4]. [75.]
Michaelmas 1676. pp.[8]. [225.]
Hilary 1676. pp.[6]. [60.]
Easter 1677. pp.[6]. [125.]
Trinity 1677. pp.[4]. [100.]
Michaelmas 1677. pp.[8]. [175.]
Hilary 1677. pp.[6]. [100.]
Easter 1678. pp.[6]. [125.]
Trinity 1678. pp.[4]. [90.]
Michaelmas 1678. pp.[8]. [175.]
Hilary 1678–1679. pp.[6]. [90.]
Easter 1679. pp.[6]. [125.]
Trinity 1679. pp.[6]. [125.]
Michaelmas 1679. pp.[10.] [175.]
Hilary 1679–1680. pp.[8]. [150.]
Easter 1680. pp.[8]. [125.]
Trinity 1680. pp.[10]. [150.]
Michaelmas 1680. pp.[10]. [175.]
Hilary 1680–1681. pp.9. [150.]
Easter 1681. pp.[8]. [150.]
Trinity 1681. pp.7. [100.]
Michaelmas 1681. pp.[10]. [150.]
Hilary 1681–1782. pp.[10]. [150.]
Easter 1682. pp.[8]. [125.]

Trinity 1682. pp.[8]. [125.]
Michaelmas 1682. pp.[12]. [200.]
Hilary 1682–1683. pp.[6]. [125.]
Easter 1683. pp.[10]. [150.]
Trinity 1683. pp.[10]. [150.]
Michaelmas 1683. pp.[12]. [125.]
Hilary 1683–1684. pp.[6]. [100.]
Easter 1684. pp.[8]. [150.]
Trinity 1684. pp.[8]. [125.]
Michaelmas 1684. pp.[12]. [200.]
Hilary 1684–1685. pp.[8]. [150.]
Easter 1685. pp.[8]. [125.]
Trinity 1685. pp.[6]. [80.]
Michaelmas 1685. pp.[10]. [150.]
Hilary 1685–1686. pp.[6]. [80.]
Easter–Trinity 1686. pp.[8]. [150.]
Michaelmas 1686. pp.[8]. [125.]
Hilary 1686–1687. pp.[4]. [50.]
Easter 1687. pp.[4]. [50.]
Trinity 1687. pp.[4]. [80.]
Michaelmas 1687. pp.[8]. [100.]
Hilary 1687–1688. pp.[6]. [75.]
Easter 1688. pp.[4]. [75.]
Trinity 1688. pp.[6]. [80.]
Michaelmas 1688. pp.[4]. [50.]
Easter 1689. pp.[18]. [300.]
Trinity 1689. pp.[10]. [150.]

Michaelmas 1689. pp.[12]. [175.]
Hilary 1689–1690. pp.[10]. [150.]
Easter 1690. pp.[6]. [100.]
Trinity 1690. pp.[8]. [100.]
Michaelmas 1690. pp.[12]. [175.]
Hilary 1690–1691. pp.[8]. [100.]
Easter 1691. pp.[8]. [125.]
Trinity 1691. pp.[8]. [100.]
Michaelmas 1691. pp.[10]. [150.]
Hilary 1691–1692. pp.[8]. [100.]
Easter 1692. pp.[6]. [80.]
Trinity 1692. pp.[8]. [100.]
Michaelmas 1692. pp.[14]. [175.]
Hilary 1692–1693. pp.[9]. [125.]
Easter 1693. pp.[8]. [150.]
Trinity 1693. pp.[7]. [100.]
Michaelmas 1693. pp.[14]. [200.]
Hilary 1693–1694. pp.[6]. [80.]
Easter 1694. pp.[6]. [80.]
Trinity 1694. pp.[8]. [100.]
Michaelmas 1694. pp.[14]. [200.]
Hilary 1694–1695. pp.[8]. [100.]
Easter 1695. pp.[6]. [80.]
Trinity 1695. pp.[8]. [100.]
Hilary 1695–1696. pp.[7]. [100.]
Easter 1696. pp.[6]. [80.]
Trinity 1696. pp.[11]. [150.]

Michaelmas 1696. pp.[8]. [100.]
Hilary 1696–1697. pp.[8]. [100.]
Easter 1697. pp.[6]. [80.]
Trinity 1697. pp.[11]. [150.]
Michaelmas 1697. pp.[11]. [150.]
Hilary 1697–1698. pp.[10]. [150.]
Easter 1698. pp.[7]. [100.]
Trinity 1698. pp.[14]. [175.]
Michaelmas 1698. pp.[13]. [175.]
Hilary 1698–1699. pp.[11]. [150.]
Easter 1699. pp.[11]. [150.]
Trinity 1699. pp.[13]. [175.]
Michaelmas 1699. pp.[14]. [175.]
Hilary 1699–1700. pp.[12]. [150.]
Easter 1700. pp.[10]. [125.]
Trinity 1700. pp.[11]. [150.]
Michaelmas 1700. pp.[14]. [175.]
Hilary 1700–1701. pp.[12]. [150.]
Easter 1701. pp.[10]. [125.]
Trinity 1701. pp.[12]. [150.]
Michaelmas 1701. pp.[12]. [150.]
Hilary 1701–1702. pp.[11]. [150.]
Easter 1702. pp.[6]. [60.]
Trinity 1702. pp.[10]. [100.]
Michaelmas 1702. pp.[12]. [150.]
Hilary 1702–1703. pp.[12]. [150.]
Easter 1703. pp.[8]. [100.]

Trinity 1703. pp.[12]. [125.]
Michaelmas 1703. pp.[16]. [200.]
Hilary 1703–1704. pp.[12]. [125.]
Easter 1704. pp.[8]. [75.]
Trinity 1704. pp.[12]. [125.]
Michaelmas 1704. pp.[11]. [100.]
Hilary 1704–1705. pp.[12]. [125.]
Easter 1705. pp.[11]. [100.]
Trinity 1705. pp.[14]. [125.]
Michaelmas 1705. pp.[12]. [100.]
Hilary 1705–1706. pp.[10]. [100.]
Easter 1706. pp.[6]. [50.]
Trinity 1706. pp.[12]. [100.]
Michaelmas 1706. pp.[9]. [100.]
Hilary 1706. pp.[8]. [80.]
Easter 1707. pp.[10]. [100.]
Trinity 1707. pp.[10]. [100.]
Michaelmas 1707. pp.[16]. [150.]
Hilary 1707. pp.[4]. [35.]
Easter–Trinity 1708. pp.[14]. [150.]
Michaelmas–Hilary 1708. pp.[19]. [250.]
Easter–Trinity 1709. pp.[13]. [175.]
Easter 1711. pp.[16]. [200.]

no more published; no copies are known to have survived of the issues lacking above; no Hilary term was kept in 1688–1689; a few issues were reprinted, in an abridged form, soon after publication.

— The term catalogues, 1668–1709 A.D.; with a number for Easter term, 1711 A.D. . . . Edited . . . by Edward Arber. 1903–1906. pp.xvi.576+x.664 +x.742. [20,000.]

privately printed.

1678–1680

A COMPLEAT catalogue of all stitch'd books and single sheets printed since the first discovery of the popish plot, (September 1678.) to January $16\frac{79}{80}$. 1680. pp.32. [650.]

— — A continuation . . . from the 1st of January $16\frac{79}{80}$ to the 25th of June 1680. 1680. pp.22. [400.]

— — A second continuation . . . from the 24th of June to Michaelmas Term 1680. 1680. pp.16. [300.]

reissued with a new collective titlepage, A general catalogue of all the stitch'd books and single sheets &c. printed the last two years, *1680; one of the British museum copies of the continuations contains additions and prices in manuscript, probably by Narcissus Luttrell; a facsimile of this copy was printed by sir Frank Francis as* Narcissus Luttrell's popish plot catalogues (*Luttrell society reprints [no.15]: Oxford 1956*).

1680

MERCURIUS librarius, or, a faithful account of all books and pamphlets published. Numb.1[–2]. April 1680. pp.[4]. [45.]

these two numbers, in the Bodleian library, are all that have survived, but the journal was still being published in November (see the Weekly advertisement of books *for 11 November 1680).*

–1693

[RANDALL TAYLOR], Bibliotheca novissima. Or a catalogue of books on divers subjects. Containing, I. Books lately printed in England. II. Books newly reprinted. III. Books now in the press. [1693]. pp.32.

V. *Eighteenth century*

a. Bibliographies

FRANCESCO CORDASCO, A register of 18th century bibliographies and references. A quarter-century survey. Chicago &c. 1950. pp.74. [523.]

includes some foreign and miscellaneous entries.

b. General

BIBLIOTHECA annua: or, the annual catalogue for

the year, 1699 [&c.]. Being an exact catalogue of all english and latin books, printed in England.

[i]. 1699–1700. By A[bel] Roper and W. Turner. pp.[iv].76. [1000.]
ii. 1700–1701. pp.[iv].76. [1000.]
iii. 1701–1702. pp.[iii].84. [600.]
iv. 1702–1704. pp.[ii].114. [1000.]
no more published.

THE MONTHLY catalogue. Numb.I[–VIII]. May–December 1714. pp.52. [1000.]
no more published?

[JOHN WILFORD], The first volume of the Monthly catalogue: containing an exact register of all books, sermons, plays, poetry, and miscellaneous pamphlets, printed and published in London, or the universities, from the beginning of March 1723, to the end of December, 1734. [1723–]1725. pp.16 and 20 parts, the first of pp.16, the rest of pp.12. [900.]

ii. 1725–1726. [1725–]1727. pp.[ii].140.[viii]. 140.[x]. [1000.]
iii. 1727–1728. [1727–]1729. pp.[ii].140.[viii]. 142.[x]. [1000.]
[iv]. 1729. pp.148.[viii]. [550.]

[WILLIAM RIDER], An historical and critical

account of the lives and writings of the living authors of Great-Britain. 1762. pp.34. [100.]

A CATALOGUE of the most esteemed modern books, that have been published for fifty years past, to this present time. 1760. pp.[ii].50. [3000.]

A CATALOGUE of all the english books that have been published for these sixty years past. 1764. pp.59. [3400.]

A COMPLEAT catalogue of all books and pamphlets published for ten years past, with their prices, and references to their characters in the Monthly review . . . May 1749, to June 1759, both inclusive. 1760. pp.v.[112]. [3000.]

— — [another edition]. A general index to the Monthly review, from its commencement to the end of the seventieth volume. . . . Vol.I., containing a catalogue of the books and pamphlets characterized. By S[amuel] Ayscough. 1786. pp.xi.715. [20,000.]

covers the period 1749–1784.

— — — A continuation . . . ending with the eighty-first volume. 1796. pp.iv.178. [5000.]

covers the period 1784–1789.

[MARSHALL], Catalogue of five hundred celebrated authors of Great Britain now living;

... including a complete list of their publications. 1788. pp.viii.[304]. [1500.]

JEREMIAS DAVID REUSS, Das gelehrte England oder lexicon der jeztlebenden [*sic*] schriftsteller in Grosbritannien, Irland und nord-Amerika, nebst einem verzeichnis ihrer schriften vom jahr 1770 bis 1790. Berlin &c. 1791. pp.xiv.459. [5000.]

— — Nachtrag und fortsetzung vom jahr 1790 bis 1803. 1804. pp.[ii].x.590+[iii].543. [12,500.]

also has an English titlepage, Alphabetical register of all the authors actually living in Great-Britain.

THE MONTHLY epitome and catalogue of new publications.

i. January–June 1797. pp.xvi.464. [1000.]
ii. 1798. pp.xvi.464.[iv]. [1000.]
iii. 1799. pp.xvi.456.[iv]. [1000.]
iv. 1800. pp.xvi.460.[iv]. [1000.]
v. 1801. pp.xiv.668.[vi]. [1000.]

[*continued as:*]

The monthly epitome, or, readers their own reviewers.

[vi]. n.s. i. 1802. pp.746.[iv]. [1000.]
[vii]. n.s. ii. 1803. pp.viii.664. [1000.]
viii. 1804. pp.[viii].658. [1000.]

[*continued as:*]

The literary magazine; or, monthly epitome

of british literature.

i. 1805. pp.iv.676. [1000.]

[ii]. 1806 (January–March). pp.216. [300.]

no more published.

[DAVID RIVERS], Literary memoirs of living authors of Great Britain . . . including a list of their works. 1798. pp.[iv].386+[iii].405. [1500.]

a copy in the Bodleian library contains ms. notes and cuttings by Thomas Park, and one in the Cambridge university library has ms. notes by Richard Gough, transcribed by John Bowyer Nichols.

A NEW catalogue of living english authors: with complete lists of their publications. . . . Vol.1. 1799. pp.v–xvi.463. [1000.]

A–Charlton only; no more published.

[JOHN WATKINS and FREDERIC SHOBERL], A biographical dictionary of the living authors of Great Britain and Ireland, comprising . . . a chronological register of their publications, with the number of editions printed. 1816. pp.viii.449. [12,500.]

FREDERIC EWEN, Bibliography of eighteenth century english literature. New York 1935. pp. [vi].29. [600.]

JAMES EDWIN TOBIN, Eighteenth century english literature and its cultural background. A bibliography. Fordham university: New York 1939. pp.vii.190. [7500.]

MARY BELL PRICE and LAWRENCE M[ARSDEN] PRICE, The publication of english humaniora in Germany in the eighteenth century. University of California: Publications in modern philology (vol.44): Berkeley 1955. pp.xxxiii.216. [2000.]*

JAMES L[OWRY] CLIFFORD, Early eighteenth-century english literature. . . . A list of reference works and selected reading. Revised edition. 1959. pp.[ii].50. [1250.]*

vi. *Nineteenth-twentieth centuries*

a. Bibliographies

BIBLIOGRAPHIES of studies in victorian literature. Urbana.

1932–1944. Edited by William D[arby] Templeman. 1945. pp.ix.450. [7500.]
1945–1954. Edited by Austin Wright. 1956. pp.[vii].312. [5000.]

b. Periodicals

FELIX SPEER, The periodical press of London, theatrical and literary (excluding the daily newspaper), 1800–1830. Useful reference series (no.60): Boston 1937. pp.58. [300.]

c. General

REVUE bibliographique du royaume des Pays-Bas et de l'étranger. Bruxelles 1822–1830.

for details of this publication see French literature, below.

THE LITERARY annual register and catalogue raisonné of new publications.

1845. pp.xxiii.230. [1000.]

1846 (January–March). pp.176. [750.]

no more published; the monthly issues were entitled Churton's literary register.

[SAMPSON LOW], Index to current literature. [Comprising a reference to every book in the english language as published, and to original literary articles of distinctive character in serial publications].

i–iv. 1859. pp.[ii].86. [7500.]

v–viii. 1860. pp.98. [8500.]

ix–xii. 1861. pp.99–170. [7500.]

no more published; reissued in one volume dated 1859–1861.

THE LITERARY gazette. A monthly record of literature. No.1[–7]. 1865. pp.260. [5000.]

no more published.

THE BOOK-BUYER's guide, being a list of the

principal books published in the various departments of literature.

i.

ii.

iii.

iv. December 1870. [Edited by Thomas J. Fenwick]. pp.xvi.52. [1750.]

v. March 1871. pp.viii.55. [2000.]

vi. June 1871. pp.xviii.50. [2000.]

vii. September 1871. pp.51. [1000.]

viii. December 1871. pp.56. [1000.]

ix. March 1872. pp.56. [1000.]

no more published.

THE BOOKSELLERS' circular and bookbuyers' guide. No.1. 1874. pp.16. [500.]

[*continued as:*]

The bookbuyer: a chronicle of, and guide to current literature. New series, No.1[–2]. 1875. pp.16.16. [1000.]

no more published.

A [*afterwards:* THE] REFERENCE catalogue of current literature, containing the full titles of books now in print and on sale, with the prices at which they may be obtained of all booksellers. 1874. pp. v–xii.[84]. [111 catalogues]. [15,000.]

— 1875. pp.viii.[104]. [71 catalogues]. [17,000.]

— 1877. pp.cciii. [107 catalogues]. [30,000.]

— 1880. pp.ccxxxvi. [87 catalogues]. [35,000.]

— [1885]. pp.xii.317. [112 catalogues]. [53,000.]

— [1889]. pp.x.404. [119 catalogues]. [68,000.]

— [1894]. pp.[x].515. [140 catalogues]. [87,000.]

— [1898]. pp. [x].576. [141 catalogues]. [100,000.]

— 1902. pp. [x].798. [168 catalogues]. [140,000.]

— 1906. pp. [ix].913. [190 catalogues]. [160,000.]

— 1910. pp. [xii].1086. [210 catalogues]. [185,000.]

— 1913. pp. xxiii.1186. [206 catalogues]. [200,000.]

— 1920. pp. xxxv.1075. [190 catalogues]. [180,000.]

— 1924. pp. xlviii.1384. [225 catalogues]. [235,000.]

— 1928. pp. xl.1429. [252 catalogues]. [240,000.]

— 1932. pp.lii.955. [213 catalogues]. [165,000.]

— 1935. pp.xcii.1204. [380,000.]

— 1938. pp.lxxii.1046 + [ii].1429.lxxiii–lxxv. [500,000.]

— 1940. pp.lxxvi.1130 + [ii].1538. [600,000.]

— 1951. pp.clii.789+[ii].1163. [300,000.]

— 1957. pp.cli.906+[ii].1345. [325,000.]

— 1961. pp.cxliv.1150+[ii].1594. [350,000.]

in progress; the issues for 1874–1932 consist of collections of publishers' catalogues, with a general index of their contents; after 1932 only the main title was retained and the catalogues were no longer issued; the method of indexing makes it almost impossible to estimate the number of works listed, and the figures given accordingly represent the number of entries in each index; since 1913 the publishers' estimate of this number has been very inaccurate; not published 1941–1950.

THE COLONIAL book circular and bibliographical record. Vol.1, no.1. 1887. pp.36. [1250.]

no more published.

THE BOOKS of to-day & the books of to-morrow. [(vol.i–)li; new series, i–v, no.4; new series, (no.1–)12; new series, no.1–8]. 1894–1952.

there were minor changes of title.

NEW book list for bookbuyers, librarians and booksellers. Compiled . . by Cedric Chivers.

1895 (October–December). pp.192. [1958.]

1896. pp.528. [5522.]

1897. pp.375. [7000.]

1898 (January–August). pp.148. [4000.]

no more published.

NEW catalogue of british literature.

1896. By Cedric Chivers. pp.[iii].292. [lxxxv]. [4847.]

1897. By C. Chivers and Armistead Cay. pp.[iii].375.[clxix]. [7295.]

no more published; this work is in part a reissue of the New book list, *above.*

INDEX of entries (literary) in the book of registry of the Stationers' company (pursuant to 5 and 6 Vict., Cap.45).

1st July, 1842, to 9th October, 1884. 1896. pp.342. [52,500.]

9th October, 1884, to 12 March, 1897. 1897. pp.508. [50,000.]

12th March, 1897, to 2nd September, 1902. 1903. pp.237. [25,000.]

2nd September, 1902, to 15th March, 1907. 1907. pp.207. [20,000.]

BUYING list of recent books recommended by the library commissions of Iowa, Minnesota, Wisconsin. Free library commission: Madison, Wis. 1901 &c.

in progress.

JOHN MATTHEWS MANLY and EDITH RICKERT. Contemporary british literature. Bibliographies and study outlines. [1922]. pp.xviii.196. [3500.]

— — Third . . . edition. By Fred B. Millett. 1935. pp.xi.556. [10,000.]

WHO's who in literature. . . . A continuance of the bibliographical section of the Literary year book. Liverpool [1933 &c.: Bootle.]

1924. Mark Meredith, editor. pp.[ix].lii.538. [35,000.]
1925. pp.[ix].lii.544. [35,000.]
1926. pp.[x].xlii.573. [40,000.]
1927. pp.[vi].xxxviii.590. [40,000.]
1928. pp.[ii].xxxiv.[x].612. [45,000.]
1929. pp.[iv].xxvii.[xviii].488. [30,000.]
1930. pp.[iv].xxii.[xx].518. [35,000.]
1931. pp.[ii].xxv.[xxi].541. [35,000.]
1932. pp.[ii].xxiii.[xxiii].526. [35,000.]
1933. pp.[ii].xxiii.[xxiii].526. [35,000.]
1934. pp.[iv].xx.[xxvi].493. [35,000.]

no more published.

ASA DON DICKINSON, The best books of our time, 1901–1925. Garden City 1928. pp.405. [1000.]

— — The best books of the decade 1926–1935. New York 1937. pp.xv.194. [400.]

— — — 1936–1945. 1948. pp.295. [1000.]

includes a few books in other languages.

WHITAKER's cumulative book list. Annual volume.

1924. pp.xx.240. [10,000.]
1925. pp.xx.240. [10,000.]
1926. pp.xvi.232. [8500.]
1927. pp.xvi.290. [10,000.]
1928. pp.xx.334. [13,981.]
1929. pp.xx.315. [12,912.]
1930. pp.xx.360. [15,849.]
1931. pp.xx.319. [14,746.]
1932. pp.xx.400. [15,279.]
1933. pp.xx.387. [14,608.]
1934. pp.xx.396. [15,436.]
1935. pp.xx.415. [16,678.]
1936. pp.xx.353. [16,944.]
1937. pp.xx.363. [17,137.]
1938. pp.xxii.343. [16,219.]
1939. pp.xvi.323. [14,904.]
1940. pp.xviii.225. [11,053.]
1941. pp.xvi.160. [7581.]
1942. pp.xvi.160. [7241.]
1943. pp.xvi.150. [6705.]
— 1939–1943. pp.iii–xx.622. [47,484.]
1944. pp.xvi.164. [6781.]
1945. pp.xx.167. [6747.]
1946. pp.xx.281. [11,411.]
1947. pp.xxiv.351. [13,046.]

— 1944–1947. pp.xxiv.588. [37,985.]
1948. pp.xxiv.432. [14,686.]
1949. pp.xxiv.496. [17,034.]
1950. pp.xxiv.462. [17,072.]
1951. pp.xxiv.483. [18,066.]
1952. pp.xxii.503. [18,741.]
— 1948–1952. pp.xxiv.1299. [85,599.]
1953. pp.xxii.490. [18,257.]
1954. pp.xxii.521. [19,188.]
1955. pp.xxii.561. [19,962.]
1956. pp.xxii.535. [19,107.]
1957. pp.xxii.585. [20,719.]
1958. pp.xxii.637. [22,143.]
1959. pp.xxii.596. [20,690.]
1960. pp.xxiv.704. [23,783.]
1961. pp.xxiv.749. [24,893.]
1962. pp.xxiv.757. [25,079.]

in progress.

THE READER's guides. [National book council:] 1928–1934.

this series was divided, by subjects, in twelve sections, each of which appeared, as a rule, four times yearly; 228 parts were published in all.

THE CUMULATIVE book index. A world list of books in the english language. New York.

xxxii. 1930. Edited by Mary Burnham. pp.

[iv].1348. [27,500.]

xxxiii. 1931. pp.[iii].1418. [30,000.]

xxxviii. 1935. pp.[iii].1492. [30,000.]

xxxix. 1936. pp.[iii].1553. [30,000.]

in progress; this publication is further cumulated, and, so far as the missing issues are concerned, replaced, by:

1928–1932. Edited by Mary Burnham. pp. [iii].2298. [125,000.]

1933–1937. pp.[vii].2680. [140,000.]

1938–1942. Edited by Mary Burnham and Regina Goldman. pp.[v].2722. [140,000.]

1943–1948. Edited by R. Goldman Grossman and Nina R. Thompson. pp.[v].2566. [135,000.]

1949–1952. pp.[vii].2023. [130,000.]

1953–1956. 1959. pp.[vii].1957. [130,000.]

1957–1958. pp.[vii].2532. [125,000.]

1959–1960. 1962. pp.[vii].2646. [130,000.]

1961. pp.viii.1062+vii.706. [65,000.]

1962. pp.[i].vi.1038+vii.710. [65,000.]

1963. pp.x.1101+

in progress; earlier issues are entered under American literature, above.

THEODORE C. EHRSAM and ROBERT H. DEILY, Bibliographies of twelve victorian authors. New York 1936. pp.362. [15,000.]

STANLEY J[ASSPON] KUNITZ and HOWARD HAYCRAFT, British author sof the nineteenth century. New York 1936. pp.[v].677. [12,500.]

BRITISH book news. A selection of books published in Britain. National book council [league].

1941. pp.[187]. [995.]
1942. pp.[160]. [1085.]
1943. pp.[168]. [1033.]
1944. pp.242. [1095.]
1945. pp.[ix].315. [1000.]
1946. pp.[viii].499. [1500.]
1947. pp.[viii].652. [2250.]
1948. pp.vi.717. [2500.]
1949. pp.vi.888. [3000.]
1950. pp.viii.888. [3000.]
1951. pp.806. [3000.]
1952. pp.694. [2500.]
1953. pp.690. [2500.]
1954. pp.714. [2500.]
1955. pp.1470. [6000.]
1956. pp.774+396. [5000.]
1957. pp.786. [3500.]
1958. pp.840. [4000.]
1959. pp.826. [4000.]
1960. pp.920. [4000.]
1961. pp.885. [3000.]

1962. pp.911. [4000.]
1963. pp.929. [4000.]
in progress.

STANLEY J[ASSPON] KUNITZ and HOWARD HAYCRAFT, Twentieth century authors. A biographical dictionary of modern literature. New York 1942. pp.vii.1577. [15,000.]

— — First supplement. Edited by S. J. Kunitz [and] Vineta Colby. 1955. pp.vii.1123. [20,000.]

ALICE PAYNE HACKETT, Fifty years of best sellers, 1895–1945. New York 1945. pp.x.140. [815.]

— — 60 years [&c.]. 1956. pp.xi.260. [1000.]

CATALOGUS tentoonstelling: het amerikaansche en engelsche boek, 1939–1946. Regeeringsvoorlichtingsdienst: ['s-Gravenhage 1946]. pp.iv.251. [5000.]

BOOKS for Germany. Agency for intellectual relief in Germany: [1947]. pp.20. [900.]

RECENT british books, 1948–1949. British council: 1949. pp.104. [2000.]

LOUISE BOGAN, Works on the humanities published in Great Britain, 1939–1946. A selective list. Library of Congress: Washington 1950. pp.iii.123. [978.]*

THE BRITISH national bibliography.

1950. Edited by A. J. Wells. pp.xi.686. [13,231.]
1951. pp.[ix].954. [15,871.]
1952. pp.[ix].1044. [17,146.]
1953. pp.[ix].993. [16,342.]
1954. pp.[ix].1040. [17,125.]
— Cumulated index 1950–1954. pp.[vi]. 1150. [79,735.]
1955. pp.[ix].1110. [17,368.]
1956. pp.xii.1135. [17,579.]
1957. pp.xii.1312. [19,054.]
1958. pp.xii.1339. [19,341.]
1959. pp.xi.1250. [17,960.]
— 1955–1959. pp.viii.1578. [19,302.]
1960. pp.xiv.1532. [.]
1961. pp.viii.1581. [.]*
1962. pp.viii.1371. [19,538.]*

in progress.

MODERN books and writers. National book league: [1951]. pp.72. [200.]

1950–1951. A thousand and one books of the year. National book league: [1951]. pp.[36]. [900.]

BRENDA MARY WALKER, The angry young men: aspects of contemporary literature. Library association: Special subject list (no.23): 1957. pp.18. [365.]*

BOOKGUIDE to books published. Editor: James Gordon [&c.]. 1957–1960.

LEWIS GASTON LEARY, *ed.* Contemporary literary scholarship. A critical review. Edited . . . for the Committee on literary scholarship and the teaching of english of the National council of the teachers of english. New York [1958]. pp.x.474. [2000.]

AN EXHIBITION in the occasion of the opening of the T. E. Hanley library. University of Texas: Research center: [Austin] 1958. pp.[ii].18. [131.]
500 copies printed.

RUDOLF JUCHHOFF and HILDEGARD FÖHL, Sammelkatalog der biographischen und literarkritischen werke zu englischen schriftstellern des 19. und 20. jahrhunderts (1830–1958). Verzeichnis der bestände in deutschen bibliotheken. Krefeld [1959]. pp.274. [13,000.]

BOOKS-in-print. Vol.i, no.1[–11]. February–December 1960. pp.[644]. [25,000.]
no more published.

TECHNICAL books-in-print. Vol.i, no.1[–11].

February–December 1960. pp.[510]. [20,000.]
no more published; the scope is wider than the title.

RICHARD D[ANIEL] ALTICK and WILLIAM R. MATTHEWS, Guide to doctoral dissertations in victorian literature 1886–1958. Urbana 1960. pp. vii.119. [2105.]

W. EASTWOOD and J. T. GOOD, Signposts. A guide to modern english literature. National book league: 1960. pp.79. [750.]

AN INDEX to book reviews in the humanities. [Detroit].*
i. 1960. pp.408. [15,000.]
ii. 1961. pp.[ii].xvi.379. [27,500.]
iii. 1962. pp.[ii].xv.304. [25,000.]
in progress?

BRITISH humanities index. Library association.
[1962]. Peter Ferriday (editor). pp.[viii].527. [6500.]
[1963]. pp.[viii].618. [7500.]
in progress.

8. *Translations &c.*

General

WILLIAM J. HARRIS, The first printed translations into english of the great foreign classics. [1909]. pp.vii.209. [1400.]

English Literature

FANNY GOLDSTEIN, A bibliography of foreign books and authors in english translations as library aids in work with the foreign born. Public library: West and branch: Boston [*c.*1940]. ff.[32]. [1000.]*

J. M. COHEN, English translators and translations. British council: British book news: Bibliographical series of supplements (no.142): 1962. pp.56. [150.]

Bantu

N. M. GRESHOFF, Some english writings by south african Bantu. University of Cape Town: School of librarianship. Bibliographical series: [Capetown] 1943 [1948]. ff.11. [87.]*

Chinese

MARTHA DAVIDSON, A list of published translations from chinese into english, french, and german. Part I: Literature, exclusive of poetry. (Tentative edition). American council of learned societies: Ann Arbor 1952. pp.xxix.179. [1512.]*

Classical languages

LEWIS WILLIAM BRÜGGEMANN, A view of the english editions, translations and illustrations of the ancient greek and latin authors. Stettin 1797. pp.xvi.838. [6000.]

— — A supplement. 1801. pp.150. [850.]

Danish

ELIAS [LUNN] BREDSDORFF, Danish literature in english translation. With a special Hans Christian Andersen supplement. A bibliography. Copenhagen 1950. pp.198. [2500.]

P[HILIP] M[ARSHALL] MITCHELL, A bibliography of english imprints of Denmark through 1900. University of Kansas: Publications: Library series (no.8): Lawrence 1960. pp.[vi].85. [394.]

Finnish

HILKKA AALTONEN, Books in english on Finland. A bibliographical list . . . including finnish literature in english translation. Turku university: Library: Publication (vol.8): Turku 1964. pp.276. [5000.]

Flemish

PROSPER ARENTS, De vlaamse schrijvers in het engels vertaald, 1481–1949. Koninklijke vlaamse academie voor taal- en letterkunde: Publicaties ([4th ser.,] no.13): Gent [1950]. pp.470. [600.]

French

CHARLES ALFRED ROCHEDIEU, Bibliography of french translations of english works: 1700–1800.

Chicago 1948. pp.xiii.387. [3500.]

German

LAWRENCE MARSDEN PRICE, English > german literary influences. . . . Part I. Bibliography. University of California: Publications in modern philology (vol.ix, no.1): Berkeley 1919. pp.110. [1015.]

BAYARD QUINCY MORGAN, A bibliography of german literature in english translation. University of Wisconsin: Studies in language and literature (no.16): Madison 1922. pp.708. [7000.]

—— Second edition. A critical bibliography of german literature in english translation, 1481– . . . 1935. Stanford university: 1938. pp.xiii.773. [12,000.]*

MARY BELL PRICE and LAWRENCE MARSDEN PRICE, The publication of english literature in Germany in the eighteenth century. University of California: Publications in modern philology (vol. xvii): Berkeley 1934. pp.viii.288. [1166.]

ANSELM SCHLÖSSER, Die englische literatur in Deutschland von 1895 bis 1934, mit einer vollständigen bibliographie der deutschen übersetzungen und der im deutschen sprachgebiet erschienenen englischen ausgaben. Forschungen zur englischen philologie (vol.v): Jena 1937. pp.[v].535. [7500.]

WALTER ROLOFF, MORTON E. MIX and MARTHA NICOLAI, German literature in british magazines, 1750–1860. Edited by Bayard Quincy Morgan and A[lexander] R[udolf] Hohlfeld. University of Wisconsin: Madison 1949. pp.viii.364. [5515.]

MARY BELL PRICE and LAWRENCE M[ARSDEN] PRICE, The publication of english humaniora in Germany in the eighteenth century. University of California: Publications in modern philology (vol.44): Berkeley &c. 1955. pp.xxxiii.216. [1250.]*

[KARLHEINZ GOLDMANN], Die literarischen und wissenschaftlichen beziehungen zwischen Nürnberg und Grossbritannien im 17. und 18. jahrhundert. Stadtbibliothek: Ausstellungs-katalog (no.18): Nürnberg [1960]. pp.[12]. [95.]

Greek

F[RANK] W[ILLIAM] TILDEN, Greek literature in english. . . . Bibliography. Indiana university: Department of Greek: Bloomington 1916. pp.57. [300.]

printed on one side of the leaf.

— — Third . . . edition. 1921. pp.82. [600.]

FINLEY MELVILLE KENDALL FOSTER, English translations from the greek. A bibliographical survey. Columbia university: Studies in english and comparative literature: New York 1918. pp.xxix.147. [1500.]

Hebrew

ISRAEL SCHAPIRO, אוצר תרגומים עברים מספרות האנגלית Bibliography of hebrew translations of english works. New York 1929. pp.[iii].43. [250.]

Hungarian

AUGUSTUS [ÁGOST] GYULAI, Bibliography of english authors' works translated into hungarian language (1620–1908). Budapest 1908. pp.28. [750.]

Indian

IMPEX reference catalogue of indian books. The list of all important indian books (in english) in print. New Delhi 1960. pp.[xxiv].468. [10,000.]

Italian

LIST of english translations of some italian classics. Library of Congress: Washington 1915. ff.5. [58.]*

MARY AUGUSTA SCOTT, Elizabethan translations from the italian. Vassar semi-centennial series: Boston &c. 1916. pp.[ii].lxxxi.560. [466.]

Japanese

DON BROWN, Japanese literature in english 1955–56. An indexed list of new and reprinted translations. Tokyo 1957. pp.40. [250.]

Latin

CLARISSA P[ALMER] FARRAR and AUSTIN P[ATTERSON]' EVANS, Bibliography of english translations from medieval sources. Records of civilisation: Sources and studies (no.39): New York 1946. pp.xiii.534. [3839.]

— — [another edition]. 1950. pp.40. [1250.]

there are several intermediate editions.

Norse

KARL LITZENBERG, The Victorians and the Vikings: a bibliographical essay on anglo-norse literary relations. University of Michigan: Contributions in modern philology (no.3): [Ann Arbor] 1947. pp.27. [100.]

Norwegian

ERLING GRÖNLAND, Norway in english. Books

on Norway and by Norwegians in english 1936–1959 . . . including a survey of norwegian literature in english translation from 1472 to 1959. Norsk bibliografisk bibliotek (vol.19): Oslo &c. 1961. pp.xvi.152. [4500.]

BOOKS in english about Norway and by norwegian authors available in the United States (1956–July, 1962). Norwegian information service: Washington [1963]. ff.[74]. [300.]*

Philippine

LEOPOLDO Y. YABES, Philippine literature in english 1898–1957. A bibliographical survey. University of the Philippines: Quezon City 1958. pp.[iv].343–434. [877.]

300 copies printed.

Polish

ELEANOR [EDWARDS] LEDBETTER, Polish literature in english translation. A bibliography. New York 1932. pp.45.

MARION MOORE COLEMAN, Polish literature in english translation. A bibliography. Cheshire, Conn. 1963. pp.[ii].ix.180. [2000.]*

Russian

NICHOLAS N. MARTIANOFF [NIKOLAI NIKOLAEVICH

MARTYANOV], Books available in english by Russians and on Russia published in the United States. New York [1935]. pp.48. [900.]

— — [seventh edition]. 1954. pp.63. [1785.]

AMREI ETTLINGER and JOAN M. GLADSTONE, Russian literature, theatre and art. A bibliography of works in english, published 1900–1945. [1946]. pp.96. [1750.]

RUSSIAN belles-lettres in english translation: a selected list. Library of Congress: Washington 1946. ff.18. [137.]*

[DZHANTEEVA and M. MORSCHINER], Современные английские и американские писатели. Библиографический указатель основных произведений и критической литературы на русском языке. Государственная центральная библиотека: Москва 1945. pp.56. [400.]

GLENDORA W. BROWN and DEMING B[RONSON] BROWN, A guide to soviet russian translations of american literature. Columbia slavic studies: New York 1954. pp.243. [1678.]

ХУДОЖЕСТВЕННАЯ литература и литературоведение. Англии: Библиографический указатель книг и статей, опубликованных в советской печати и в печати зарубежных стран. Всесоюзная государственная библиотека иностранной литературы: Москва 1957. pp.227. [3055.]

MAURICE B[ERNARD] LINE, A bibliography of russian literature in english translation to 1900 (excluding periodicals). Library association: Bibliographies (no.4): 1963. pp.74. [500.]

Spanish and portuguese

ANGEL FLORES, Spanish literature in english translation. A bibliographical syllabus. New York 1926. pp.82. [1000.]

WILLIAM H. FLETCHER and WILLIAM W. LYMÁN, A guide to the spanish-american literature in translation. Los Angeles junior college: Los Angeles 1936. pp.115.

ZELMARA BIAGGI and F. SÁNCHEZ, English translations from the spanish, 1932 to April 1938. Stonington 1939. pp.18. [300.]

JAMES A[LBERT] GRANIER, Latin american belles-lettres in english translation. A selective and annotated guide. Library of Congress: Hispanic foundation bibliographical series (no.1): Washington 1942. pp.iii.31. [60.]*

— — [Second revised edition]. 1943. pp.ii.33. [60.]*

WILLIS KNAPP JONES, Latin american writers in english translation. A tentative bibliography. Pan american union: Bibliographic series (no.30): Washington 1944. ff.vi.45.45a–141. [2500.]*

CATÁLOGO de exposição de livros portuguêses traduzidos de inglês. Instituto britânico em Portugal: [Lisbon] 1944. pp.39. [402.]

REMIGIO UGO PANE, English translations from the spanish, 1484–1943. A bibliography. Rutgers university studies in spanish (no.2): New Brunswick 1944. pp.vi.218. [2682.]

Swedish

NILS AFZELIUS A bibliographical list of books in english on Sweden and literary works translated into english from swedish. Stockholm 1936. pp.36. [700.]

8. *Miscellaneous*

GEORGE BALLARD, Memoirs of several ladies of Great Britain, who have been celebrated for their writings. Oxford 1752. pp.xvii.474. [1000.]

— — [another edition]. Memoirs of british

ladies [&c.]. London 1775. pp.viii.320. [viii]. [1000.]

HORACE WALPOLE, EARL OF ORFORD, A catalogue of the royal and noble authors of England, with lists of their works. Strawberry-Hill 1758. pp. [vi].ix.223+[ii].215.[vi]. 1500.]

there are several issues of this edition, one or more having an 18-page postscript; a copy in the Bodleian library contains ms. notes by William Cole.

— — The second edition. 1759. pp.[vi].ix.247. [iv]+[ii].250.[vi]. 1500.]

a copy in the Bodleian library contains ms. notes by Michael Lort and Philip Yorke, 2nd earl of Hardwicke.

— — The third edition. Dublin 1759. pp.166. [ii]+[ii].147–288.[iv]. [1500.]

American literature.

[under this heading is included only the literature of the United States, and of Canada when it is included with that of the United States; when the literature of the United States is included with that of Great Britain, it is entered under English literature; the literature of other american countries and in other languages is entered under the several countries and languages; and that of latin America as a whole under America, 2.vii.]

1. *Bibliographies*

SOME bibliographies which list works published in the United States during the war years. Library of Congress: Washington 1947. ff.4. [36.]*

[KLAUS LANZINGER and GEORGE STEINER], Ausgewähltes verzeichnis der im bereich der Österreichischen nationalbibliothek, der österreichischen universitäten und der amerikanischen bibliothek in Österreich vorhandenen zeitschriften, jahrbücher und nachschlagwerke zum studium der amerikanischen literatur und des amerikanischen englisch. Universität: Amerika-institut: [Innsbruck 1959]. pp.[iii].38. [100.]

2. *Manuscripts*

KATHERINE H. DAVIDSON, Preliminary inventory of the records of the Federal writers' project, Work projects administration, 1935–44. National archives (no.57): Washington 1953. pp.v.15. [large number.]*

AMERICAN literary manuscripts. A checklist of holdings in academic, historical and public libraries in the United States. Modern language association of America: American literature group: Committee on manuscript holdings: Austin [1960]. pp.xxviii.421. [large number.]

3. *General*

A CATALOGUE of all the books printed in the

United States. Boston 1804. pp.79. [1500.]

reprinted by A[dolf] Growoll, Book-trade bibliography in the United States *(New York 1898).*

ALEXANDER V. BLAKE, The american bookseller's complete reference trade list, and alphabetical catalogue of books published in this country. Claremont, N.H. 1847. pp.232. [5000.]

— — Supplement. 1848. pp.[viii].235–351. [2500.]

O[RVILLE] A[UGUSTUS] ROORBACH, Bibliotheca americana. Catalogue of american publications, including reprints and original works, from 1820 to 1848, inclusive. New York 1849. pp.xi.360. [6000.]

— — Supplement. 1850. pp.vii.124. [2000.]

— — [another edition]. 1852. pp.xi.652. [10,000.]

— — — Supplement. 1855. pp.vii.220. [3500.]

— — — Addenda. 1858. pp.257. [3500.]

— — — Vol. IV. of the Bibliotheca &c. 1861. pp.vii.162. [2000.]

— — [continuation]. The american catalogue of books . . . published in the United States. . . . Compiled . . . by James Kelly. New York &c.

[i] 1861–1866. 1866. pp.[iv].303. [6000.]

ii. [1866–1870]. 1871. pp.[iii].488. [10,000.]

[TRÜBNER & CO.], Trübner's Bibliographical guide to american literature; being a classified list of books . . . published in the United States of America during the last forty years. 1855. pp.xxxii. 108. [3000.]

— — [another edition]. 1859. pp.x.cxlix.554. [10,000.]

SAMPSON LOW, SON & CO., The american catalogue of books: or, english guide to american literature, giving the full title of original works published in the United States since the year 1800, with especial reference to books of interest to Great Britain. 1856. pp.viii.190. [3500.]

HENRY STEVENS, Catalogue of american books in the library of the British museum, Christmas 1856. Vol. I. 1859. pp.[ii].449+[ii].451–628. [12,000.]

— — [a reissue]. 1866. pp.xxxii.628. [12,000.]

UNIFORM trade list circular. Philadelphia.

i. 1866–1867. pp.336. [10,000.]
ii. nos.1–3. 1867. pp.128. [3000.]

no more published.

THE PRINCE library. The american part of the collection which . . . Thomas Prince . . . bequeathed to the Old South church, and now deposited in the Public library. Boston [1868]. pp.70. [1500.]

— [another edition]. Catalogue of the american portion of the library [&c.] 1868. pp.xxv.166. [1500.]

printed, in smaller format, from the same type as the catalogue first entered, with the omission of cross-references.

— — [another edition]. Boston 1870. pp.xvii. 160. [6000.]

THE AMERICAN catalogue of books for 1869. New York 1870. pp.xxi. coll.5–104. [2500.]

[*continued as:*]

The trade circular annual for 1871, including the American catalogue of books published in the United States during the year 1870. 1871. pp.vii.240+26 catalogues. [20,000.]

[*continued as:*]

The annual american catalogue [catalog]. Publishers' weekly.

1871. pp.xii.91. [3000.]
1886. pp.xx.199.128. [5000.]
1887. pp.xx.193.136. [5000.]
1888. pp.xviii.195.128. [5000.]
1889. pp.xviii.182.132. [5000.]
1890. pp.xviii.184.136. [5000.]
1891. pp.xx.213.144. [5000.]

1892. pp.xviii.227.144. [5000.]
1893. pp.xviii.217.146. [5000.]
1894. pp.xx.213.142. [5000.]
1895. pp.xx.237.162. [5000.]
1896. pp.xviii.229.164. [5000.]
1897. pp.xviii.219.158. [5000.]
1898. pp.xviii.223.148. [5000·]
1899. pp.xxiv.241.166. [5500.]
1900. pp.xxxii.267.302. [6500]
1900–1901. pp.xlii.480 [14,500]
1900–1902. pp.xliii.683. [22,000]
1900–1903. pp.lviii.930 [30,000]
1904. [*not published separately.*]
1905. pp.xxxvii.378–329. [8112.]
1906. pp.xxxvii.356.352. [7000.]
1907. [*not published separately.*]
1908. pp.xlix.494.379. [9500.]
1909. pp.xlix.639. [11,000.]

— — [consolidated issues]. The american catalogue [catalog]. Under the direction of [founded by] F[rederick] Leypoldt. [Publishers' weekly:] New York.

Books in print . . . 1876. Compiled by Lynds E[ugene] Jones. [1879–] 1880–1881. pp. 28.13.837.112+xx.492. [300,000.[

includes a supplement of books published 1876–1879.

1876–1884. Compiled by A[ugusta] I[sabella] Appleton pp.xxxii.448+ [ii].260 [15,000.]

1884–1890. pp.[ii].xxxiv.584 + [iv].318. [20,000.]

1890–1895. Compiled under the editorial direction of R[ichard] R[ogers] Bowker. 1896. pp.xxxvi.503+[iv].142. [17,500.]

1895–1900. pp.xxxvi.564+[iv].301. [20,000.]

1900–1905. pp.lxiv.1233. [22,500.]

1905–1907. pp.lxvi.1164. [22,500.]

1908–1910. pp.lxxxviii.1541. [30,000.]

no more published; not published for 1872–1885; a facsimile of the issues for 1876–1900 was published New York 1941.

THE UNIFORM trade list annual, embracing the full trade lists of american publishers. New York 1873.

[*continued as:*]

The publishers' trade list annual. 1874 &c.

details of this publication are not given, for it consists merely of the publishers' lists bound up without collective index.

— Books in print. An author-title-series index to the Publishers' trade list annual.

1948. Edited by B. A. Uhlendorf. pp.1201. [80,000.]

1949. pp.xiv.1313. [90,000.]

1950. pp.xiv.1429. [100,000.]
1951.
1952.
1953.
1954.
1958. Edited by Sarah L. Prakken. pp.xxxi. 1798. [125,000.]
1959.
1960. pp.xxxi.2050. [140,000.]
1961.
1962.
1963.
1964. pp.xxiii.2673. [178,000.]

in progress.

— Subject guide to books in print.
1957. Edited by Sarah L. Prakken.
1958.
1959.
1960.
1961.
1962. pp.xxiv.1842. [120,000.]
1963.
1964. pp.xxvii.2112. [133,500.]

SAMUEL F[OSTER] HAVEN, Catalogue of american publications in what is now the United States, 1639–1775. Albany 1874. pp.[ii].358. [7500.]

THE TITLE-SLIP registry [monthly]. Supplementary to The library journal and The publishers' weekly. Vol. I. New York 1879. pp.127. [2500.]
printed on one side of the leaf.

HOWARD CHALLEN, A record of the new books, published November, 1878–June, 1879. Philadelphia 1879. pp.[xi]. ff.[37]. [1500.]
no more published.

OSCAR FAY ADAMS, A brief handbook of american authors. Boston 1884. pp.x.188. [1500 authors.]
— — Fifth edition. A dictionary of american authors. Boston &c. 1905. pp.x.588. [25,000.]

CATALOGUE of copyright entries. Treasury department [1906 &c.: Library of Congress: Copyright office]: Washington 1891 &c.
in progress; the title and composition of this work have varied; the second series is made up of six sections, published independently and at varying intervals: part 1, group 1: books; group 2: pamphlets (including maps); group 3: plays and motion pictures; part 2: periodicals; part 3: music; part 4: works of art (including photographs); the current third series (from 1947) comprises the following parts: 1A: books; 1B: pamphlets, serials and contributions to periodicals; 2: periodicals; 3–4: dramas and works intended for oral delivery; 5A: published music; 5B: unpublished

music; 5C: renewal registrations of music; 6: maps and atlases; 7–11A: works of art, reproductions of works of art, scientific and technical drawings, photographic works, prints and pictorial illustrations; 11B: commercial prints and labels; 12–13: motion pictures and filmstrips.

P[ATRICK] K[EVIN] FOLEY, American authors, 1795–1895. A bibliography. Boston 1897. pp.xvi. 350. [6000.]

500 copies printed.

A CUMULATED index to the books of 1898–1899, being the record of the 'Cumulative book index' for two years, revised and enlarged under the direction of M[arion] E. Potter. Minneapolis 1900. pp.607. [22,500.]

— 1900. pp.3–400. [15,000.]

— 1901. pp.[iv].508. [17,500.]

[*continued as:*]

The cumulative book index. . . . Annual cumulation. Minneapolis [New York].

[vi]. 1902–1903. pp.827. [20,000.]

vii. 1904. pp.640. [15,000.]

viii. 1905. pp.[iv].505. [15,000.]

ix. 1906. pp.[iv].574. [17,500.]

x. 1907. pp.[iv].761. [25,000.]

xi. 1908. pp.[iv].678. [22,500.]

xii. 1909. pp.[iv].746. [25,000.]

xiii. 1910. Compiled under the editorial supervision of M. E. Potter and Emma L. Teich. pp.[vi].640. [20,000.]

xiv. 1911. Compiled by E. L. Teich. pp.[ii]. 624. [17,500.]

xv. 1912. Compiled by M. E. Potter and E. L. Teich. pp.[vi].830. [22,500.]

xvi. 1913. pp.[vi].834. [22,500.]

xvii. 1914. Compiled by M. E. Potter [*and others*]. pp.[iv].840. [22,500.]

xviii. 1915. pp.[iv].851. [22,500.]

xix. 1916. pp.[v].894. [20,000.]

xix. [*sic*, xx]. 1917. pp.[v].790. [17,500.]

xxi. 1918–1919. Compiled by E. L. Teich. pp.[v].943. [20,000.]

xxii. 1919–1920. Compiled by E. L. Teich and others. pp.[v].677. [15,000.]

xxiii. 1920–1921. [*not published.*]

xxiv. 1921–1922. Edited by Eleanor E. Hawkins. pp.[v].806. [17,500.]

xxv. 1922–1923. pp.[v].819. [17,500.]

xxvi. 1923–1924. [*not published*].

xxvii. 1924–1925. Edited by Mary Burnham. pp.[v].787. [17,500.]

xxviii. 1925–1926. Edited by M. Burnham and Ida M. Lynn. pp.[v].1395. [27,500.]

xxix. 1927. Edited by Ida Lynn. pp.[iv].879. [17,500.]

xxx. 1928. Edited by M. Burnham. pp.[iv]. 980. [20,000.]

xxxi. 1928–1929. pp.[iv].1920. [40,000.]

xxxii. 1930. pp.[iv].1347. [27,500.]

xxxiii. 1931. pp.[iii].1418. [27,500.]

xxxiv. 1932. [*not published*].

xxxv. [*omitted in the numbering*].

xxxvi. 1933. pp.[iii].1188. [22,500.]

xxxvii. 1933–1934. pp.[iii].2437. [50,000.]

xxxviii. 1935. pp.[iii].1492. [30,000.]

xxxix. 1936. pp.[iii].1553. [30,000.]

[xl]. 1937. pp.xiii.1059. [20,000.]

xli. 1938. Edited by M. Burnham and Regina Goldman. pp.[iii].1534. [30,000.]

xlii. 1938–1939. pp.[iii].2969. [60,000.]

xliii. 1940. pp.[iii].1491. [30,000.]

xliv. 1941. pp.[iii].1409. [27,500.]

xlv. 1942. pp.[iii].1268. [25,000.]

[xlvi–xlviii], 1943–June 1945. pp.[iii].2229. [45,000.]

[xlviii–xlix]. July 1945–1946. pp.[v].1567. [30,000.]

l. 1947. Edited by R. Goldman and Nina R. Thompson. pp.[iii].1343. [25,000.]

li. 1948. [*not published.*]

[lii–liii]. 1949–1950. Edited by R. Goldman Grossman and N. R. Thompson. pp.[iii]. 2448. [50,000.]

[liv]. 1951. pp.[v].871+vi.590. [27,500.]

[lv]. 1952. pp.x.875+v.577. [27,500.]

[lvi]. 1953. pp.v.789+iv.550. [25,000.]

[lvii]. 1954. pp.[ii].vii.795+v.556. [25,000.]

[lviii]. 1955. pp.[ii].viii.866 + viii.589. [26,000.]

[lix]. 1956. pp.[ii].vii.838+ix.628. [26,000.]

[lx]. 1957. pp.viii.910+vi.609. [27,000.]

[lxi]. 1958. pp.viii.856+ix.630. [27,000.]

[lxii]. 1959. pp.viii.901+vii.598. [27,000.]

[lxiii]. 1960. pp.vii.924+vii.680. [27,000.]

[lxiv]. 1961. pp.viii.1062+vii.706. [28,000.]

[lxv]. 1962. pp.[i].vi.1038+vii.710. [28,000.]

in progress; notwithstanding its title this confused publication is in part the annual cumulation of a nominally monthly list of new publications, in part an independent work listing books in print, in part a supplement to the United States catalog; *at first it covered only the publications of the United States and Canada, later it is described as 'a world list of books in the english language', but does not exclude works in foreign languages published in the United States.*

THE UNITED STATES catalog. Books in print,

1899. Edited by George Flavel Danforth [and] Marion E. Potter. Minneapolis [1900]. pp.viii. 755+3–361. [80,000.]

— Second edition. Edited by Marion E. Potter. New York 1906. pp.1130. [90,000.]

— Third edition. Books in print January 1, 1912. pp.[vi].2837. [150,000.]

— — Supplement . . . 1912–1917. Edited by M. E. Potter, Emma L. Teich and Louise Teich. pp.[iv].2298. [100,000.]

— — — 1918–1921. Edited by Eleanor E. Hawkins. pp.[vii].2185. [50,000.]

— — — 1921–1924. pp.[vii].2161. [50,000.]

— Fourth edition. Books in print January 1, 1928. Edited by Mary Burnham. pp.[iii].3164. [150,000.]

the continuation of this work is entered under English literature, The cumulative book index; *the period for 1924–1927 is covered by the 'annual' edition of the same work, which is entered next above.*

THE AMERICAN literary yearbook. A biographical and bibliographical dictionary of living north american authors. Vol.1. Edited by Hamilton Traub, Henning, Minn. 1919. pp.viii.3–276. [12,500.]

no more published.

WHO'S who among north american authors. Los Angeles.

[i. 1921]. pp.vi.441. [8500.]
ii. 1925–1926. Edited by A[lberta] Lawrence. pp.xv.472. [10,000.]
iii. 1927–1928. pp.vii.1088. [2900.]
iv. 1929–1930. pp.vii.1378. [30,000.]
v. 1931–1932. pp.xi.1230. [30,000.]
vi. 1933–1935. pp.viii.1270. [30,000.]

STANLEY J[ASSPON] KUNITZ and HOWARD HAYCRAFT, American authors, 1600–1900. A biographical dictionary of american literature. New York 1938. pp.vi.846. [20,000.]

W[ILLIAM] J[EREMIAH] BURKE and WILL D[AVID] HOWE, American authors and books, 1640–1940. New York 1943. pp.x.858. [50,000.]

—— Augmented . . . by Irving R. Weiss [1962]. pp.834. [50,000.]

LITERARY history of the United States. . . . Bibliography. New York 1949. pp.xxii.817. [20,000.]

WILLIAM STEWART WALLACE, Dictionary of north american authors deceased before 1950. Toronto 1951. pp.viii.525. [authors: 26,250.]

SYLVIA SAIFER, Available books of all publishers: 1953–1954. A reference guide to books available from american publishers, agents & distributors. Philadelphia.*

A–Ayres. [1954]. pp.[iv].li.236. [6000.]

no more published.

JACOB NATHANIEL BLANCK, Bibliography of american literature. Bibliographical society of America: New Haven.

i. A–B. 1955. pp.l.474. [2328.]

ii. C–D. 1957. pp.xix.534. [2759.]

iii. E–Harte. 1959. pp.xxi.482. [2482.]

iv. Hawthorne-Ingraham. 1963. pp.xxii.495. [4125.]

in progress.

ÁNGEL MINCHERO VILASARÓ, Diccionario universal de escritores. I. Estados Unidos. San Sebastian 1957. pp.3–639. [10,000.]

RICHARD M. LUDWIG, *ed.* Literary history of the United States. Bibliography supplement. New York 1959. pp.xix.268. [6000.]

AMERICAN book publishing record. New York 1960 &c.

in progress.

4. *Select*

WILEY & PUTNAM, American book circular. Classified list of some of the most important and recent american publications. New York 1843. pp.64. [1172.]

SELDEN L[INCOLN] WHITCOMB, Chronological outlines of american literature. New York 1894. pp.x.286. [2500.]
reprinted in 1906.

BEST [*afterwards:* A selection from the best] books of 1897 [&c.] [Best books selected for a small public library]. University of the state of New York: State library [*afterwards:* New York state library]: Bulletin (Bibliography no.12 [&c.]): Albany.

1897. [By Martha T. Wheeler]. . . . (no.12): 1899. pp.581–603. [205.]
1898 . . . (no.18): 1899. pp.581–603. [205.]
1899 . . . (no.21): 1900. pp.3–26. [225.]
1900 . . . (no.29): 1901. pp.923–950. [250.]
1901 . . . (no.34): 1902. pp.169–193. [250.]
1902 . . . (no.35): 1903. pp.199–230. [250.]
1903 . . . (no.37): 1904. pp.421–461. [250.]
1904 . . . (no.39): 1905. pp.503–543. [250.]
1905 . . . (no.40): 1906. pp.549–590. [250.]
1906 . . . (no.43): 1907. pp.83–126. [250.]
1907 . . . (no.44): 1908. pp.3–55. [250.]
1908 . . . (no.45): 1909. pp.3–48. [250.]
1909 . . . (no.49): 1910. pp.3–54. [250.]
1910 . . . (no.50): 1911. pp.3–54. [250.]
1911 . . . (no.51): 1912. pp.3–65. [250.]

1912. [By Mary E. Eastwood] . . . (no.53): 1913. pp.3–63. [250.]
1913 . . . (no.54): 1914. pp.3–60. [250.]
1914 . . . (no.56): 1915. pp.5–58. [250.]
1915 . . . (no.58): 1916. pp.5–65. [250.]
1916 . . . (no.61): 1917. pp.5–67. [250.]
1917 . . . (no.62): 1918. pp.5–77. [250.]
1918 . . . (no.66): 1919. pp.3–64. [250.]
1919 . . . (no.67): 1920. pp.3–65. [250.]
1920 . . . (no.70): 1921. pp.5–58. [250.]
1921 . . . (no.72): 1922. pp.5–57. [250.]
1922 . . . (no.73): 1923. pp.3–52. [250.]
1923 . . . (no.74): 1924. pp.3–57. [250.]
1924 . . . (no.75): 1925. pp.3–58. [250.]
1925 . . . (no.76): 1926. pp.3–58. [250.]

no more published, but continued in a similar form in New York libraries.

A.L.A. booklist. [A guide to the best new (to new; to current) books]. American library association: Boston [Chicago].

i–ii. 1904–1906. pp.xlii.144+256. [2000.]
iii. 1907. pp.[ii].xxx.238. [1000.]
iv. 1908. pp.[ii].xlvi.317. [900.]
v. 1909. pp.[ii].xxxviii.197. [750.]
vi. 1909–1910. pp.[ii].lxvix [*sic*, lxix].424. [1500.]

vii. 1910–1911. pp.[ii].lxxiii.456. [1500.]
viii. 1911–1912. pp.[ii].lviii.424. [1500.]
ix. 1912–1913. pp.[ii].lxxi.467. [1500.]
x. 1913–1914. pp.[ii].lxxv.427. [1500.]
xi. 1914–1915. pp.[ii].lxxiv.476. [1500.]
xii. 1915–1916. pp.[ii].lxxxviii.496. [2000.]
xiii. 1916–1917. pp.[ii].lxxxii.462. [2000.]

[*continued as:*]

The Booklist [and subscription books bulletin].

xiv. 1917–1918. pp.[ii].lxx.348. [1500.]
xv. 1918–1919. pp.[ii].lxxxii.466. [2000.]
xvi. 1919–1920. pp.[ii].lxxviii.358. [2000.]
xvii. 1920–1921. pp.[ii].lxxxiii.358. [2000.]
xviii. 1921–1922. pp.[ii].lxxviii.382. [2500.]
xix. 1922–1923. pp.[ii].lvii.342. [2000.]
xx. 1923–1924. pp.[ii].lxiv.398. [2500.]
xxi. 1924–1925. pp.[ii].lvi.400. [2500.]
xxii. 1925–1926. pp.[ii].lxi.446. [2500.]
xxiii. 1926–1927. pp.[ii].lxxviii.454. [2500.]
xxiv. 1927–1928. pp.[ii].lxii.421. [2500.]
xxv. 1928–1929. pp.lxx.421. [2000.]
xxvi. 1929–1930. pp.[ii].490. [2000.]
xxvii. 1930–1931. pp.[ii].614. [2500.]
xxviii. 1931–1932. pp.[ii].547. [2500.]
xxix. 1932–1933. pp.[ii].410. [2000.]
xxx. 1933–1934. pp.[iv].409. [2000.]
xxxi. 1934–1935. pp.[iv].444. [2000.]

xxxii. 1935–1936. pp.[iii].xli.354. [2000.]
xxxiii. 1936–1937. pp.[iii].xliv.364. [2000.]
xxxiv. 1937–1938. pp.[ii].xliv.422. [2500.]
xxxv. 1938–1939. pp.[ii].xlix.396. [2500.]
xxxvi. 1939–1940. pp.[ii].xlvii.456. [3000.]
xxxvii. 1940–1941. pp.[ii].li.580. [3500.]
xxxviii. 1941–1942. pp.[ii].liv.448. [3000.]
xxxix. 1942–1943. pp.[ii].502.xlix. [3000.]
xl. 1943–1944. pp.[ii].404.l. [3000.]
xli. 1944–1945. pp.[ii].xlii.354. [3000.]
xlii. 1945–1946. pp.[ii].xlv.381. [3000.]
xliii. 1946–1947. pp.[ii].xliv.374. [3000.]
xliv. 1947–1948. pp.[ii].lii.392. [3000.]
xlv. 1948–1949. pp.[ii].459. [3000.]
xlvi. 1949–1950. pp.[ii].407. [3000.]
xlvii. 1950–1951. pp.[ii].459. [3000.]
xlviii. 1951–1952. pp.[ii].440. [3000.]
xlix. 1952–1953. pp.[ii].434. [3000.]
l. 1953–1954. pp.[ii].516. [3000.]
li. 1954–1955. pp.[ii].540. [3000.]
lii. 1955–1956. pp.[ii].552. [3000.]
liii. 1956–1957. pp.[ii].653. [4000.]
liv. 1957–1958. pp.[ii].717. [4000.]
lv. 1958–1959. pp.[ii].698. [4000.]
lvi. 1959–1960. pp.[ii].759. [4000.]
lvii. 1960–1961. pp.[ii].778. [4000.]

in progress.

THE BOOK review digest. New York.

i. 1905. pp.396. [3000.]

ii. 1906. By Justina Leavitt Wilson, Clara Elizabeth Fanning. pp.[iv].389. [2000.]

iii. 1907. pp.[iv].491. [2500.]

iv. 1908. pp.[iv].492. [2000.]

v. 1909. pp.[iv].502. [2500.]

vi. 1910. pp.[iv].463. [2500.]

vii. 1911. pp.[iv].560. [3000.]

viii. 1912. By J. L. Wilson, Mary Katharine Reely, C. E. Fanning, pp.[iv].537. [3000.]

ix. 1913. By C. E. Fanning, M. K. Reely. pp.[ii].680. [4000.]

x. 1914. pp.648. [3000.]

xi. 1915. Edited by C. E. Fanning, Margaret Jackson and M. K. Reely. pp.556. [2500.]

xii. 1916. By Margaret Jackson, M. K. Reely. pp.[ii].680. [4000.]

xiii. 1917. pp.[iv].699. [3000.]

xiv. 1918. Edited by M. K. Reely. pp.[iv]. 556. [2000.]

xv. 1919. pp.[iv].634. [3000.]

xvi. 1920. Edited by M. K. Reely and Pauline H. Rich. pp.[iv].657. [3000.]

xvii. 1921. Edited by Marion H. Knight and Mertice M[ay] James. pp.[iv].725. [2500.]

xviii. 1922. pp.[iv].650. [2500.]
xix. 1923. pp.[iv].638. [2500.]
xx. 1924. pp.[iv].723. [2400.]
xxi. 1925. pp.[iv].858. [2500.]
xxii. 1926. pp.[iv].1059. [2755.]
xxiii. 1927. Edited by M. A. Knight, M. M. James and Matilda L. Berg. pp.[iv].946. [3000.]
xxiv. 1928. pp.[iv].972. [3125.]
xxv. 1929. pp.[iv].1188. [3500.]
xxvi. 1930. Edited by M. A. Knight, M. M. James and Ruth N. Lechlitner. pp.[iv].1288. [3800.]
xxvii. 1931. Edited by M. A. Knight, M. M. James and Dorothy Brown. pp.[ii].1632. [3900.]
xxviii. 1932. pp.[iv].1187. [3800.]
xxix. 1933. pp.v.1177. [3400.]
xxx. 1934. pp.v.1183. [3500.]
xxxi. 1935. pp.v.1252. [4000.]
xxxii. 1936. pp.v.1601. [4000.]
xxxiii. 1937–1938. pp.v.1222. [4400.]
xxxiv. 1938–1939. Edited by M. M. James and Dorothy Brown. pp.[v].1216. [4200.]
xxxv. 1939–1940. pp.vi.1216. [4200.]
xxxvi. 1940–1941. pp.vi.1158. [4000.]
xxxvii. 1941–1942. pp.vi.1551. [3800.]

xxxviii. 1942–1943. pp.vi.974. [3700.]

xxxix. 1943–1944. pp.vi.1015. [3700.]

xl. 1944–1945. pp.vi.940. [3300.]

xli. 1945–1946. pp.vi.895. [2850.]

xlii. 1946–1947. pp.vi.1345. [3500.]

xliii. 1947–1948. pp.vi.1114. [4050.]

xliv. 1948–1949. pp.vi.1067. [3700.]

xlv. 1949–1950. Edited by M. M. James, D. Brown and Gladys M. Dunn. pp.iv.1134. [4000.]

xlvi. 1950–1951. Edited by M. M. James and D. Brown. pp.iv.1119. [4000.]

xlvii. 1951–1952. pp.iv.1448. [4000.]

xlviii. 1952–1953. Edited by Nina R. Thompson, Jeannette Meyers and Eva L. Reiman. pp.iv.1107. [4000.]

xlix. 1953–1954. pp.ii.1157. [4000.]

l. 1954–1955. Edited by M. M. James and Dorothy Brown. pp.[ii].ii.1103. [4000.]

li. 1955–1956. pp.[ii].ii.1129. [4000.]

lii. 1956–1957. pp.[ii].ii.1533. [5000.]

liii. 1957–1958. pp.iv.1148. [4000.]

liv. 1958–1959. pp.iv.1258. [4000.]

lv. 1959–1960. Edited by Dorothy P. Davison . . . Martha Welday Young. pp.vi.1207. [3000.]

lvi. 1960–1961. pp.vi.1617. [5000.]

lvii. 1961–1962. pp.vi.2135. [7000.]
lviii. 1962–1963. pp.vi.1491. [4500.]

in progress; only the annual cumulations are set out; each fifth volume contains a cumulative index of the preceding five volumes.

A TENTATIVE selection from the books of 1909. New York state library: Bibliography (no.48): Albany 1910. pp.3–60. [1289.]

ZAIDEE BROWN, Buying list of books for small libraries. New edition revised by Caroline Webster. New York state library (Bibliography no.52). Albany 1912. pp.3–64. [900.]

—— Edition three. Compiled by Caroline Webster . . . (no.65): 1920. pp.3–144. [1250.]

LIST of books for prison libraries. New York state library: Bulletin (no.57): Albany 1916. pp.5–49. [517.]

JOHN MATTHEWS MANLY and EDITH RICKERT, Contemporary american literature. Bibliographies and study outlines. [1922]. pp.xix.188. [2500.]

—— Revision by Fred B. Millett. New York 1929. pp.viii.378. [6000.]

ALUMNI reading and study in literature. Book list on american literature. Amherst college:

Amherst 1923. pp.26. [400.]

APPROVED library lists. Bureau of education: Manila 1928. pp.xvii.595. [4000.]

THE LITERATURE of the United States of America. . . . Compiled . . . by the English-speaking union. National book council: Bibliography (no.114): 1929. pp.[4]. [250.]

limited to books published since 1900.

HARRIET [EMILY] SMITH POTTER, A check list of books in the Julian Willis Abernethy library of american literature. Middlebury college: [Bulletin (vol.xxv, no.2):] Middlebury, Vt. [1930]. pp.238. [4500.]

— — [second edition]. A check-list, Abernethy [&c.]. Compiled by Viola C[hittenden] White. 1940. pp.ix.291. [6000.]

B[RADFORD] M[ORTON] FULLERTON, Selective bibliography of american literature 1775–1900. A brief estimate of the more important american authors and a description of their representative works. New York 1932. pp.xiii.327. [900.]

J. DUNCAN SPAETH and JOSEPH E. BROWN, American life and letters. A reading list. Princeton 1934. pp.vi.57. [750.]

[MARY] ELOISE RUE, Subject index to readers. American library association: Chicago 1938. pp. xviii.174. [400.]

— — Second [*sic*] edition. Subject index to books for primary grades. Compiled by Mary K. Eakin and Eleanor Merritt. 1961. pp.vii.167. [750.]

this is the second edition of the book under its new title.

FRED B. MILLETT, Contemporary american authors. 1940. pp.xiii.716. [5000.]

WILLIAM T[HOMSON] HASTINGS, Syllabus of american literature. [Third edition]. Chicago 1941. pp.xii.141. [2000.]

SELECTED list of books in english by U.S. authors. American library association: Committee on library cooperation with latin America: Books for latin America project: Chicago 1942. pp.167. [1279.]*

— Supplement. December 31, 1942. pp.[3]. [31.]

KATALOG der amerikanischen büchersammlung. Schweizerische landesbibliothek: [Bern 1943]. pp.55. [1250.]

BOOKS published in the United States. . . . A

selected list [A selection] for reference libraries. American library association: International relations board: Committee on aid to libraries in war areas: Chicago.

1939–1943. [By Charles Flowers McCombs]. pp.xii.86. [1406.]
1944. [By Foster McCrum Palmer]. pp.42. [468.]
1945. pp.38. [396.]
no more published.

CATALOGUE of american books. British council: Scottish-american centre: Edinburgh 1944. pp.16.

THE UNITED STATES quarterly book list [book review]. Library of Congress: Washington.

i. 1944–1945. [Edited by Joseph Patrick Blickensderfer]. pp.[369]. [500.]
ii. 1945–1946. pp.18.356. [500.]
iii. 1946–1947. pp.22.424. [600.]
iv. 1947–1948. pp.[ii].ix.522.25. [1000.]
v. 1948–1949. pp.[ii].ix.560. [1000.]
vi. 1949–1950. pp.[ii].ix.522.22. [1000.]
vii. 1950–1951. pp.25.441. [800.]
viii. 1951–1952. pp.[ii].25.457. [800.]
ix. 1953. pp.[ii].28.512. [900.]
x. 1954. pp.vii.639. [1200.]
xi. 1955. pp.vii.570. [1000.]

xii, nos.1–2. March-June 1956. pp.viii.269. [600.]

no more published.

3000 AMERICAN books, 1940–1944, selected for norwegian libraries. Royal norwegian embassy: Washington 1945. ff.ix.190. [3000.]*

FOSTER MCCRUM PALMER, Books published in the United States, 1944. A selection for reference libraries. American library association: International relations board: Committee on aid to libraries in war areas: Chicago 1946. pp.42. [468.]

REPRESENTATIVE recent additions to the American library. United States information service: 1950. pp.40. [200.]*

THE FREE book. Fort Worth 1950. pp.40. [750.]*
— [another edition]. 1951. pp.30. [500.]

BIBLIOGRAPHY of professional and scientific books. Care book program: New York 1951. pp.[xv].224. [2600.]*
— [another edition]. 1954. ff.[ii].v.241. [3500.]*

EXHIBIT of outstanding books from America. United States information agency: Zagreb 1953. pp.112. [1000.]

HOWARD MUMFORD JONES, Guide to american literature and its backgrounds since 1890. Cambridge [Mass.] 1953. pp.[vii].151. [1500.]

— — Third edition. [By] H. M. Jones and Richard M. Ludwig. 1964. pp.xiii.240. [2500.]

THE GREAT DECADE in american writing 1850–1860. Emerson, Hawthorne, Melville, Thoreau, Whitman. Books and manuscripts; with paintings by friends and contemporaries of the authors. American academy of arts and letters and National institute of arts and letters: New York [1954]. pp.29. [96.]

A GUIDE to basic books. American booksellers association: [Chicago 1955]. pp.256. [1500.]

AMERICAN literature catalogue. United states information service: Library: 1956. pp.100. [1750.]

LES ANNÉES vingt. Les écrivains américains à Paris et leurs amis 1920–1930. Exposition. Centre culturel américain: [1959]. pp.3–142. [590.]

CATALOGUE of an exhibition of historical and literary Americana from the collections of Thomas W[inthrop] Streeter and C. Waller Barrett together with addition from the American antiquarian society and the Yale university library.

Grolier club: New York 1960. pp.48. [104.]

SCHOLARLY books in America. A quarterly bibliography of university press publications. [Chicago] 1959 &c.

in progress.

D. D. ZINK, Eleven nineteenth century american authors. Air force academy: Library: Special bibliography series (no.7): [Denver] 1959. pp.ii.65.

SYLVIA SCHÜTZE, Amerikanische literatur der gegenwart. Ein auswahlverzeichnis. Städtische volksbüchereien: Völker im spiegel der literatur (no.8): Dortmund 1962. pp.112. [750.]

CONTEMPORARY authors. The international bio-bibliographical guide to current authors and their works. Detroit.

i. 1962. pp.246. [5000.]

in progress.

BOOKS. New York 1964 &c.

in progress.

5. *Regional*

ALEXANDER NICHOLAS DE MENIL, The literature of the Louisiana territory. St. Louis 1904. pp.354. [1000.]

the name Louisiana is issued in the widest sense and

covers the present states of Louisiana, Missouri, Iowa, Minnesota, Kansas, Colorado, Nebraska, Arkansas, South Dakota and Oklahoma.

CHARLES N. BAXTER and JAMES M. DEARBORN, Confederate literature. A list of books and newspapers, maps, music, and miscellaneous matter printed in the south during the Confederacy, now in the Boston athenæum. Boston athenæum: Publications of the Robert Charles Billings fund (vol.v): Boston 1917. pp.[iv].214. [1250.]

RALPH LESLIE RUSK, The literature of the middle western frontier. Columbia university studies in english and comparative literature: New York 1925. pp.xiii.457+vi.419. [2500.]
sets out the works published in the middle west.

RICHARD BARKSDALE HARWELL, Confederate belles-lettres. A bibliography and a finding list of the fiction, poetry, drama, songsters, and miscellaneous literature published in the confederate states of America. Heartman's historical series (no.56): Hattiesburg 1941. pp.79 [128.]
199 copies printed.

DOROTHY RITTER RUSSO and THELMA LOIS SULLIVAN, Bibliographical studies of seven authors of Crawfordville, Indiana: Lew and Susan Wallace,

Maurice and Will Thompson, Mary Hannah and Caroline Virginia Krout, and Meredith Nicholson. Indiana historical society: Indianapolis 1952. pp.xv.486. [400.]

NORTHWEST books. Inland empire council of teachers of english: Portland, Or. [1942]. pp.356. [3500.]

a preliminary duplicated edition was issued in 1933.

— First supplement. Bibliography of northwest writing, 1942–1947. Lincoln, Neb. 1949. pp.xiv.278. [3500.]

FREDERICK R[ICHMOND] GOFF, The first decade of the federal act of copyright, 1790–1800. Library of Congress: Washington 1951. pp.28. [80.]

consists in large part of a list of Pennsylvania registrations.

CLYDE H[ULL] CANTRELL and WALTON R. PATRICK, Southern literary culture. A bibliography of masters' and doctors' theses. [University, Ala. 1955]. pp.xiv.124. [2529.]*

HAZEL E. MILLS, *ed.* Who's who among Pacific northwest authors. Pacific northwest library association: Reference section: [Bozeman, Mont.] 1957. ff.114. [1000.]*

WILLIAM COYLE, *ed.* Ohio authors and their

books . . . 1796–1950. Cleveland &c. [1962]. pp.xxiv.741. [10,000.]

6. *Translations &c.*

H[ERMAN] H[ERBERT] B[ERNARD] MEYER, List of references on immigrant literature in the United States (german-yiddish). Library of Congress: [Washington 1916]. ff.3. [75.]

STURGIS E[LLENO] LEAVITT, Hispano-american literature in the United States. A bibliography of translations and criticisms.

[1837–1931]. Harvard council on hispano-american studies: Cambridge 1932. pp.x. 54. [1108.]

reprinted in vol.ii of Bibliographies of the belles-lettres of hispanic America *(Cambridge [1947]).*

1932–1934. Chapel Hill 1935. pp.[iv].21. [351.]

a supplement for 1935 appeared in Hispania *(May 1936), xix.201–210.*

JOHN E[UGENE] ENGLEKIRK, Bibliografía de obras norteamericanas on traducción española. México 1944. pp.119. [1250.]

FÉLIX ANSERMOZ-DUBOIS, L'interprétation française de la littérature américaine d'entre deux guerres (1919–1939). Essai de bibliographie. Lausanne 1944. pp.xviii.237. [1100.]

VERZEICHNIS amerikanischer bücher in deutscher übersetzung erschienen in Deutschland seit 1945. Frankfurt a.M. 1951. pp.63. [1000.]

— [another edition]. United States information agency: 1954. pp.[ii].294. [2500.]*

— — Nachtrag. Embassy of the United States of America: Bonn.*

[i]. 1954–1956. pp.[v].108. [750.]
ii. 1956–1958. pp.[v].93. [650.]
iii. 1958–1960. pp.[v].114. [1000.]

LIVRES américains traduits en français et livres français sur les États-Unis d'Amérique. (Répertoire d'ouvrages disponibles en librairie). Services américains d'information: Paris [1951]. pp.xiv. 125. [1498.]

— [another edition]. Bibliothèque Benjamin Franklin: 1956. pp.85. [1200.]

— — Additif. 1958. pp.44. [500.]

GLENORA W. BROWN and DEMING B[RONSON] BROWN, A guide to soviet russian translations of american literature. Columbia slavic studies: New York 1954. pp.243. [1678.]

[JOSÉ PORTER *and others*], Exposición de libros

españoles antiguos y modernos referentes a los Estados Unidos y de obras de autores norteamericanos traducidas y publicadas en España. Instituto de estudios norteamericanos and Casa americana: [Barcelona 1956]. pp.80. [1300.]

[ILO REMER *and others*]. A provisional bibliography of United States books translated into spanish. Library of Congress: Hispanic foundation: Bibliographical series (no.3): Washington 1957. pp.ix.471. [4500.]*

[ILO REMER *and others*]. A provisional bibliography of United States books translated into portuguese. Library of Congress: Hispanic foundation: Bibliographical series (no.2): Washington 1957. pp.[ii].vii.182. [1750.]*

RUDOLPH GJELSNESS, The american book in Mexico. A bibliography of books by authors of the United States of America published in Mexico, 1952–55. University of Michigan: Department of library science: Studies (no.4): Ann Arbor 1957. pp.xii.92. [650.]*

AMERICAN books in arabic translation. Catalog. United States information service: [Beirut] 1958. pp.[ii].110. [300.]*

RICHARD MUMMENDEY, Die schöne literatur der Vereinigten Staaten von Amerika in deutschen übersetzungen. Eine bibliographie. Bonner beiträge zur bibliotheks- und bücherkunde (vol.5): Bonn 1961. pp.ix.199. [1887.]

also published by the Bibliographical society of the university of Virginia.

SPANISH and portuguese translations of United States books, 1955–1962. A bibliography. Library of Congress: Hispanic foundation: Bibliographic series (no.8): Washington 1963. pp.xv.506. [5000.]*

7. *Writings on american literature*

LIST of references on the development of american literature. Library of Congress: Washington 1914. ff.10. [125.]*

WILLIAM B. CAIRNS, British criticisms of american writings. University of Wisconsin: Studies in language and literature (no.1 &c.): Madison.

1783–1815. . . . (no.1): 1918. pp.97. [250.]
1815–1833. . . . (no.14): 1922, pp.319. [750.]

A LIST of some books on current american literature. Library of Congress: Washington 1930. ff.6. [50.]*

A SELECTED list of recent books on current american literature. Library of Congress: Washington 1938. ff.10. [91.]*

REVIEW. A quarterly guide to professional reviews. [Chicago].

i. 1941. Edited by Louis Kaplan, Clarence S[ibley] Paine. pp.100. [4213.]

ii. 1942. pp.98. [3946.]

iii. 1943. pp.27.26.30.37. [3433.]

iv. 1944. pp.27.22.20.42. [3199.]

no more published.

FRANK G. NELSON, A guide to american literature. Oslo 1946. pp.36. [350.]

LEWIS [GASTON] LEARY, Articles on american literature appearing in current periodicals, 1920–1945. Duke university publications: Durham, N. C. 1947. pp.x.337. [6500.]

— — [another edition]. Articles . . . 1900–1950. pp.xv.437. [14,000.]

HOWARD MUMFORD JONES, Guide to american literature and its backgrounds since 1890. Cambridge [Mass.] 1953. pp.[iii].151. [1500.]

— — Second edition. 1959. pp.[ix].192. [2000.]

JAMES LESLIE WOODRESS, Dissertations in american literature 1891–1955. Durham, N.C. 1957. pp.x.100. [3000.]

— — 1891–1961. 1962. pp.xii.138. [3000.]

CLARENCE [LOUIS FRANK] GOHDES, Bibliographical guide to the study of the literature of the U. S. A. Durham, N.C. [1959]. pp.xii.ff.102. [1000.]

— — Second edition. [1963]. pp.xiii.125. [1500.]

[KLAUS LANZINGER and GEORGE STEINER], Ausgewähltes verzeichnis der im bereich der Österreichischen nationalbibliothek, der österreichischen universitäten und der amerikanischen bibliotheken in Österreich vorhandenen zeitschriften, jahrbücher und nachschlagewerke zum studium der amerikanischen literatur und des amerikanischen englisch. Universität: Amerika-institut: [Innsbruck 1959]. pp.[iii].38. [90.]

THOMAS H. JOHNSON [*and others*], Literary history of the United States. New York 1962. pp. xxiv.790+iii–xix.268. [25,000.]

8. *Miscellaneous*

SUBSCRIPTION books bulletin. Vol.1 [–24]. American library association: Chicago 1930–1953.
merged into The Booklist.

NELLIE MAE LOMBARD, Looking at life through american literature. Los Angeles county: Office of superintendent of schools: Los Angeles 1940. ff.[vi].88. [1250.]*

— — [another edition]. Stanford university [1944]. pp.x.91. [1750.]

DAVID [MARTIN], American catholic convert authors. A bio-bibliography. Detroit [1944]. pp.[ii].259. [1750.]

AMERICAN books once in the collections of the British museum but destroyed by enemy action during World war II. 1946. pp.[276.] [7500.]

consists of slips reproduced by photostat.

OLGA PERAGALLO, Italian-american authors and their contribution to american literature. . . . Edited by Anita Peragallo. New York [1949]. pp.iii–xii.3–242. [500.]

KATHERINE H. DAVIDSON, Preliminary inventory of the records of the Federal writers' project, Works projects administration, 1935–44. National archives: Preliminary inventories (no.69): Washington 1953. pp.v.15. [large number.]*

EDITIONS for the Armed services . . . with the complete list of . . . books published for american armed forces overseas. New York [1948]. pp.139. [1324.]

Addison, Joseph.

A. R. HUMPHREYS, Steele, Addison and their periodical essays. British council: British book news: Bibliographical series of supplements (no.109): 1959. pp.46. [100.]

Ade, George.

DOROTHY RITTER RUSSO, A bibliography of George Ade, 1866–1944. Indiana historical society: Committee on bibliography (no.2): Indianapolis 1947. pp.xv.314. [2000.]

Ainsworth, William Harrison.

HAROLD LOCKE, A bibliographical catalogue of the published novels and ballads of William Harrison Ainsworth. 1925. pp.68. [200.]

Alcott, Louisa May.

LUCIE GULLIVER, Louisa May Alcott. A bibliography. Boston 1932. pp.[iv].71. [500.]

Aldrich, Thomas Bailey.

ANNETTE PERSIS WARD, Annotated list of the works of Thomas Bailey Aldrich. Church of the ascension: Parish library: New York 1907. pp.[7].

FREDERIC FAIRCHILD SHERMAN, A check list of first editions of the works of Thomas Bailey Aldrich. New York 1921. pp.15. [70.]
125 copies privately printed.

Aldridge, James.

I. M. LEVIDOVA, Джеймс Олдридж. Всесоюзная государственная библиотека иностранной литературы: Прогрессивные писатели стран капитализма: Москва 1953. pp.16. [50.]

Aldington, Richard.

ALISTER KERSHAW, A bibliography of the works of Richard Aldington from 1915 to 1948. 1950. pp.ix.57. [231.]

Aldiss, Brian Wilson.

MARGARET MANSON, Item forty-three. Brian W. Aldiss: a bibliography 1954–1962. [Wisbech 1963]. pp.[24]. [122.]
500 copies printed.

Allingham, William.

P[ATRICK] S[ARSFIELD] O'HEGARTY, A bibliography of William Allingham. Dublin 1945. pp.12. [30.]

35 copies privately printed.

Anderson, Isabel Weld Perkins.

[ELEANOR WILBUR POMEROY], Bibliography of the works of Isabel Anderson. . . . Third edition. Medford, Mass. 1935. pp.[18]. [50.]

Anderson, Maxwell.

MARTHA COX, Maxwell Anderson bibliography. University of Virginia: Bibliographical society: Charlottesville 1958. pp.[viii].119. [1250.]*

Anderson, Sherwood.

EUGENE P[AUL] SHEEHY and KENNETH A. LOHF, Sherwood Anderson. A bibliography. Los Gatos 1960. pp.vii–125. [845.]

Anstey, F., *pseud.*

MARTIN JOHN TURNER, A bibliography of the works of F. Anstey [Thomas Anstey Guthrie]. 1931. pp.vii.44. [55.]

150 copies privately printed.

Arnold, Matthew.

THOMAS BURNETT SMART, The bibliography of Matthew Arnold. 1892. pp.x.90. [540.]

KENNETH ALLOTT, Matthew Arnold. British book news: Bibliographical series of supplements: 1955. pp.44. [100.]

Aron, Willy.

A BIBLIOGRAPHICAL essay, containing an account of books . . . written by Willy Aron. German-jewish publishers of America: New York 1935. pp.10. [40.]

Ascham, Roger.

SAMUEL A[ARON] and DOROTHY R. TANNENBAUM, Roger Ascham. (A concise bibliography). Elizabethan bibliographies (no.37): New York 1946. ff.[iii].27. [356.]*

Ashe, William Willard.

WILLIAM A[DAMS] DAYTON, William Willard Ashe. [Washington 1936]. pp.22. [167.]*

Ashkenazi, Touvia.

A BIBLIOGRAPHICAL list of writings, 1922–1954, with published biographical notes. Washington 1954. ff.2–103. [150.]*

Atwood, Wallace Walter.

THE BIBLIOGRAPHY of Wallace W. Atwood, Clark university: Library: Publications (vol.ix. no.6): Worcester, Mass. 1945. pp.16. [223.]

Auden, Wystan Hugh.

RICHARD HOGGART, W. H. Auden. British council: British book news: Bibliographical series of supplements (no.93): 1957. pp.48. [75.]

— — New edition. 1961. pp.48. [100.]

EDWARD CALLAN, An annotated check list of the works of W. H. Auden. Denver [1958]. pp.26. [307.]

Austen, Jane.

PROVISIONAL list of Jane Austen's letters, showing the location of the originals, or (if these are untraced) the best authority for the text. Revised proof. [*s.l.* 1925]. pp.17. [138.]

[SIR] GEOFFREY [LANGDON] KEYNES, Jane Austen: a bibliography. 1929. pp.xxvi.289. [371.]

R[OBERT] W[ILLIAM] CHAPMAN, Jane Austen. A critical bibliography. Oxford 1953. pp.viii.62. [180.]

— — Second edition. 1955. pp.viii.63. [180.]

Austin, Mary Hunter.

JOSEPH GAER, *ed.* Mary Austin, bibliography and biographical data. California literary research: Monograph (no.2): [*s.l.* 1934]. ff.[i].43. [400.]*

Bacon, Francis, viscount St. Albans.

W[ILLIAM] H. WYMAN, The bibliography of the Bacon-Shakespeare literature. [Cincinnati 1882]. pp.8. [63.]

privately printed.

— — [another edition]. Bibliography of the Bacon-Shakespeare controversy. Cincinnati. 1884. pp.124. [255.]

BACON. British museum: Catalogue of printed books: 1884. pp.[ii].coll.24. [500.]

G[EORGE] WALTER STEEVES, Francis Bacon. A sketch of his life, works and literary remains;

chiefly from a bibliographical point of view. 1910. pp.xv.232. [250.]

PARKER WOODWARD, Francis Bacon's works (acknowledged, vizarded, or suspected). 1912. pp.[iii].105. [200.]

A SELECTED list of references on Francis Bacon, viscount St. Albans (1561–1626). Library of Congress: Washington 1930. ff.5. [48.]*

R[EGINALD] W[ALTER] GIBSON, Francis Bacon: a bibliography of his works and of Baconiana to the year 1750. Oxford 1950. pp.xvii.369. [700.]

a duplicated supplement appeared in 1959.

J. MAX PATRICK, Francis Bacon. British council: British book news: Bibliographical series of supplements (no.131): 1961. pp.43. [100.]

CATALOGUE of exhibition organised by the St. Albans city council . . . to commemorate the 400th anniversary of the birth of Francis Bacon. [St. Albans 1961]. pp.24. [54.]

Bagehot, Walter.

NORMAN ST JOHN-STEVAS, Walter Bagehot. British council: British book news: Bibliographical series: 1963. pp.42. [100.]

Baretti, Giuseppi.

LUIGI PICCIONI, Bibliografia analitica di Giuseppi Baretti. Torino 1942. pp.iii–xi.151. [332.]

Baring, Maurice.

LESLIE CHAUNDY, A bibliography of the first editions of the works of Maurice Baring. 1925. pp.48. [75.]

250 copies printed.

Barlow, Joel.

JOEL BARLOW, 1754–1812: a bibliographical list. Library of Congress: Washington 1935. ff.26. [186.]*

Barrie, sir James Matthew.

HERBERT GARLAND, A bibliography of the writings of sir James Matthew Barrie. 1928. pp.146. [900.]

B[RADLEY] D[WYANE] CUTLER, Sir James M. Barrie. A bibliography. New York 1931. pp.[ix]. 242. [125.]

ANDREW BLOCK, Sir J. M. Barrie. First editions and their values (no.3): 1933. pp.xvi.48. [75.]

500 copies printed.

Barton, Bruce.

A LIST of writings by Bruce Barton. Library of Congress: Washington 1937. ff.12. [233.]*

Baum, Lyman Frank.

JOAN BAUM and ROLAND [ORVIL] BAUGHMAN, L. Frank Baum. . . . An exhibition of his published writings. Columbia university: Libraries: New York 1956. pp.50. [108.]

Baxter, Richard.

ALEXANDER B[ALLOCH] GROSART, Annotated list of the writings of Richard Baxter. Edinburgh [printed] 1868. pp.56. [200.]

150 copies privately printed; issued as an appendix to Grosart's edition of Baxter's What we must do to be saved.

[STEPHEN W. LAWLEY], Private collection of Baxter's works. Exeter [printed] 1895. ff.20. [120.]

A[RNOLD] G[WYNNE] MATTHEWS, The works of Richard Baxter. An annotated list. Oxted, Surrey [1932]. pp.52. [200.]

ROGER THOMAS, The Baxter treatises: a catalogue of the Richard Baxter papers (other than letters) in Dr. William's library. Dr. Williams's library: Occasional paper (no.8): 1959. pp.31 [400.]

Baynes, Norman Hepburn.

[J. M. H.], An address presented to Norman Hepburn Baynes, with a bibliography of his writings. Oxford 1942. pp.38. [275.]

privately printed.

Beaumont, Francis.

ALFRED CLAGHORN POTTER, A bibliography of Beaumont and Fletcher. Library of Harvard university: Bibliographical contributions (no.39): Cambridge, Mass. 1890. pp.20. [425.]

SAMUEL A[ARON] TANNENBAUM, Beaumont & Fletcher. (A concise bibliography). Elizabethan bibliographies (no.3): New York 1938. pp.x.94. [1628.]

300 copies printed.

— — Supplement . . . by S. A. Tannenbaum and Dorothy R. Tannenbaum. ff.[ii].23. [280.]*

Beazley, John Davidson.

A LIST of the published writings of John Davidson Beazley. Oxford 1951. pp.27. [200.]

Bede, the venerable.

CHARLES W[ILLIAM] JONES, Bedae pseudepigrapha: scientific writings falsely attributed to Bede. Ithaca, N.Y. 1939. pp.xv.154. [225.]

M[AX] L[UDWIG] W[OLFRAM] LAISTNER and H[ENRY] H[ALL] KING, A hand-list of Bede manuscripts. Ithaca. N.Y. 1943. pp.x.168. [1000.]

Beecher, Henry Ward.

LIST of references relating to Henry Ward Beecher. Library of Congress: Washington 1946. ff.6. [61.]*

Beeching, Henry Charles.

SIR SIDNEY LEE, Henry Charles Beeching. . . . Annotated bibliography by Geor[ge] A[rthur] Stephen. Norwich 1919. pp.12. [100.]

Beerbohm, sir Max.

A[LBERT] E[UGENE] GALLATIN, Sir Max Beerbohm. Bibliographical notes. Cambridge, Mass. 1944. pp.xiii.127. [400.]
400 copies printed.

SIR MAX BEERBOHM, Notes on a exhibition of books, caricatures, manuscripts [&c.]. Grolier club: New York [1944]. pp.9. [50.]
16 copies printed.

A[LBERT]E[UGENE] GALLATIN and L[ESLIE] M[AHIN] OLIVER, A bibliography of the works of Max Beerbohm. Soho bibliographies (no.3): 1952. pp.x.60. [150.]

Belloc, Joseph Hilaire Pierre.

PATRICK CAHILL, The english first editions of Hilaire Belloc. A chronological catalogue. 1953. pp.52. [153.]
privately printed.

RENÉE HAYNES, Hilaire Belloc. British council: British book news: Bibliographical series of supplements (no.35): 1953. pp.35. [150.]

Bennett, Enoch Arnold.

FRANK SWINNERTON, Arnold Bennett. British council: British book news: Bibliographical series of supplements: 1950. pp.32. [100.]

Bentham, Jeremy.

[THOMAS WHITTAKER], Report on the Bentham mss. at University college, London. [1892]. pp.20. [2000.]

[AGNES C. DOYLE], Jeremy Bentham. Selected bibliography. [Boston 1899]. pp.[8]. [100.]

— SIEGWART, Benthams werke und ihre publikation. Bern 1910. pp.119. [125.]

A[LEXANDER] TAYLOR MILNE, Catalogue of the manuscripts of Jeremy Bentham in the library of University college, London. 1937. pp.iii–xi.147. [2000.]*

— — Second edition. 1962. pp.xi.104. [large number.]

almost all copies of the first edition were destroyed by enemy action.

Bentley, Richard.

A[UGUSTUS] T[HEODORE] BARTHOLOMEW and J[OHN] W[ILLIS] CLARK, Hand-list of the works of

Richard Bentley, D.D.; and of the pamphlets written in his defence or against him. Under revision. Cambridge 1906. pp.16. [190.]
privately printed.

— — [second edition]. Richard Bentley, D.D. A bibliography of his works and of all the literature called forth by his acts or his writings. By A. T. Bartholomew. Cambridge 1908. pp.xix.115. [310.]

Beowulf.

CHAUNCEY B[REWSTER] TINKER, The translations of Beowulf. A critical bibliography. Yale studies in english (vol.xvi): New York 1903. pp.151. [50.]

Berkeley, George.

H[ERMAN] RALPH MEAD, A bibliography of George Berkeley, bishop of Cloyne. University of California: Library bulletin (no.17): Berkeley 1910. pp.46. [550.]

T[HOMAS] E[DMUND] JESSOP, A bibliography of George Berkeley. . . . With an inventory of Berkeley's manuscript remains by A[rthur] A[ston] Luce. 1934. 1934. pp.xvi.100. [800.]

CATALOGUE of manuscripts, books and Berkeleiana exhibited in the library of Trinity college. [Dublin 1953]. pp.37. [130.]

T. E. JESSOP, George Berkeley. British council: British book news: Bibliographical series of supplements (no.113): 1959. pp.36. [75.]

Bernard, Richard.

JOHN INGLE DREDGE, The writings of Richard Bernard. . . . A bibliography. Horncastle 1890. ff.[i].25. [60.]

50 copies privately printed.

— — [another issue]. Lincolnshire bibliographies (no.1): 1890. pp.[iii].25.[60.]

75 copies privately printed.

Besant, Annie.

THEODORE [DEODATUS NATHANIEL] BESTERMAN, A bibliography of Annie Besant. 1924. pp.114. [448.]

the British museum pressmarks are added in ms. to one of the copies in that library.

Bierce, Ambrose Gwinett.

VINCENT STARRETT, Ambrose Bierce. A bibliography. The centaur bibliographies [of modern

american authors] (no.9): Philadelphia 1929. pp. 117. [150.]
300 copies printed.

JOSEPH GAER, *ed.* Ambrose Gwinett Bierce. Bibliography and biographical data. California literary research: Monograph (no.4): [*s.l.* 1935]. ff.102. [1250.]*

Blake, William.

CATALOGUE of books, engravings, water-colors & sketches by William Blake exhibited at the Grolier club. New York 1905. pp.xix.147. [89.]

WILLIAM BLAKE. An exhibition. Grolier club: New York 1919. pp.vii.12. [40.]

[SIR] GEOFFREY [LANGDON] KEYNES, A bibliography of William Blake. Grolier club: New York 1921. pp.xvi.517. [775.]
250 copies printed.

— — [another edition of one section]. William Blake's illuminated books. A census compiled by G. Keynes and Edwin Wolf 2nd. Grolier club: New York 1953. pp.xviii.124. [200.]

[ELIZABETH MONGAN and EDWIN WOLF], William Blake, 1757–1827. A descriptive catalogue of an exhibition . . . selected from collections in the

United States. Museum of art: Philadelphia 1939. pp.xxi.175. [283.]

KATHLEEN RAINE, William Blake. British council: British book news: Bibliographical series of supplements: 1950. pp.40. [100.]

KERRISON PRESTON, William Blake 1757–1827. Notes for a catalogue of the Blake library at the Georgian house, Merstham. Cambridge 1960 [1961]. pp.47. [500.]

— — Second edition. 1962. pp.48. [500.]

GERALD EADES BENTLEY and MARTIN K. NURMI, A Blake bibliography. Annotated lists of works, studies, and Blakeana. Minneapolis [1964]. pp. xix.393.

Blake, William Phipps.

PUBLISHED writings of William Phipps Blake. [Tucson] 1910. pp.[21]. [250.]

Blakey, Roy Gillispie, ***and*** **Gladys McAlpin Campbell Blakey.**

LISTS of publications of Roy G. Blakey and Gladys Blakey. University of Minnesota: [Minneapolis] 1948. ff.[i].14. [175.]*

Bloodgood, Joseph Colt.

EDITH HOLT BLOODGOOD and VICTOR H. LONG, Index to the writings of Joseph Colt Bloodgood. Baltimore [1936]. pp.[ii].51. [750.]

Bloxam, Matthew Holbeche.

[M. H. BLOXAM], A fardel of antiquarian papers and books, written by Matthew Holbeche Bloxam. Rugby [printed] [1888]. pp.vi.44. [210.]
privately printed.

Blunden, Edmund.

ALEC M. HARDIE, Edmund Blunden. British council: British book news: Bibliographical series of supplements (no.93 [*sic*, 92]): 1958. pp.43. [75.]

Bobbin, Tim.

J[OHN] P[OTTER] BRISCOE, The literature of Tim Bobbin; being a chronologically arranged list of the various editions of the writings of 'Tim Bobbin'. Manchester 1872. pp.12. [43.]

Bode, Boyd H.

RUTH E[STHER] SEEGER, Writtings by and about Boyd H. Bode. A bibliography. Ohio state university: College of education: Columbus 1951. pp.[iii].15. [200].

Bolt, Richard Arthur.

PUBLICATIONS and addresses, including editorials and radio script . . . 1900–1955. University of California: School of public health: Berkeley 1955. pp.[iv].72. [719.]

Boreman, Thomas.

WILBUR MACY STONE, The Gigantick histories of Thomas Boreman. Portland, Maine, 1933. pp. 43. [10.]

250 copies printed.

Borrow, George Henry.

THOMAS J[AMES] WISE, A bibliography of the writings in prose and verse of George Henry Borrow. 1914. pp.xxii.319. [100.]

100 copies privately printed.

Boswell, James.

FREDERICK ALBERT POTTLE, The literary career of James Boswell, esq., being the bibliographical materials for a life of Boswell. Oxford 1929. pp. xliv.335. [750.]

CATALOGUE of an exhibition of the private papers of James Boswell from Malahide castle. Grolier club: New York 1931. pp.[216]. [581.]

FREDERICK A[LBERT] and MARION S. POTTLE, The private papers of James Boswell from Malahide castle in the collection of lt.-colonel Ralph Heyward Isham. A catalogue. 1931. pp.xxv.[231]. [698.]

415 copies printed.

CLAUDE COLLEER ABBOTT, A catalogue of papers relating to Boswell, Johnson & sir William Forbes found at Fettercairn house, a residence of . . . lord Clinton. Oxford 1936. pp.xxvii.258. [1607.]

P. A. W. COLLINS, James Boswell. British council: British book news: Bibliographical series of supplements (no.77): 1956. pp.48. [150.]

Boyd, Julian P.

JULIAN P. BOYD. A bibliographical record. Princeton 1950. pp.xiv.62. [250.]

Boyle, Robert.

CATALOGUS librorum tractatuumq; philosophicorum, a dom. Roberto Boyle . . . scriptorum . . . cui accessit librorum etiam theologicorum, qui ab eodem authore exarati sunt, nomenclatura. Londini 1688. pp.29. [100.]

— [another edition]. Catalogue of the philosophical books and tracts, written by the honourable Robert Boyle esq.; . . . to which is added a catalogue of the theological books, written by the same author. 1689. pp.22. [100.]

— [another edition]. 1690. pp.[ii].14. [100.]

— [another edition]. 1692. pp.[ii].17. [100.]

J[OHN] F[ARQUHAR] F[ULTON], The honourable Robert Boyle. A handlist of his works. 1932. ff.[13]. [280.]

[JOHN] F[ARQUHAR] FULTON, A bibliography of the honourable Robert Boyle. Oxford [1932]. pp.172. [450.]

— — Addenda to a bibliography of the honourable Robert Boyle. Oxford [1934]. ff.[i]. 27. [50.]

printed on one side of the leaf; further addenda by the author appear in the Oxford bibliographical society publications *(1948), new ser.i.33–38.*

— — Second edition. 1961. pp.[ii].xxvi.219. [750.]

Brackenridge, Hugh Henry.

CHARLES F[REDERICK] HEARTMAN, A bibliography of the writings of Hugh Henry Brackenridge prior to 1825. Heartman's historical series (no.29): New York 1917. pp.37. [42.]

59 copies printed.

Bradford, Gamaliel.

HELEN F. BRADFORD, Index to publications of Gamaliel Bradford VI, 1863–1932. [Wellesley, Mass. 1942]. pp.20. [250.]

Brainerd, writers named.

[ERASTUS BRAINERD], Bibliography of the name of Brainerd. Seattle, Wash. 1904. pp.18. [200.]

privately printed.

Brande, William Thomas.

A[LAN] J[OHN] HORNE, A bibliography of William Thomas Brande (1788–1866). Royal institution: Library: 1955. ff.[ii].17. [115.]*

Brennan, Christopher John.

WALTER W. STONE and HUGH ANDERSON, Christopher John Brennan. A comprehensive bibliography. Studies in australian bibliography (no.9): Cremorne 1959. pp.[iii].55. [500.]*

150 copies printed.

Brent, Charles Henry.

BISHOP Charles Henry Brent. A register of his papers in the Library of Congress. Washington 1959. pp.[ii].10. [3000.]*

Breton, Nicholas.

SAMUEL A[ARON] TANNENBAUM and DOROTHY R. TANNENBAUM, Nicholas Breton. (A concise bibliography). Elizabethan bibliographies (no.39): New York 1947 [on cover: 1946]. ff.[ii].i.34. [521.]*

Brice, Andrew.

T[HOMAS] N[ADAULD] BRUSHFIELD, The life and bibliography of Andrew Brice. 1888. pp.64. [12.]

privately printed.

Bridges, Robert Seymour.

[LESLIE CHAUNDY and EUAN HILLHOUSE METHVEN COX], Robert Bridges. Bibliographies of modern authors (no.1): 1921. pp.[iii].8. [75.]

GEORGE L. MCKAY, A bibliography of Robert Bridges. New York &c. 1933. pp.xii.215. [160.]

JOHN SPARROW, Robert Bridges. British council: British book news: Bibliographical series of supplements (no.147): 1962. pp.36. [50.]

Brigham, Albert Perry.

BIBLIOGRAPHY of Albert Perry Brigham. [Hamilton, N.Y. 1929]. pp.[7]. [80.]

Bright, Timothie.

[SIR] GEOFFREY [LANGDON] KEYNES, Dr. Timothie Bright... with a bibliography of his writings. Wellcome historical medical library: Publications (n.s. i): 1962. pp.[vii].47. [23.]

Brinton, Daniel Garrison.

[D. G. BRINTON], Analytical catalogue of works and scientific articles by Daniel G. Brinton. [Media, Pa. 1892]. pp.14. [125.]

— — [another edition]. [1894]. pp.16. [150.]

[D. G. BRINTON], Bibliography. Daniel G. Brinton. [Media 1898]. pp.9. [150.]

[D. G. BRINTON], A record of study in aboriginal american languages by Daniel G. Brinton. Media, Pa. 1898. pp.24. [71.]
privately printed.

STEWART CULIN, Bibliography of Daniel G. Brinton. Philadelphia 1900. pp.28. [250.]

Brontë, family of.

BUTLER WOOD, A bibliography of the works of the Brontë family, including a list of books and magazine articles on the Brontës. Brontë society: Publications (Part i): Bradford [printed] 1895. pp.34. [500.]

— — Supplement. . . . (Part vi): 1897. pp.19. [300.]

JOHN ALBERT GREEN, Catalogue of the Gleave Brontë collection at the Moss Side free library, Manchester. Moss Side 1907. pp.32. [243.]

— — List of additions, 1907–1916. 1916. pp. [ii].24. [200.]

THOMAS J[AMES] WISE, A bibliography of the writings in prose and verse of the members of the Brontë family. 1917. pp.xv.259. [150.]

100 copies privately printed.

J. ALEX[ANDER] SYMINGTON, Catalogue of the museum & library. The Brontë society: Haworth 1927. pp.3–200. [1000.]

[T. J. WISE], A Brontë library. A catalogue of printed books, manuscripts and autograph letters by the members of the Brontë family collected by Thomas James Wise. 1929. pp.xxiii.84. [150.]

30 copies privately printed.

CATALOGUE of the Bonnell collection in the Brontë parsonage museum. Brontë society: Haworth 1932. pp.90. [500.]

M. L. PARRISH, Victorian lady novelists. George Eliot, mrs. Gaskell, the Brontë sisters. First editions in the library at Dormy house, Pine Valley, New Jersey. 1933. pp.xii.160. [Brontë: 20.]

PHYLLIS BENTLEY, The Brontë sisters. British council: British book news: Bibliographical series of supplements: 1950. pp.44. [50.]

I. M. LEVIDOVA, Шарлотта Бронте. Всесоюзная государственная библиотека иностранной литературы: Писатели зарубежных стран: Москва 1956. pp.26. [80.]

Brooke, Rupert Chawner.

[SIR] GEOFFREY [LANGDON] KEYNES, A bibliography of Rupert Brooke. Soho bibliographies (vol.iv): 1954. pp.147. [400.]

— — Second edition. 1959. pp.158. [500.]

Brooks, Charles Timothy

FANNIE MAE ELLIOTT and LUCY CLARK, Charles Timothy Brooks. A checklist of printed and manuscript works . . . in the library of the university of Virginia. Charlottesville 1960. pp.9.

Brougham and Vaux, Henry Peter Brougham, 1st baron.

[RALPH THOMAS], A bibliographical list of lord Brougham's publications. . . . By the author of 'The handbook of fictitious names'. 1873. pp.[ii]. 24. [134.]

100 copies privately printed.

Brown, Thomas Edward.

WILLIAM CUBBON, Thomas Edward Brown, the manx poet. Manx museum: Douglas 1934. pp.64. [500.]

Browne, John Ross.

E[MMA] MIRIAM LONE, Check-list of first editions of the works of John Ross Browne. New York 1930. pp.16. [52.]

Browne, sir Thomas.

W[ILLIAM] A[LEXANDER] GREENHILL, Browne's Religio medici. [1883]. pp.6.7 [*soc*, 9]. [50.]

a copy with ms. additions is in the Bodleian library; the last leaf, wrongly numbered 7, is a supplement.

CHARLES WILLIAMS, The bibliography of the 'Religio medici'. Norwich 1905. pp.[ii].16. [60.]

— — Second edition. A Bibliography [&c.].

1907. pp.22. [66.]
privately printed.

T. K. MONRO, Notes on the early editions of sir Thomas Browne. Glasgow 1923. pp.19. [50.]

[SIR] GEOFFREY [LANGDON] KEYNES, A bibliography of sir Thomas Browne. Cambridge 1924. pp.xii.256. [510.]
500 copies printed.

GEO[RGE] A[RTHUR] STEPHEN, Sir Thomas Browne. A catalogue of works by and about sir Thomas Browne in the Norwich public libraries. Norfolk celebrities (no.iii): Norwich 1925. pp.[6]. [75.]

OLIVIER LEROY, A french bibliography of sir Thomas Browne. 1931. pp.[ix].97. [138.]
225 copies printed.

PETER GREEN, Sir Thomas Browne. British council: British book news: Bibliographical series of supplements (no.108): 1959. pp.39. [75.]

Browning, Elizabeth Barrett *and* **Robert.**

FREDERICK J[AMES] FURNIVALL, A bibliography of Robert Browning from 1833 to 1881. . . . Third edition. Browning society: Papers (no.2): 1881. pp.21–170. [750.]

the earlier editions appeared in the same year.

H[ARRY] BUXTON FORMAN, Elizabeth Barrett Browning and her scarcer books. A bio-bibliographical note. [Ashley library]: 1896. pp.31. [8.]
30 copies privately printed.

THOMAS J[AMES] WISE, A complete bibliography of the writings in prose and verse of Robert Browning. 1897. pp.9.245. [1500.]
50 copies privately printed.

CATALOGUE of the library of the Browning society. Boston 1897. pp.47. [500.]

SPECIAL reading list, Robert Browning. Free public library: Worcester, Mass. 1899. pp.8. [150.]

THOMAS J[AMES] WISE, A bibliography of the writings in prose and verse of Elizabeth Barrett Browning. 1918. pp.xv.251. [155.]
100 copies privately printed.

ROBERT BROWNING, 1812–1889. A list of books and of references to periodicals in the Brooklyn public library. Brooklyn 1912. pp.48. [350.]

AURELIA E[MMA] BROOKS, Browningiana in Baylor university. Baylor university: Baylor bulletin (vol.xxiv, nos.5–6): Waco, Tex. 1921. pp. vii.405. [10,000.]

[T. J. WISE], A Browning library. A catalogue of printed books, manuscripts and autograph letters by Robert Browning and Elizabeth Barrett Browning collected by Thomas James Wise. 1929. pp.xxxii.128. [200.]

30 copies privately printed.

A. JOSEPH ARMSTRONG, Browning the world over, being Baylor university Browning interests . . . Browning's international influence and . . . a bibliography of foreign Browningiana. Baylor university: Baylor bulletin (vol.xxxvi, nos.3–4): Waco, Tex. 1933. pp.5–190. [1000.]

META FÖRSTER and WINIFRED M. ZAPPE, Robert Browning bibliographie. Halle 1939. pp.35. [750.]

ROBERT BROWNING. An excerpt from the General catalogue of printed books in the British museum. 1939. pp.[ii].coll.28. [450.]

LESLIE NATHAN BROUGHTON, CLARK SUTHERLAND NORTHUP and ROBERT PEARSALL, Robert Browning: a bibliography, 1830–1950. Cornell studies in english (vol.xxxix): Ithaca, N.Y. 1953. pp.xv.446. [8341.]

LIVIO JANNATTONI, Elizabeth Barrett Browning,

con un saggio di bibliografia italiana. Amor di libro (vol.13): [Firenze 1953]. pp.53.

JOHN BRYSON, Robert Browning. British council: British book news: Bibliographical series of supplements (no.106): 1959. pp.44. [100.]

[LACHLAN PHIL KELLEY], Elizabeth Barrett Browning 1806–1861 . . . Catalogue of the centenary exhibition. Public library: St Marylebone [1961]. pp.22.[iv]. [144.]

Bryant, Thomas.

J. H. E. WINSTON, Bibliography of the published writings (1856–1902) of Thomas Bryant. Bibliographies of Guy's men (no.6): 1915. pp.24. [350.]

Bryant, William Cullen.

HENRY C[ADY] STURGES, Chronologies of the life and writings of William Cullen Bryant, with a bibliography of his works in prose and verse. New York 1903. pp.cxxvii. [250.]

Brydges, sir Egerton Samuel.

A CATALOGUE of all the works printed at the private press at Lee priory. . . . [A catalogue of other works written, or edited, by sir Egerton Brydges]. Geneva 1824. pp.10. [101.]

Buchan, John, first baron Tweedsmuir.

ARCHIBALD HANNA, John Buchan, 1875–1940. A bibliography. Hamden, Conn. 1953. pp.xi.135. [800.]

[B. C. WILMOT], Checklist of works by and about John Buchan in the John Buchan collection. Queen's university [Kingston, Ont.]: Douglas library: Boston 1961. pp.[v].38.24. [334.]*

Buckman, S. S.

[S. S. BUCKMAN], Thirty years' contributions by S. S. Buckman. Cheltenham [printed] [1907]. pp.7. [100.]

Bunyan, John.

[GEORGE HENRY MOORE and SAMUEL AUSTIN ALLIBONE], Bunyan's Pilgrim's progress, &c. Lenox library: Contributions to a catalogue (no.iv): New York 1879. pp.49. [427.]

FRANK MOTT HARRISON, A bibliography of the works of John Bunyan. Bibliographical society: Transactions: Supplement (no.vi): 1932. pp. xxviii.83. [57.]

CATALOGUE of the John Bunyan library (Frank Mott Harrison collection). Public library: Bedford 1938. pp.44. [800.]

JOHN BUNYAN. An excerpt from the General catalogue of printed books in the British museum. 1939. pp.[ii].coll.74. [1000.]

FRANK MOTT HARRISON, A handlist of editions of the first part of the Pilgrim's progress. [Hove] 1941. ff.[115]. [1750.]

25 copies reproduced from typewriting, in the main on one side of the leaf.

CYRIL HARGREAVES and M[ARGARET] GREENSHIELDS, Catalogue of the Bunyan meeting library and museum. Bedford 1955. pp.44. [600.]

HENRI A[NTOINE] TALON, John Bunyan. British book news: Bibliographical series of supplements (no.73): 1956. pp.40. [100.]

Burke, Edmund.

FRANCESCO CORDASCO, Edmund Burke: a handlist of critical notices & studies. 18th century bibliographical pamphlets (no.12): New York 1950. pp. 12. [106.]

THOMAS W[ELLSTED] COPELAND and MILTON SHUMWAY SMITH, A check list of the correspondence of Edmund Burke. Index society: [New York] 1955. pp.xviii.481. [5000.]

T. E. UTLEY, Edmund Burke. British council:

British book news: Bibliographical series of supplements (no.87): 1957. pp.36. [75.]

Burke, Oliver Joseph.

JAMES COLEMAN, Bibliography of Thomas O'Neill Russell [and Oliver Joseph Burke]. Bibliographical society of Ireland; Bibliographies of irish writers series: Dublin [printed] 1919. pp.4. [Burke: 7.]

Burney, Fanny.

FANNY BURNEY (Madame Frances d'Arblay), 1752–1840. A bibliographical list. Library of Congress: [Washington] 1930. ff.15. [188.]*

Burns, Robert.

WILLIAM GOWANS, A bibliography of all the american editions of the work of Robert Burns, and books relating to him or his works. New York 1859 [1870]. pp.214. [50.]

reproduced (?) from handwriting on paper dated 1868; the copy or original inspected is in the Library of Congress.

[EDWARD CLEMENTS BIGMORE], Descriptive list of a collection of original manuscript poems by

Robert Burns. 1861. pp.24. [100.]

a list of the mss. sold by auction in May 1861; 25 copies privately printed.

CATALOGUE of manuscripts, ... in Burns' monument museum. Edinburgh 1864. pp.11. [30.]

[JAMES M'KIE], Bibliotheca burnsiana. Life and works of Burns: title pages and imprints of the various editions in the private library of James M'Kie. Kilmarnock 1866. pp.43. [478.]

not limited to editions in M'Kie's library.

[JAMES M'KIE], Bibliotheca burnsiana. Life and works of Burns: list of the various editions in the private library of James M'Kie. Kilmarnock 1866. pp.12. [115.]

[JAMES M'KIE], The Burns calendar: a manual of Burnsiana. Kilmarnock 1874. pp.[81]. [1000.]

[JAMES GIBSON], The bibliography of Robert Burns. Kilmarnock 1881. pp.xi.340. [1500.]

CATALOGUE of the McKie Burnsiana library. Kilmarnock 1883. pp.iv.64. [600.]

—— [another edition]. Compiled by David Sneddon. 1909. pp.vi.170. [1250.]

[WILLIAM BROWN], List of documentary relics of Robert Burns exhibited by William Brown.

Edinburgh bibliographical society: Papers (session 1891–1892, no.i): Edinburgh 1891. pp.2. [17.]

CATALOGUE of the Burns exhibition. Royal Glasgow institute of fine arts: Glasgow 1896. pp. 502. [1750.]

[JAMES DUNCAN and ALEXANDER BALHARRIE], Catalogue of the Burns, Scott and Shakespeare exhibition, . . . from the collection of A[lexander] C[rawford] Lamb. Victoria galleries: Dundee [1896]. pp.115. [500.]

MEMORIAL catalogue of the Burns exhibition held in the galleries of the Royal Glasgow institute of the fine arts . . . 1896. Glasgow 1898. pp.xxiv. 506. [1750.]

W[ILLIAM] CRAIBE ANGUS, The printed works of Robert Burns. A bibliography in outline. Glasgow 1899. pp.xl.134. [1000.]

60 copies privately printed.

J[AMES] C[AMERON] EWING, A selected list of editions of the works of Robert Burns, and of books upon his life & writings. 1899. pp.14. [50.]

50 copies printed.

JAMES CAMERON EWING, Bibliography of Robert Burns, 1759–1796. Edinburgh 1909. pp.[v].16. [18.]

36 copies privately printed.

JAMES GRANT WILSON, American editions of Robert Burns's poems. New York 1900. pp.[3]. [140.]

JAMES CAMERON EWING, Robert Burns's letters addressed to Clarinda: Edinburgh 1921. pp.[v]. 26. [30.]
[50 copies] privately printed.

LIST of selected books by and on Robert Burns. Public libraries: Glasgow 1926. pp.8. [70.]

DAVIDSON COOK, Burns manuscripts in the Honresfield collection of sir Alfred James Law. Glasgow 1928. pp.35. [29.]
100 copies privately printed.

THE BURNS COTTAGE, Alloway. Catalogue of manuscripts . . . in the cottage and the museum. Ayr 1937. pp.54. [250.]

ROBERT BURNS's literary correspondents, 1786–1796. A chronological list of letters addressed to the poet. [Edited by James Cameron Ewing]. Burns monument trustees: Alloway 1938. pp.xv. ff.28.pp.29–48. [300.]

ROBERT BURNS. An excerpt from the General catalogue of printed books in the British museum. 1939. pp.[ii].coll.40. [750.]

LIST of selected books by and on Robert Burns. Corporation public libraries: Glasgow 1950. pp. 12. [100.]

MARION E. WALDEN, A selected list of songs of Burns. Corporation public librarie): Glasgow 1950. pp.12. [100.]

NANCIE CAMPBELL, The Murison Burns collection. Public libraries: Dunfermline 1953. pp.140. [1500.]

ROBERT BURNS exhibition. Manuscripts, letters, books and relics of the poet, his family and associates. Arranged . . . in Lady Stair's house. Edinburgh 1953. pp.17. [120.]

the relics are not listed.

WILLIAM AITKENHEAD, A selected list of books on and by Robert Burns. Public libraries: Glasgow [1956]. pp.15. [125.]

DAVID DAICHES, Robert Burns. British book news: Bibliographical series of supplements (no.88): 1957. pp.39. [35.]

[ANTHONY G. HEPBURN, A. HUNTER and D. R. YOUNGER], Catalogue of Robert Burns collection in the Mitchell library. Glasgow 1959. pp.vii.217. [3500.]

A SPLORE in honor of the two-hundredth anniversary of the birth of Robert Burns. University of Texas: Humanities research center: [Austin 1959]. pp.15. [76.]

G[EORGE] ROSS ROY, Robert Burns. An exhibition in the Noble H. Getchell library. University of Nevada: Bibliographical series (no.1): [Reno] 1962. pp.27. [113.]

Burroughs, Edgar Rice.

BRADFORD M. DAY, Edgar Rice Burroughs biblio. Woodhaven, N.Y. 1956. pp.29.*

— — [another edition]. Edgar Rice Burroughs. A bibliography. [1962]. pp.47.*

HENRY HARDY HEINS, A golden anniversary bibliography of Edgar Rice Burroughs. Albany 1962. pp.122. [300.]*

— — Complete edition. West Kingston, R.I. 1964. pp.[ii].418. [1000.]*

Burton, sir Richard Francis.

NORMAN M[OSLEY] PENZER, An annotated bibliography of sir Richard Francis Burton. 1923. pp. xvi.351. [500.]

500 copies printed.

Burton, Robert.

PAUL JORDAN-SMITH, Bibliographia burtoniana. A study of the Anatomy of melancholy, with a bibliography of Burton's writings. Stanford university 1931. pp.xiv.120. [130.]

Burton, Theodore Elijah.

THEODORE ELIJAH BURTON, 1851–1929: a bibliographical list. Library of Congress: Washington 1932. ff.21. [215.]*

Bury, John Bagnell.

NORMAN H[EPBURN] BAYNES, A bibliography of the works of J. B. Bury. Cambridge 1929. pp.[v]. 184. [369.]

Butler, Howard Crosby.

HOWARD SEAVOY LEACH, A bibliography of Howard Crosby Butler, 1872–1922. Princeton 1924. pp.24. [125.]

Butler, Nicholas Murray.

MILTON HALSEY THOMAS, Bibliography of Nicholas Murray Butler. New York 1934. pp.ix. 439. [3500.]

Butler, Samuel, 1835–1902.

HENRY FESTING JONES and A[UGUSTUS] T[HEODORE] BARTHOLOMEW, The Samuel Butler collection at Saint John's college, Cambridge. A catalogue. Cambridge 1921. pp.ix.60. [500.]

A. J. HOPPÉ, A bibliography of the writings of Samuel Butler. [1925]. pp.xvi.184. [225.]
500 copies printed.

[CARROLL A. WILSON], Catalogue of the collection of Samuel Butler . . . in the Chapin library. Williams college. Portland, Me. 1945. pp.vii.35. [250.]

STANLEY B. HARKNESS, The career of Samuel Butler, 1835–1902. A bibliography. 1955. pp.154. [1500.]

Bynner, Edwin Lassetter.

LUCY T[RIMBLE] CLARK, The Barrett library Edwin Lassetter Bynner. A checklist of printed and manuscript works . . . in the library of the university of Virginia. Charlottesville 1961. pp. [vii].9. [40.]*

Byrne, Donn.

WINTHROP WETHERBEE, (Brian Oswald) Donn Byrne. A bibliography. Boston 1938. pp.25. [300.]

WINTHROP WETHERBEE, Donn Byrne. A bibliography. Public library: New York 1949. pp.xi.89. [500.]

Byron, George Gordon Noel, 6th baron.

[PAUL LE BRETHON], Catalogue des ouvrages de Byron conservés au Département des imprimés. Bibliothèque nationale: 1905. pp.[ii].coll.34. [266.]

[HARRY NELSON GAY], List of the first thousand works acquired by the Keats-Shelley memorial, Rome. 1910. pp.115. [Byron: 150.]

[—] List of the second thousand works . . . 1913. pp.99. [150.]

SHORT bibliographies of Wordsworth, Coleridge, Byron, Shelley, Keats. English association: Leaflet (no.23): 1912. pp.13. [250.]

O. INTZE, Byroniana. Birmingham [printed] 1914. pp.24. [175.]

CATALOGUE of the Byron exhibition. Mechanics' institution: Nottingham 1915. pp.42. [400.]

R[EGINALD] H[ARVEY] GRIFFITH and H[OWARD] M[UMFORD] JONES, A descriptive catalogue of an exhibition of manuscripts and first editions of

Lord Byron held in the library of the university of Texas. Austin 1924. pp.xiii.106. [200.]
307 copies printed.

BIBLIOGRAPHICAL catalogue of first editions, proof copies & manuscripts of books by lord Byron exhibited . . . by the First edition club. 1925. pp.xvii.97. [75.]
500 copies printed.

[T. J. WISE], A Byron library. A catalogue of printed books, manuscripts and autograph letters by George Gordon Noel, baron Byron, collected by Thomas James Wise. 1928. pp.xxvii.146. [250.]
30 copies privately printed.

THOMAS JAMES WISE, A bibliography of the writings in verse and prose of George Gordon Noel, lord Byron. 1932–1933. pp.xxvii.142+xxxii.134. [500.]
180 copies privately printed.

THE ROE-BYRON collection, Newstead abbey. Compiled by the staff of Nottingham public libraries. Corporation of Nottingham: 1937. pp. 188. [750.]
the collection of Herbert Charles Roe is now the property of the corporation.

[RICARDO QUINTANA], Byron, 1788–1938. An exhibition at the Huntington library. San Marino 1938. pp.16. [32.]

BYRON. An excerpt from the General catalogue of printed books in the British museum. 1939. pp.[ii].coll.78. [1000.]

WILLIS W. PRATT, Lord Byron and his circle. A calendar of manuscripts in the university of Texas library. Austin 1947. pp.60. [293.]

HERBERT READ, Byron. British council: British book news: Bibliographical series of supplements: 1950. pp.43. [150.]

Cabell, James Branch.

MERLE [DE VORE] JOHNSON, A bibliographic check-list of the works of James Branch Cabell, 1904–1921. New York 1921. pp.28. [25.]

250 copies printed.

GUY HOLT, A bibliography of the writings of James Branch Cabell. The centaur bibliographies [of modern american authors] (no.3): Philadelphia 1924. pp.73. [200.]

500 copies printed.

I[SIDORE] R[OSENBAUM] BRUSSEL, A bibliography of the writings of James Branch Cabell. The centaur bibliographies [of modern american authors] (no.11): Philadelphia 1932. pp.132. [300.]

350 copies printed.

FRANCES JOAN BREWER, James Branch Cabell. A bibliography of his writings, biography and criticism. Charlottesville, Va. 1957. pp.[ii].206. [533.]

—— Part II. Notes on the Cabell collections at the university of Virginia, by Matthew J. Bruscoli. 1957. pp.178. [750.]

Caldwell, Charles.

EMMET FIELD HORINE, Biographical sketch and guide to the writings of Charles Caldwell. Brooks, Ky. 1960. pp.x.157. [293.]

300 copies printed.

Calvert, George Henry.

HAMILTON B[ULLOCK] TOMPKINS, Bibliography of the works of George Henry Calvert. Newport, R.I. 1900. pp.15. [70.]

30 copies printed.

Campbell, Joseph.

P[ATRICK] S[ARSFIELD] O'HEGARTY, A bibliography of Joseph Campbell (SeosAṁ mAċ CAṫṁAoil)]. Dublin 1940. pp.6. [10.]

35 copies privately printed.

Campbell, William Wallace.

PUBLISHED writings of William Wallace Campbell. [*s.l. c.*1900]. pp.9. [224.]

Carlyle, Thomas.

[RICHARD HERNE SHEPHERD], The bibliography of Carlyle. [1881]. pp.xi.60. [200.]

MARY EUNICE WEAD, A catalogue of the dr. Samuel A[rthur] Jones Carlyle collection, with additions from the general library. University of Michigan: General library: Publications (no.1): Ann Arbor 1919. pp.xi.119. [600.]

ISAAC WATSON DYER, A bibliography of Thomas Carlyle's writing and ana. Portland, Me. 1928. pp.xii.587. [7500.]

Carman, William Bliss.

FREDERIC FAIRCHILD SHERMAN, A check list of first editions of the works of Bliss Carman. New York 1915. pp.16. [88.]
75 copies privately printed.

WILLIAM INGLIS MORSE, Bliss Carman: bibliography, letters, fugitive verses and other data. Windham, Conn. 1941. pp.86. [200.]

Carpenter, Edward.

A BIBLIOGRAPHY of the writings of Edward Carpenter. 1916. pp.14. [225.]
150 copies printed.

A BIBLIOGRAPHY of Edward Carpenter. A catalogue of books, manuscripts, letters, etc. by and about Edward Carpenter in . . . the Central library. Sheffield 1949. pp.ix.83. [1000.]

Carpenter, William Henry.

A BIBLIOGRAPHY of the writings of William Henry Carpenter. New York 1925. pp.[viii].19. [150.]
privately printed.

Carroll, Lewis [*pseud.* **Charles Lutwidge Dodgson].**

SIDNEY HERBERT WILLIAMS, A bibliography of the writings of Lewis Carroll. 1924. pp.xiii.142. [220.]

A LIST of writings of Lewis Carroll . . . collected by M[orris] L[ongstreth] Parrish. [New York] 1928. pp.viii.148 [*sic,* 152]. [300.]

— A supplementary list. 1933. pp.ix.116. [200.]

66 copies privately printed; a copy in the British museum contains manuscript notes by Maurice Buxton Forman.

SIDNEY HERBERT WILLIAMS and FALCONER MADAN, A handbook of the literature of the rev. C. L. Dodgson. 1931. pp.xxiv.336. [873.]

— — Supplement . . . by F. Madan. 1935. pp.24. [50.]

CATALOGUE of an exhibition at Columbia university to commemorate the one hundredth anniversary of the birth of Lewis Carroll. New York 1932. pp.[ix].155. [415.]

FALCONER MADAN, The Lewis Carroll centenary in London, 1932. Including a catalogue of the exhibition. 1932. pp.xix.140. [643.]

400 copies printed.

—— Additional exhibits. pp.[10]. [48.]

FLORA V. LIVINGSTON, The Harcourt Amory collection of Lewis Carroll in the Harvard college library. Cambridge, Mass. 1932. pp.xiii.190. [500.]

65 copies privately printed.

OLIVER WILSON, Alice's adventures in wonderland. A survey of the important editions and issues. Rara libri (no.1): Seattle 1937. pp.ix.42. [20.]

DEREK HUDSON, Lewis Carroll. British council: British book news: Bibliographical series of supplements (no.96): 1958. pp.38. [100.]

THE PARODIES of Lewis Carroll and their originals. Catalogue of an exhibition. Florida state university: Library: [Tallahassee] 1960. ff.14. [15.]*

Carson, Hampton Lawrence.

BIBLIOGRAPHY of Hampton Carson, esq. of the Philadelphia bar, 1874–1913. Philadelphia 1913. pp.32. [200.]

Carver, Jonathan.

JOHN THOMAS LEE, A bibliography of Carver's Travels. State historical society of Wisconsin: Madison 1910. pp.[ii].143–183. [34.]

Cary, Joyce.

WALTER ALLEN, Joyce Cary. British council: British book news: Bibliographical series of supplements (no.41): 1953. pp.32. [25.]

Casavis, Jakosos Nikolaos.

J. N. CASAVIS, My writings, 1913–1937. New York 1938. pp.16. [783.]

Casement, sir Roger David.

P[ATRICK] S[ARSFIELD] O'HEGARTY, A bibliography of Roger Casement. Dublin 1949. pp.6. [15.]

40 copies privately printed.

Castlemon, Harry. [*pseud.* **Charles Austin Fosdick.**]

JACOB [NATHANIEL] BLANCK, Harry Castlemon, boys' own author: appreciation and bibliography. New York 1941. pp.xviii.142. [100.]

Caxton, William.

WILLIAM CAXTON. An excerpt from the General catalogue of printed books of the British museum. 1926. pp.8. [175.]

Chalmers, Thomas.

HUGH WATT, The published writings of dr. Thomas Chalmers (1780–1847). A descriptive list. Edinburgh 1943. pp.86. [208.]

privately printed.

Channing, Edward.

GEORGE W[ASHINGTON] ROBINSON, Bibliography of Edward Channing. Cambridge [Mass.] 1932. pp.20. [125.]

Chapman, George.

SAMUEL A[ARON] TANNENBAUM, George Chapman. (A concise bibliography). Elizabethan bibliographies (no.5): New York 1938. pp.viii.40. [668.]

— — Supplement. By S. A. and Dorothy R. Tannenbaum. 1946. ff.17. [177.]*

Chapman, Herman Haupt.

BIBLIOGRAPHY of Herman Haupt Chapman. [New Haven] 1943. ff.[i].17. [400.]*

— [another edition]. [1956]. ff.[i].40. [1000.]*

Chapman, John.

A LIST of references on John Chapman, 1775–1847, 'Johnny Appleseed'. Library of Congress: Washington 1935. ff.4. [43.]*

ROBERT PRICE, John Chapman. A bibliography of 'Johnny Appleseed' in american history, literature and folklore. Paterson, N.J. 1944. pp.vi.40. [500.]

Chatterton, Thomas.

W[ILBERFORCE] R[OSS] BARKER, A catalogue of the autograph manuscripts and other remains of Thomas Chatterton. Museum of antiquities: Bristol 1907. pp.54. [41.]

[SIR] FRANCIS ADAMS HYETT and [WILLIAM] BAZELEY, Chattertoniana, being a classified catalogue of . . . printed matter, relating to the life or works of Chatterton, or to the Rowley controversy. Gloucester 1914. pp.44. [450.]

E[DWARD] R[OBERT] NORRIS MATHEWS, Thomas Chatterton. A bibliography. Public libraries. Reference library: [Bristol 1916]. pp.28. [500.]

Chaucer, Geoffrey.

ALBERT S[TANBOROUGH] COOK, A bibliography of Chaucer. University of California: [*s.l.* 1886]. pp.[ii].40. [3000.]

[A. H.] JOHN KOCH, The chronology of Chaucer's writings. Chaucer society [2nd ser., vol.xxvii]: 1890. pp.[ii].iv.89. [1000.]

SOPHIE JEWETT, Chaucer: outlines and references. 1896. pp.32. [400.]

[—] — [third edition]. English literature: Chaucer, Selected references. [Revised by Martha Hale Shackford]. Wellesley college: Department of english literature: [Wellesley, Mass.] 1918. pp. [iv].56. [1250.]

WALTER W[ILLIAM] SKEAT, The Chaucer canon. With a discussion of the works associated with the name of Geoffrey Chaucer. Oxford 1900. pp.xi. 168. [100.]

AN EXHIBITION of original and other editions . . . of Geoffrey Chaucer. Grolier club: New York 1900. pp.45. [38.]

ELEANOR PRESCOTT HAMMOND, Chaucer: a bibliographical manual. New York 1908. pp.x.579. [2500.]

— — [supplement]. Dudley David Griffith, A bibliography of Chaucer, 1908–1924. University of Washington: Publications in language and literature (vol.iv, [no.1]): Seattle 1926. pp.148. [1650.]

— — [supplement]. Willard E[dgar] Martin, A Chaucer bibliography, 1925–1933. Duke university: Durham, N.C. 1935. pp.xii.97. [1000.]

— — — [another edition]. Bibliography . . . 1908–1953. . . . (vol.13): 1955. pp.xviii.398. [5000.]*

CAROLINE F[RANCES] E[LEANOR] SPURGEON, Chaucer devant la critique en Angleterre et en France depuis son temps jusqu'à nos jours. 1911. pp.ix.422. [400.]

CHAUCER. An excerpt from the General catalogue of printed books in the British museum. 1943. pp.[ii].coll.46. [650.]

NEVILL COGHILL, Geoffrey Chaucer. British council: British book news: Bibliographical series of supplements (no.79): 1956. pp.67. [100.]

CHARLES MUSCATINE, The book of Geoffrey Chaucer. An account of . . . Chaucer's works . . . to modern times. Book club of California: [San Francisco] 1963. pp.[v].64. [30.]

Chauncy, Charles.

[PAUL LEICESTER FORD], Bibliotheca chaunciana.

A list of writings of Charles Chauncy. Elzevir club series (no.6): Brooklyn, N.Y. 1884. ff.[v].31. [88.]

10 copies privately printed.

Cheever, Ezekiel.

JOHN T. HASSAM, Ezekiel Cheever. The Cheever mss. and letters. Boston 1903. pp.13. [50.]

Chesterfield, Philip Dormer Stanhope, fourth earl of.

SIDNEY L[EWIS] GULICK, A Chesterfield bibliography to 1800. Bibliographical society of America: Papers (vol.xxix): Chicago 1935. pp. 114. [181.]

Chesterton, Gilbert Keith.

CHRISTOPHER HOLLIS, G. K. Chesterton. British council: British book news: Bibliographical series of supplements: 1950. pp.32. [100.]

JOHN SULLIVAN, G. K. Chesterton. A bibliography. [1958]. pp.208. [1000.]

Childers, Robert Erskine.

P[ATRICK] S[ARSFIELD] O'HEGARTY, A bibliography of the books of Erskine Childers. Dublin 1948. pp.6. [13.]

40 copies privately printed.

Churchill, sir Winston Leonard Spencer.

BENJAMIN FRANKLIN, Winston Churchill. An exhibition. University of Pennsylvania: University museum: Philadelphia [1951]. pp.55. [Churchill: 100.]

JOHN CONNELL [*pseud.* JOHN HENRY ROBERTSON], Winston Churchill. British book news: Bibliographical series of supplements (no.80): 1956. pp. 43. [60.]

BERNARD J[AMES] FARMER, Bibliography of the work of sir Winston S. Churchill. 1958. pp.[iii]. 62.[v]. [750.]

privately reproduced from typewriting; a copy in the British museum contains manuscript additions.

FREDERICK WOODS, A bibliography of the works of sir Winston Churchill. 1963. pp.340. [1000.]

Ciardi, John.

WILLIAM WHITE, John Ciardi bibliography. Detroit 1959. pp.67. [500.]

Clarke, sir Fred.

MARY CLARKE FIELD, A provisional bibliography of the works of sir Fred Clarke. University of London: Institute of education: Education libraries bulletin (supplement 4): 1962. pp.[ii].19. [200.]*

Clough, Arthur Hugh.

BIBLIOGRAPHY of Arthur Hugh Clough. Library of Congress: Washington 1922. ff.7. [86.]*

Cobbett, William.

MORRIS LEONARD PEARL, William Cobbett. A bibliographical account of his life and times. 1953. pp.vii.266. [289.]

Cohen, Morris Raphael.

MARTIN A. KUHN, Morris Raphael Cohen: a bibliography. City college of New York: Library: Lancaster, Pa. &c. [1957]. pp.[iii].44. [300.]

Cohn, William.

[GEORGE HILL], Bibliography. Dr. William Cohn in honour of his seventy-fifth birthday. Oxford [1955]. pp.39. [232.]

Cole, George Watson.

[G. W. COLE], A list of the printed productions of George Watson Cole, 1870–1936. With comments by friends. Bulletin of bibliography: Pamphlets (no.33): Boston 1936. pp.28. [100.]

Cole, John.

[J. TAYLOR], Catalogue of a unique collection of historical mss., antiquarian & topographical publications, of John Cole . . . collected by John Taylor. [Northampton 1883]. pp.9. [100.]
printed on one side of the leaf.

Coleman, John Winston.

A BIBLIOGRAPHY of the writings of John Winston Coleman, jr. Lexington, Ky. 1953. pp.[iii].19. [50.]

Colenso, John William.

B. D. FRASER, John William Colenso. A bibliography. University of Cape Town: School of librarianship: [Capetown] 1952. pp.[iii].iv.26. [187.]*

Coleridge, Samuel Taylor.

W[ILLIAM] HALE WHITE, A description of the Wordsworth & Coleridge manuscripts in the possession of mr. T. Norton Longman. 1897. pp.vi.72. [25.]

RICHARD HERNE SHEPHERD, The bibliography of Coleridge. A bibliographical list . . . of the . . . writings in verse and prose of Samuel Taylor Coleridge. . . . Revised . . . by W. F. Prideaux. 1900. pp.xi.95. [250.]

JOHN LOUIS HANEY, A bibliography of Samuel Taylor Coleridge. Philadelphia 1903. pp.xv.144. [1250.]

330 copies privately printed.

SHORT bibliographies of Wordsworth, Coleridge, Byron, Shelley, Keats. English association: Leaflet (no.23): 1912. pp.13. [250.]

THOMAS J[AMES] WISE, A bibliography of the writings in prose and verse of Samuel Taylor Coleridge. Bibliographical society: 1913. pp.xii. 316. [500.]

— — Supplement. Coleridgeiana. 1919. pp.40. [60.]

500 copies printed.

[T. J. WISE], Two lake poets. A catalogue of printed books, manuscripts and autograph letters by William Wordsworth and Samuel Taylor Coleridge collected by Thomas James Wise. 1927. pp.xxiii.136. [250.]

30 copies privately printed.

S. T. COLERIDGE. . . . Centenary exhibition organised by the University college of the south west of England. Royal Albert memorial museum: Exeter 1934. pp.20. [48.]

VIRGINIA WADLOW KENNEDY and MARY NEILL

BARTON, Samuel Taylor Coleridge. A selected bibliography of the best available editions of his writings, of biographies and criticisms of him, and of references showing his relations with contemporaries. Enoch Pratt free library: Baltimore 1935. pp.vii.151. [1250.]

COLERIDGE. An excerpt from the General catalogue of printed books in the British museum. 1947. pp.[ii].coll.36. [500.]

KATHLEEN RAINE, Coleridge. British council: British book news: Bibliographical series of supplements (no.43): 1953. pp.44. [100.]

Collier, John Payne.

HENRY B[ENJAMIN] WHEATLEY, Notes on the life of John Payne Collier; with a complete list of his works, and an account of such Shakespeare documents as are believed to be spurious. 1884. pp.67. [125.]

Collins, Michael.

P[ATRICK] S[ARSFIELD] O'HEGARTY, A bibliography of the books of Arthur Griffith, Michael Collins and Kevin O'Higgins. Dublin 1937. [Collins: 2.]

30 copies privately printed; interleaved.

Collins, Wilkie.

M[ORRIS] L[ONGSTRETH] PARRISH and ELIZABETH V. MILLER, Wilkie Collins and Charles Reade. First editions (with a few exceptions) in the library at Dormy house. 1940. pp.x.356. [Collins: 150.]
150 copies printed.

FRANCESCO CORDASCO and KENNETH W. SCOTT, Wilkie Collins and Charles Reade: a bibliography of critical notices and studies. Brooklyn 1949. pp.vi.7. [104.]

Collins, William.

THOMAS GRAY, . . . and William Collins, Winchester college library: [Winchester 1947]. pp.11. [Collins: 35.]

Collitz, Klara Hechtenberg.

[K. H. COLLITZ], A bibliography of the writings of Klara H. Collitz. [Oxford] 1938. pp.26. [37.]
privately printed.

Congreve, William.

BONAMY DOBRÉE, William Congreve. British council: British book news: Bibliographical series: 1963. pp.35. [50.]

Conrad, Joseph [Teodor Józef Konrad Korzeniowski .

THOMAS J[AMES] WISE, A bibliography of the writings of Joseph Conrad. 1920. pp.111. [82.]
150 copies privately printed.
— — Second edition. 1921. pp.xv.128. [100.]
170 copies privately printed.

[T. J. WISE], A Conrad library. A catalogue of printed books, manuscripts and autograph letters by Joseph Conrad (Téodor Josef Konrad Korzeniowski) collected by Thomas James Wise. 1928. pp.xix.67. [150.]
25 copies privately printed.

[G. T. KEATING], A Conrad memorial library. The collection of George T. Keating. Garden Cisy, N.Y. 1929. pp.xvi.451. [304.]

RICHARD CURLE, A handlist of the various books, pamphlets, prefaces, notes . . . written about Joseph Conrad by Richard Curle. Brookville, Penn. 1932. pp.[iii].23. [66.]

JOSEPH CONRAD, 1857–1924. Library of Congress: Washington 1932. ff.3. [25.]*

OLIVER WARNER, Joseph Conrad. British council: British book news: Bibliographical series of supplements: 1950. pp.39. [100.]

[JANINA ZABIELSKA], Joseph Conrad (1857–1924). Polish library: 1956. pp.[iii].24. [202.]*
an exhibition catalogue.

KENNETH A. LOHF and EUGENE P[AUL] SHEEHY, Joseph Conrad at mid-century. Editions and studies 1895–1955. Minneapolis [1957]. pp.xiii.114. [1275.]

Conwell, Russell Herman.

MAURICE F[ALCOLM] TAUBER, Russell Herman Conwell, 1843–1925. A bibliography. Temple university: Library: Philadelphia 1935. ff.[ii].ii.40. [183.]*

Conybeare, Frederick Cornwallis.

LOUIS MARIÈS, Frederick Cornwallis Conybeare. . . . Notice biographique et bibliographie critique. 1926. pp.[iv].155. [275.]

Cooke, John Esten.

OSCAR WEGELIN, A bibliography of the separate writings of John Esten Cooke. Heartman's historical series (no.43): Metuchen, N.J. 1925. pp.20. [34.]
51 copies printed.

— — Second edition, revised . . . (no.44): Hattiesburg 1941. pp.13. [34.]
99 copies printed.

Coolidge, John Calvin.

ADDRESSES of president Coolidge issued as government documents. Library of Congress: Washington 1930. ff.5. [69.]*

Coomaraswamy, Ananda K.

S. DURAI-RĀJA-ṢIṄGAM. Coomaraswamiana. A bibliography of gurudev Ananda K. Coomaraswamy's writings. [Kuantan 1949]. pp.5. [200.]*

Cooper, C. Purton.

THE POLITICAL and party publications of mr. Purton Cooper during the last seven years. 1857. pp.13. [55.]

Cooper, James Fenimore.

ROBERT E[RNEST] SPILLER and PHILIP C[ONKLIN] BLACKBURN, A descriptive bibliography of the writings of James Fenimore Cooper. New York 1934. pp.xiii.260. [250.]

Cooper, Peter.

C[HARLES] SUMNER SPALDING, Peter Cooper. A critical bibliography of his life and works. Public library: New York 1941. pp.25. [300.]

Coppard, Alfred Edgar.

JACOB SCHWARTZ, The writings of Alfred Edgar Coppard. A bibliography. 1931. pp.[vii].73. [150.]

GILBERT H. FABES, The first editions of A. E. Coppard, A. P. Herbert and Charles Morgan. 1933. pp.[vi].154. [Coppard: 38.]

Cowper, William.

LODOWICK [CHARLES] HARTLEY, William Cowper. A list of critical and bibliographical studies published from 1895 to 1949. North Carolina state college of agriculture and engineering: State college record (vol.xlix. no.6): Raleigh 1950. pp. 24. [241.]

LODWICK [CHARLES] HARTLEY, William Cowper. The continuing revaluation. An essay and a bibliography of cowperian studies from 1895 to 1960. Chapel Hill 1960. pp.xi.159. [1028.]

NORMAN NICHOLSON, William Cowper. British council: British book news: Bibliographical series of supplements (no.121): 1960. pp.40. [75.]

NORMA RUSSELL, A bibliography of William Cowper to 1837. Oxford bibliographical society:

Publications (n.s., vol.12): Oxford 1963. pp. xxvi.339. [531.]

also issued independently.

Cox, Watty.

SÉAMUS Ó CASAIDE, Watty Cox and his publications. Bibliographical society of Ireland (vol.v, no.2): Dublin 1935. pp.[ii].19–38. [30.]

reissued in 1954.

Crabbe, George.

R. L. BRETT, George Crabbe. British council: British book news: Bibliographical series of supplements (no.75): 1956. pp.43. [50.]

Crane, Hart.

H[ERSHEL] D. ROWE, Hart Crane. A bibliography. Denver [1955]. pp.30. [400.]

Crane, Stephen.

VINCENT STARRETT, Stephen Crane. A bibliography. Centaur bibliographies of modern american authors (no.2): Philadelphia 1923. pp.46. [70.]

300 copies printed.

B[ENJAMIN] J[OHN] R[EEMAN] STOLPER, Stephen Crane. A list of his writings and articles about him. Stephen Crane association: Newark, N.J. 1930. pp.30. [350.]

AMES W[ILLIAM] WILLIAMS and VINCENT STARRETT, Stephen Crane. A bibliography. Glendale, Cal. 1948. pp.xi.161. [750.]

HERBERT FAULKNER WEST, A Stephen Crane collection. Dartmouth college: Library: Hanover, N.H. 1948. pp.xiii.31. [113.]

350 copies printed; a catalogue of the George Matthew Adams collection at Dartmouth.

JOAN H. BAUM, Stephen Crane (1871–1900). An exhibition of his writings . . . with appendixes contributing to the bibliography of Stephen Crane. Columbia university: Library: New York [1956]. pp.[ii].61. [296.]

Crane, Thomas Frederick.

[T. F. CRANE], Bibliography of Thomas Frederick Crane. [Ithaca 1925]. pp.42. [334.]

Crashaw, Richard.

MARGARET WILLY, Three metaphysical poets. British council: British book news: Bibliographical series of supplements (no.134): 1961. pp.48. [150.]

Crowne, John.

GEORGE PARKER WINSHIP, The first Harvard playwright. A bibliography of the restoration dramatist John Crowne. Cambridge [Mass.] 1922. pp.22. [48.]

Cummings, Edward Estlin.

PAUL LAUTER, E. C. Cummings. Index to first lines and bibliography of works by and about the poet. Denver 1955. ff.[ii].44. [1000.]*

— — Supplement one, compiled by P. Lauter and S. V. Baum. [1955]. ff.3. [20.]*

GEORGE J[AMES] FIRMAGE, E. E. Cummings: a bibliography. Middletown, Conn. [1960]. pp.ix. 130. [393.]

Curle, Richard.

RICHARD CURLE, A handlist of the various books, pamphlets, prefaces, notes . . . written about Joseph Conrad by Richard Curle. Brookville, Penn. 1932. pp.[iii].23. [66.]

Cushing, Harvey Williams.

A BIBLIOGRAPHY of the writings of Harvey Cushing. Prepared . . . by the Harvey Cushing society. Menasha [printed] 1939. pp.iii–xv.110. [658.]

Cynewulf.

KARL JANSEN, Die schriften zu und über Cynewulf. Bonn 1907. pp.[iii].54. [419.]

— — [another edition]. Die Cynewulf-forschung von ihren anfängen bis zur gegenwart.

Bonner beiträge zur Anglistik (no.xxiv): Bonn 1908. pp.[ii].127. [422.]

additions by Carleton Brown appear in Englische Studien *(1921), xlv.98–101.*

Daniel, Samuel.

SAMUEL A[ARON] TANNENBAUM, Samuel Daniel. (A concise bibliography). Elizabethan bibliographies (no.25): New York 1942. pp.ix.37. [673.]

300 copies printed.

Davis, Richard Harding.

HENRY COLE QUIMBY, Richard Harding Davis. A bibliography. New York 1924. pp.xxi.294. [1000.]

Deacon, Thomas.

CHARLES W[ILLIAM] SUTTON, The writings of 'doctor' Thomas Deacon of Manchester, 1718 to 1747, and of his opponent the rev. J. Owen, of Rochdale. A bibliographical note. Manchester 1879. pp.18. [25.]

De Beer, sir Gavin Rylands.

PUBLICATIONS 1922–1952. Saint Ives 1952. pp.16. [200.]

— 1952–1960. [1961]. pp.17–24. [100.]

120 copies privately printed.

De Costa, Benjamin Franklin.

[B. F. DE COSTA], The titles of fifty-five separately printed works. New York 1899. pp.[11]. [55.]
privately printed.

Defoe, Daniel.

[MACHELL STACE], An alphabetical catalogue of an extensive collection of the writings of Daniel De Foe; and of the different publications for and against that very extraordinary writer. 1829. pp. 48. [500.]

AUGUST KIPPENBERG, Robinson in Deutschland bis zur Insel Felsenburg (1731–43). Hannover 1892. pp.[v].122.xix. [55.]
also issued as a thesis.

HERMANN ULLRICH, Robinson und Robinsonaden. . . . Teil I. Bibliographie. Litterar-historische forschungen (vol.vii): Weimar 1898. pp.xxiii.248. [1250.]
a supplement appears in the Zeitschrift für bücherfreunde *(1908), xi.444–456, 489–498.*

[WILLIAM SUPPLEE LLOYD], Catalogue of various editions of Robinson Crusoe and other books by and referring to Daniel Defoe. Philadelphia [printed] 1915. pp.43. [400.]

HENRY CLINTON HUTCHINS, Robinson Crusoe and its printing, 1719–1731. A bibliographical study. New York 1925. pp.xix.201. [25.]

350 copies printed.

OTTO DENEKE, Robinson Crusoe in Deutschland. Die frühdrucke 1720–1780. Göttingische nebenstunden (no.11): Göttingen 1934. pp.[iv].39. [15.]

DANIEL DEFOE. An excerpt from the General catalogue of printed books. British museum: 1953. coll.122. [1500.]

JAMES SUTHERLAND, Defoe. British council: British book news: Bibliographical series of supplements (no.51): 1954. pp.36. [100.]

CLARENCE S[AUNDERS] BRIGHAM, Bibliography of american editions of Robinson Crusoe to 1830. American antiquarian society: Worcester, Mass. 1958. pp.[ii].137–183. [125.]

JOHN ROBERT MOORE, A checklist of the writings of Daniel Defoe. Indiana university: Humanities series (no.47): Bloomington 1960. pp.xviii.254. [547.]

DANIEL DEFOE 1660–1731. Commemoration in Stoke Newington of the tercentenary of his birth.

An exhibition. Public libraries committee: [Stoke Newington 1960]. pp.40. [389.]
— Addenda. [1960]. pp.4. [15.]*

Dekker, Thomas.

LIST of references on Thomas Dekker. Library of Congress: Washington 1916. ff.2. [17.]*

SAMUEL A[ARON] TANNENBAUM, Thomas Dekker. (A concise bibliography). Elizabethan bibliographies (no.7): New York 1939. pp.[viii]. 47. [728.]
300 copies printed.

De La Mare, Walter John.

LIST of references on Walter De La Mare. Library of Congress: Washington 1923. ff.3. [46.]*
— Later references. 1925. ff.2. [15.]*

KENNETH HOPKINS, Walter de la Mare. British council: British book news: Bibliographical series of supplements (no.36): 1953. pp.44. [100.]

[LEONARD CLARK], Walter de la Mare. A check-list prepared on the occasion of an exhibition of his books and mss at the National book league. Cambridge 1956. pp.xiii.55. [339.]

De Leon, Daniel.

JOSEPH CARLETON BORDEN, A bibliographical list of writings of Daniel De Leon issued by the Socialist labor party of America from 1892 to 1936. Columbia university: School of library service: New York 1936. ff.45.ii. [79.]*

Denis, Ferdinand.

PAUL ALEXANDER MCNEIL, Notes on the works of Ferdinand Denis, 1798–1890, Americanist, in the Oliveira Lima collection, Catholic university of America. Washington 1941. pp.[8].

De Quincey, Thomas.

J[OHN] A[LBERT] GREEN, Thomas de Quincey. A bibliography based upon the De Quincey collection in the Moss Side library. Manchester 1908. pp.vii.110. [783.]

WILLIAM E[DWARD] A[RMYTAGE] AXON, The canon of De Quincey's writings, with references to some of his unidentified articles. 1912. pp.[ii]. 46. [40.]

Derleth, August William.

100 books by August Derleth. Sauk City, Wis. 1962. pp.121. [100.]

De Voto, Bernard Augustine.

THE PAPERS of Bernard De Voto. A description and a checklist of his works. [Stanford university: 1960]. pp.62. [750.]

Dewey, John.

MILTON HALSEY THOMAS and HERBERT WALLACE SCHNEIDER, A bibliography of John Dewey. New York 1929. pp.xxi.151. [1000.]

— — [another edition]. John Dewey. A centennial bibliography. Chicago [1962]. pp.xiii.370. [1600.]

— — [third edition]. John Dewey. A centennial bibliography [1962]. pp.xiii.370. [3000.]

Dibdin, Charles.

E[DWARD] R[IMBAULT] DIBDIN, A Charles Dibdin bibliography. Liverpool 1937. pp.[viii].146.[xix]. [600.]

30 copies privately printed.

Dibdin, Thomas Frognal.

FRANCESCO CORDASCO, A bibliography of Thomas Frognal Dibdin. 18th century bibliographical pamphlets (no.6): Brooklyn 1950. pp.12. [38.]

Dickens, Charles John Huffam.

JAMES COOK, Bibliography of the writings of Charles Dickens. 1879. pp.88. [150.]

[RICHARD HERNE SHEPHERD], The bibliography of Dickens. [1880]. pp.viii.107. [200.]

CHARLES PLUMPTRE JOHNSON, Hints to collectors of original editions of the works of Charles Dickens. 1885. pp.56. [94.]

FRED[ERIC] G[EORGE] KITTON, Dickensiana. A bibliography of the literature relating to Charles Dickens and his writings. 1886. pp.xxxii.511. [584.]

DICKENSIANA, Illustrated catalogue of works by and literature relating to Charles Dickens in library of E[dmund] S[chofield] Williamson. Toronto [1896]. pp.[35]. [100.]
100 copies printed.

FREDERIC G[EORGE] KITTON, The novels of Charles Dickens. A bibliography and a sketch. Book-lover's library: 1897. pp.xi.247. [15.]

FREDERIC G[EORGE] KITTON, The minor writings of Charles Dickens. A bibliography and a sketch. Book-lover's library: 1900. pp.xi.260. [300.]

FREDERIC G[EORGE] KITTON, The Dickens exhibition held at the Memorial hall, London . . . Catalogue. [1903]. pp.66.

W. H. SAUNDERS, List of books . . . exhibited at Dickens' birthplace museum. Postsmouth 1904. pp.61. [108.]

J[OSEPH] C[HARLES] THOMSON, Bibliography of the writings of Charles Dickens. Warwick 1904. pp.108. [115.]

WILLIAM CLYDE WILKINS, First and early american editions of the works of Charles Dickens. Cedar Rapids 1910. pp.51. [50.]

200 copies privately printed.

DICKENS exhibition. South Kensington museum: 1912. pp.63. [350.]

CHARLES DICKENS, 1812–1870. A list of books and of references to periodicals in the Brooklyn public library. Brooklyn 1912. pp.68. [750.]

AN EXHIBITION of books . . . manuscripts & letters commemorative of the centenary of Charles Dickens. Franklin club: St. Louis 1912. pp.vi.50. [300.]

[RUTH S. GRANNISS], Catalogue of an exhibition of the works of Charles Dickens. Grolier club:

New York 1913. pp.[vii].220. [342.]

— [another edition]. 1913. pp.xxvi.321. [342.]

300 copies printed.

JOHN C. ECKEL, The first editions of the writings of Charles Dickens and their values. A bibliography. 1913. pp.xviii.296. [100.]

— — Revised and enlarged. New York &c. 1932. pp.xvii.272. [100.]

250 copies printed.

A[BRAHAM] S. W[OLF] ROSENBACH, A catalogue of the writings of Charles Dickens in the library of Harry Elkins Widener. Philadelphia 1918. pp. [vii].111. [200.]

privately printed; the collection now forms part of Harvard university library.

A[LAIN] DE SUZANNET, Catalogue d'un choix de livres imprimés, lettres autographes . . . provenant de ma bibliothèque. . . . I. Œuvres de Charles Dickens. Biarritz 1925. pp.83. [250.]

56 copies printed.

CHARLES DICKENS. An excerpt from the general catalogue of printed books in the British museum. 1926. pp.29. [1150.]

CHARLES DICKENS. List of works, criticisms, etc., Dickensiana, biography and illustrations in books and periodicals in the libraries. Municipal libraries: Subject list (no.1): Bath 1926. pp.[4]. [350.]

CHARLES DICKENS, A selected list of books dealing with dickensian literature compiled . . . by the Dickens fellowship. Second edition. [National book council]: Bibliography (no.47): 1928. pp.[2]. [50.]

JOHN C. ECKEL, Prime Pickwicks in parts. Census with complete collation. New York &c. 1928. pp.[xiv].91.

440 copies printed.

CORTES W[IRT] CAVANAUGH, Charles Dickens, his life as traced by his works. . . . Early american editions of the works of Charles Dickens, by Herman Le Roy Edgar and R[obert] W[illiam] [Glenroie] Vail. Public library: New York 1929. pp.31. [100.]

THOMAS HUTTON and ARTHUR H. CLEAVER, A bibliography of the periodical works of Charles Dickens. 1933. pp.xix.384. [13.]

A DICKENS library. Exhibition catalogue of the [Charles James] Sawyer collection of the works of Charles Dickens. 1936. pp.108. [500.]

privately printed.

W[ILLIAM] MILLER and E. H. STRANGE, A centenary bibliography of the Pickwick papers. [1936]. pp.[vi].223.

a description of the first edition.

CATALOGUE of books, portraits, illustrations and miscellaneous exhibits . . . to commemorate publication of Pickwick papers. Public libraries and Coming museum: Southwark [1936]. pp.27. [200.]

GUIDE to the books, autographs, letters and pictures exhibited in celebration of the centenary of the . . . Pickwick papers. Public library, museum and national gallery of Victoria: Melbourne 1936. pp.18.

DICKENS exhibition, 1936. Public library, museums, and national gallery, of Victoria: Melbourne 1936. pp.20. [47.]

M. L. PARRISH, A list of the writings of Charles Dickens. Compiled from the collection at Dormy house, Pine Valley, New Jersey. Philadelphia 1938. pp.[18.]

THE LIFE and works of Charles Dickens, 1812–1870. An exhibition from the collection of William M[cIntire] Elkins. Free library: Philadelphia 1946. pp.iii–xii.58. [167.]

YO. B. FRIDLENDER, Чарльз Диккенс. Указатель важнейшей литературы на русском языке (1838–1954). Библиотека им. М. Е. Салтыкова-Щедрина: Ленинград 1946. pp.3–128. [300.]

WILLIAM MILLER, The Dickens student and collector. A list of writings relating to Charles Dickens and his works, 1836–1945. 1946. pp.xii.351. [3250.]

— — Supplement. Brighton 1947. pp.12. [175.] *privately printed.*

K. J. FIELDING, Charles Dickens. British council: British book news: Bibliographical series of supplements (no.37): 1953. pp.47. [150.]

— — New edition. 1960. pp.48. [150.]

JOHN D[OZIER] GORDAN, Reading for profit: the other career of Charles Dickens. An exhibition from the Berg collection. Public library: New York 1958. pp.30. [90.]

DICKENS. An excerpt from the General catalogue of printed books in the British museum. 1960. pp.[ii].coll.237–378. [2000.]

MARY CALLISTA CARR, Catalogue of the Dickens collection at the university of Texas. University of Texas: Bibliographical series (no.1): Austin 1961. pp.x.197. [788.]

YU. V. FRIDLENDER and I[GOR] M[AKSIMILIANOVICH] KATARSKY, Чарльз Диккенс. Библиография русских переводов и критической литературы на русском языке, 1838–1960. Всесоюзная государственная библиотека иностранной литературы [&c.]: Москва 1962. pp.328. [2256.]

Dickins, Bruce.

[B. DICKINS], A list of books & papers, 1912–1953. Cambridge [1953]. pp.7. [100.]
privately printed.

Dickinson, Emily.

ALFRED LEETE HAMPSON, Emily Dickinson. A bibliography. Northampton, [Mass.] 1930. pp.36. [150.]
500 copies printed.

EMILY DICKINSON. . . . A bibliography. Jones library: Publication (no.2): Amherst, Mass. 1930. pp.63. [400.]
— — Second edition. 1930 [1931]. pp.63. [400.]

Disraeli, Benjamin, 1st earl of Beaconsfield.

PAUL BLOOMFIELD, Disraeli. British council:

British book news: Bibliographical series of supplements (no.138): 1961. pp.39. [75.]

Dobson, Henry Austin.

FRANCIS EDWIN MURRAY, A bibliography of Austin Dobson. Derby 1900. pp.xix.347. [650.]

ALBAN [TABOR AUSTIN] DOBSON, A bibliography of the first editions of published and privately printed books and pamphlets by Austin Dobson. First edition club [vol.viii]: 1925. pp.xiv.89. [68.]

500 copies printed.

[ALBAN TABOR AUSTIN DOBSON], Catalogue of the collection of the works of Austin Dobson. University of London: Library: 1960. pp.[v].62. [2000.]

AUSTIN DOBSON. [Central library. Ealing 1962]. pp.16. [75.]*

Dock, George.

BIBLIOGRAPHY of the writings of dr. George Dock. Barlow society for the history of medicine: Los Angeles 1950. pp.[16]. [158.]

300 copies printed; a duplicated supplement has been issued.

Donne, John.

[SIR] GEOFFREY [LANGDON] KEYNES, Bibliography of the works of dr. John Donne. Baskerville club [Publication no.2]: Cambridge 1914. pp.xii.168. [154.]

300 copies printed.

— — Third edition. 1958. pp.xix.286. [1000.]

WILLIAM WHITE, John Donne since 1900. A bibliography of periodical articles. Boston 1942. pp.v.23. [750.]

printed largely on one side of the leaf.

FRANK KERMODE, John Donne. British council: British book news: Bibliographical series of supplements (no.86): 1957. pp.48. [100.]

— — [another edition]. 1961. pp.48. [125.]

Dos Passos, John Roderigo.

JACK POTTER, A bibliography of John Dos Passos. Chicago 1950. pp.3–95. [1500.]

365 copies printed.

Douglas, Lady Eleanor.

C[HRISTOPHER] J[OSEPH] HINDLE, A bibliography of the printed pamphlets and broadsides of lady Eleanor Douglas, the 17th century prophetess. Edinburgh 1934. pp.[ii].20. [42.]

— — Revised edition. Edinburgh bibliographical society: 1936. pp.34. [53.]

Douglas, Norman.

EDWARD D. MCDONALD, A bibliography of the writings of Norman Douglas. Centaur bibliographies [of modern american authors] (no.7): Philadelphia 1927. pp.165. [500.]

300 copies printed.

CECIL WOOLF and ALAN ANDERSON, Memorial exhibition of works by Norman Douglas. Central library: Edinburgh 1952. pp.8. [64.]

CECIL WOOLF, A bibliography of Norman Douglas. Soho bibliographies (vol.vi): 1954. pp. 201. [150.]

CECIL WOOLF, Notes on the bibliography of Norman Douglas. Edinburgh 1955. pp.[iii].9. [40.]

95 copies privately printed.

Doyle, sir Arthur Conan.

HAROLD LOCKE, A bibliographical catalogue of the writings of sir Arthur Conan Doyle. Tunbridge Wells 1928. pp.84. [450.]

EDGAR W[ADSWORTH] SMITH, Baker street inventory. A sherlockian bibliography. Summit, N.J. 1945. pp.3–81.[xiii]. [650.]
300 copies printed.

SHERLOCK HOLMES. Catalogue of an exhibition. Public libraries committee: St. Marylebone [1951]. pp.[iv].iv.60. [200.]

NATHAN L. BENGIS, The "signs" of our times. An irregular bibliography. New York 1956. ff.[i].29. [125.]*
a bibliography of The sign of four.

Drayton, Michael.

SAMUEL A[ARON] TANNENBAUM, Michael Drayton. (A concise bibliography). Elizabethan bibliographies (no.22): New York 1941. pp.ix.54. [983.]
300 copies printed.

Dreiser, Theodore.

EDWARD D[AVID] MCDONALD, A bibliography of the writings of Theodore Dreiser. Centaur bibliographies [of modern american authors] (no.8): Philadelphia 1928. pp.130. [300.]
350 copies printed.

[FAIR TEACHOUT] VREST ORTON, Dreiserana. A book about his books. Chocorua bibliographies: New York 1929. pp.ix.85. [300.]

RALPH N. MILLER, A preliminary checklist of books and articles on Theodore Dreiser. Western Michigan college library: [Kalamazoo] 1947. ff.11. [250.]*

Drinkwater, John.

TIMOTHY D'ARCH SMITH, John Drinkwater 1882–1937. Catalogue of an exhibition . . . to mark the twenty-fifth anniversary of his death. 1962. pp.51.

Dryden, John.

CATALOGUE of an exhibition of first and other editions of the works of John Dryden (1631–1700). Grolier club: New York 1900. pp.[ii].97. [115.]

200 copies printed.

— — [another edition]. Exhibition [&c.]. 1900. pp.88. [115.]

LIST of Dryden's plays. Library of Congress: Washington [*c.*1920]. ff.4. [39.]*

PERCY J[OHN] DOBELL, John Dryden. Bibliographical memoranda. 1922. pp.[vii].30. [30.]

100 copies printed.

[T. J. WISE], A Dryden library. A catalogue of printed books, manuscripts and autograph letters by John Dryden, . . . collected by Thomas James Wise. 1930. pp.xxiv.92. [150.]

160 copies privately printed; the collection contains no manuscripts; according to an erratum slip the subtitle should have been A catalogue of the plays, poems, and prose writings of John Dryden.

HUGH MACDONALD, John Dryden. A bibliography of early editions and of Drydeniana. Oxford 1939. pp.[ii].xiv.359. [500.]

SAMUEL HOLT MONK, John Dryden. A list of critical studies published from 1895 to 1948. Minneapolis [1950]. pp.v.52. [768.]

BONAMY DOBRÉE, John Dryden. British council: British book news: Bibliographical series of supplements (no.70): 1956. pp.48. [150.]

— — Revised edition. pp.48. [150.]

Dublin, Louis Israel.

PUBLICATIONS and addresses, 1903 to 1952, by Louis I. Dublin. [*s.l.* 1952]. pp.[ii].50. [660.]*

Dugdale, sir William.

FRANCIS MADDISON, DOROTHY STYLES and

ANTHONY WOOD, Sir William Dugdale, 1605–1686. A list of his printed works and of his portraits. Warwickshire county council: Records and museum committee: [Warwick] 1953. pp.92. [150.]

Dunbar, Paul Laurence.

ESTHER W. KLAPHAAK, Author bibliography of Paul Laurence Dunbar. [*s.l.* *c.*1950]. ff.[i].22. [250.]*

Dunlap, William.

OSCAR WEGELIN, A bibliographical check list of the plays and miscellaneous writings of William Dunlap (1766–1839). Bibliographica americana (vol.i): New York 1916. ff.[14]. [54.]

Duns, Joannes.

URIËL SMEETS, Lineamenta bibliographiae scotisticae. Commissio scotistica: Romae 1942. pp. xvi.184. [1312.]

EFREM BETTONI, Vent'anni di studi scotisti (1920–1940). Saggio bibliografico. [Università cattolica del sacro cuore:] Quaderni della Rivista di filosofia neoscolastica: Milano [1943]. pp.iii.106. [500.]

ODULF SCHÄFER, Johannes Duns Scotus. Bibliographische einführung in das studium der philosophie (no.22): Bern 1953. pp.34. [700.]

ODULF SCHÄFER, Bibliographia de vita operibus et doctrina Iohannis Duns Scoti . . . saec. XIX–XX. Romae 1955. pp.iii–xxv.223. [4506.]

Durrell, Lawrence.

ROBERT A. POTTER and BROOKE WHITING, Lawrence Durrell: a checklist. University of California: Library: Los Angeles 1961. pp.[ii].50. [311.]

Dutton, Ann.

J[OHN] C[UDWORTH] WHITEBROOK, Ann Dutton. A life and bibliography. Oxford [1921]. pp.20. [60.]

Duvoison, Roger Antoine.

IRVIN KERLAN, A Roger Duvoison bibliography. University of Virginia: Bibliographical society: Secretary's news sheet (no.39): Charlottesville 1958. pp.16. [100.]*

Eastwick, E. B.

[E. B. EASTWICK], Statement of the services and writings . . . of E. B. Eastwick. [*c.*1880]. pp.11. [25.]

Eddy, Mary Baker.

LIST of writings in the Library of Congress by mrs. Mary Baker G. Eddy. Library of Congress: Washington 1907. ff.7. [69.]*

CATALOGUE of works on christian science by Mary Baker Eddy. Boston [1944]. pp.32. [150.]

Edgeworth Maria.

BERTHA COOLIDGE SLADE, Maria Edgeworth, 1767–1849. A bibliographical tribute. 1937. pp. xxxii.254. [50.]
250 copies printed.

Edwards, Jonathan.

THOMAS H[ERBERT] JOHNSON, The printed writings of Jonathan Edwards, 1703–1758. A bibliography. Princeton university library: Publications: Princeton 1940. pp.xiv.136. [346.]
later editions are also recorded.

Egle, William Henry.

A[MMON] MONROE AURAND, Notes and queries. . . . The works of dr. William Henry Egle. A bibliography. Harrisburg, Pa. 1934. pp.64. [200.]
160 copies privately printed.

Ekwall, Eilert.

OLOF VON FEILITZEN, The published writings of Eilert Ekwall. A bibliography. Lund studies in english (no.30): Lund [1961]. pp.3–52. [369.]

Eliot, George, *pseud.*

P[ERCIVAL] H[ORACE] MUIR, A bibliography of the first editions of books by George Eliot (Mary Ann Evans) (1819–1880). Bookman's journal: Supplement: [1927]. pp.41–58. [19.]

M[ORRIS] L[ONGSTRETH] PARRISH, Victorian lady novelists. George Eliot, mrs. Gaskell, the Brontë sisters. First editions in the library at Dormy house, Pine Valley, New Jersey. 1933. pp.xii.160. [George Eliot: 110.]

150 copies printed.

LETTICE COOPER, George Eliot. British council: British book news: Bibliographical series of supplements: 1951. pp.46. [100.]

Eliot, John.

[WILBERFORCE EAMES], Bibliographic notes on Eliot's indian Bible and on his other translations and works in the indian language of Massachusetts. Washington 1890. pp.[ii].58. [30.]

Eliot, Thomas Stearns.

DONALD C[LIFFORD] GALLUP, A catalogue of english and american first editions of writings by T. S. Eliot exhibited in the Yale university library. New Haven 1937. pp.42. [275.]

DONALD GALLUP, A bibliographical check-list of the writings of T. S. Eliot, including his contributions to periodicals and translations of his work into foreign languages. Yale university: Library New Haven 1947. pp.128. [750.]
— — [another edition]. T. S. Eliot. A bibliography. London 1952. pp.xi.177. [977.]

M. C. BRADBROOK, T. S. Eliot. British council: British book news: Bibliographical series of supplements [no.8]: 1950. pp.62. [150.]
— — [third edition]. 1955. pp.64. [150.]

AN EXHIBITION of manuscripts and first editions of T. S. Eliot. University of Texas: Humanities research center: [Austin 1961]. pp.46. [200.]

HANS W[ILLI] BENTZ, Thomas Stearns Eliot in übersetzungen. Weltliteratur in übersetzungen: Britische autoren (vol.i): Frankfurt am Main [1963]. pp.xiii.59. [222.]*

Elliott, Ebenezer.

EBENEZER ELLIOTT (the corn-law rhymer), 1781–1849. Sheffield city libraries and Rotherham public library: Sheffield [printed] [1949]. pp.36. [175.]

Elliott, Mary Belson.

PHILIP D[ILLON] JORDAN and DANIEL C[ARL] HASKELL, The juvenilia of Mary Belson Elliott. Public library: New York 1936. pp.18. [178.]

Ellwood, Charles Abram.

MARY VIE CRAMBLITT, A bibliography of the writings of Charles Abram Ellwood. Durham, N.C. 1944. ff.[iv].viii.34.*

Emerson, Ralph Waldo.

GEORGE WILLIS COOKE, A bibliography of Ralph Waldo Emerson. Boston &c. 1908. pp.ix.342. [4000.]

KENNETH WALTER CAMERON, Ralph Waldo Emerson's reading. A guide... to the one thousand volumes which he withdrew from libraries. Raleigh, N.C. 1941. pp.3–144. [1000.]

INDEX to early american periodical literature, 1728–1870. No.4. Ralph Waldo Emerson. New York university: New York 1942. pp.40. [500.]

BUNSHŌ JUGAKU, A bibliography of Ralph Waldo Emerson in Japan from 1878 to 1935. Kyoto 1947. pp.xx.70. [228.]
500 copies printed.

JOHN D[OZIER] GORDAN, Ralph Waldo Emerson, 1803–1882. Catalogue of an exhibition from the Berg collection. Public library: New York 1953. pp.47. [125.]

JACKSON R. BRYER and ROBERT A. REES, A checklist of Emerson criticism 1951–1961. Hartford [1964]. ff.53. [420.]*

Ethelred, saint.

ANSELM HOSTE, Bibliotheca aelrediana. A survey of the manuscripts, old catalogues, editions and studies concerning st. Aelred of Rievaulx. Instrvmenta patristica (vol.ii): Steenbrvgis 1962. pp. 3–206. [750.]

Evans, sir John.

L. FORRER, Sir John Evans. . . . Biographie et bibliographie. Chalon-sur-Saône 1909. pp.[iii].36. [250.]

Evelyn, John.

[(SIR) GEOFFREY LANGDON KEYNES and AUGUSTUS THEODORE BARTHOLOMEW]. A handlist of the works of John Evelyn . . . and of books connected with him. Cambridge 1916. pp.2.ff.18.pp.19–20. [117.]

25 copies printed.

[SIR] GEOFFREY [LANGDON] KEYNES, John Evelyn. A study in bibliography & a bibliography of his writings. Cambridge 1937. pp.xix.310. [180.]

also issued by the Grolier club; 300 copies printed.

Ewen, C. L'Estrange.

[C. L'E. EWEN], Anthropological, biographical, genealogical, nautical, philatelic and topographical works by C. L'Estrange Ewen. Paignton 1940. pp.8. [30.]

Fairburn, Arthur Rex Dugard.

OLIVE [A.] JOHNSON, A. R. D. Fairburn 1904–1957. A bibliography of his published work. University of Auckland: Monograph series (no.3): [Auckland] 1958. pp.117. [764.]

Farquhar, Francis Peloubet.

SUSANNA BRYANT DAKIN, The published writings of Francis Peloubet Farquhar. San Francisco 1954. pp.[iii].vii.17. [125.]

Farrell, James Thomas.

EDGAR [MARQUESS] BRANCH, A bibliography of James T. Farrell's writings 1921–1957. Philadelphia [1959]. pp.xxi.17–142. [1350.]*

Faulkner, William.

ROBERT W[OODHAM] DANIEL, A catalogue of the writings of William Faulkner. Yale university library: New Haven 1942. pp.32. [300.]

WILLIAM FAULKNER biography and criticism, 1951–1954. University of Oregon: Library: [Eugene] 1955. ff.11.*

JAMES B. MERIWETHER, William Faulkner: a check list. Princeton university: Library: Princeton 1957. pp.23. [300.]

WILLIAM FAULKNER. An exhibition of manuscripts. University of Texas: Research center: [Austin 1959]. pp.16. [75.]

IRENE LYNN SLEETH, William Faulkner: a bibliography of criticism. Swallow pamphlets (no.13): Denver [1962]. pp.28. [1000.]

Federn, Paul.

JOS. I. MEIERS, Selected bibliography of the writings and publications of Paul Federn. New York 1949. ff.6. [75.]*

Ferguson, John.

ELIZABETH H. ALEXANDER, A bibliography of John Ferguson. [Glasgow] 1920. pp.[iii].32. [89.]

— — A further bibliography of the late John Ferguson. 1934. pp.[iii].47. [140.]

Fergusson, Robert.

JOHN A. FAIRLEY, Bibliography of Robert Fergusson. Glasgow 1915. pp.50. [94.]

100 copies printed.

Field, Eugene.

FIRST EDITIONS, Manuscripts, letters, &c., of Eugene Field. Collectors' club: New York 1915. pp.30. [217.]

LIST of writings relating to Eugene Field. Library of Congress: Washington 1920. ff.3. [32.]*

Field, Henry.

HENRY FIELD, Bibliography: 1926–1958. [Coconut Grove, Fla.] 1958. pp.91. [458.]*

— — 1926–1964. [Miami] 1964. pp.vii.112. [594.]*

Fielding, Henry.

FRANCESCO CORDASCO, Henry Fielding. A list of critical studies published from 1895 to 1946. Eighteenth century bibliographical pamphlets (no.5): Brooklyn 1948. pp.[ix].224. [224.]

JOHN BUTT, Fielding. British council: British book news: Bibliographical series of supplements (no.57): 1954. pp.35. [100.]

I. M. LEVIDOVA, Генри Фильдинг. Био-библиографический указатель к двухстапятидесятилетию со дня рождения. Всесоюзная государственная библиотека иностранной литературы: Писатели зарубежных стран: Москва 1957. pp.28. [200.]

Figgis, Darrell.

P[ATRICK] S[ARSFIELD] O'HEGARTY, A bibliography of the books of Darrell Figgis. Dublin 1937. pp.[ii].10. [27.]

30 copies privately printed.

Firbank, Arthur Annesley Ronald.

P[ERCIVAL] H[ORACE] MUIR, A bibliography of the first editions of books by Arthur Annesley Ronald Firbank (1886–1926). Bookman's journal: Supplement: 1927. pp.8. [11.]

MIRIAM J[EANNETTE] BENKOVITZ, A bibliography of Ronald Firbank. Soho bibliographies (vol.xvi): 1963. pp.103. [100.]

Firth, sir Charles.

[SIR CHARLES FIRTH], A bibliography of the writings of sir Charles Firth. Oxford 1928. pp. v.46. [650.]

Fitzgerald, Edward.

W[ILLIAM] F[RANCIS] PRIDEAUX, Notes for a bibliography of Edward FitzGerald. 1901. pp. xi.88. [75.]

EDWARD FITZGERALD, 1809–1883. A list of books, with references to periodicals, in the Brooklyn public library. Brooklyn 1909. pp.12. [150.]

JOANNA RICHARDSON, Edward Fitzgerald. British council: British book news: Bibliographical series of supplements (no.125): 1960. pp.42. [75.]

Fitzgerald, Francis Scott Key.

BERNARD H. PORTER, The first publications of F. Scott Fitzgerald. Denver [1960]. pp.11. [275.]

Fitzgerald, Percy Hetherington.

[P. H. FITZGERALD], An output. A list of writings on many diverse subjects . . . by Perce Fitzgerald. [1912]. pp.40. [150.]
privately printed.

Fletcher, Andrew.

ROBERT A[NDREW] SCOTT MACFIE, A bibliography of Andrew Fletcher of Saltoun, 1653–1716. Edinburgh 1901. pp.[iii].32. [50.]
30 copies privately printed.

Fletcher, John.

ALFRED CLAGHORN POTTER, A bibliography of Beaumont and Fletcher. Library of Harvard university: Bibliographical contributions (no.39): Cambridge, Mass. 1890. pp.20. [425.]

SAMUEL A[ARON] TANNENBAUM, Beaumont & Fletcher. (A concise bibliography). Elizabethan bibliographies (no.3): New York 1938. pp.x.94. [1628.]

Forbes, John.

T[HOMAS] G[RAVES] LAW, Bibliography of two scottish Capucins, John Forbes and George Lesley, both named in religion father Archangel. Bibliographical society: Edinburgh 1891. pp.4. [Forbes: 6.]

Force, Peter.

NEWMAN F. MAC GIRR, Bio-bibliography of Peter Force, 1790–1868. Heartman's historical series (no.57): Hattiesburg 1941. pp.30. [246.]
150 copies printed.

Ford, Ford Madox.

KENNETH YOUNG, Ford Madox Ford. British council: British book news: Bibliographical series of supplements (no.74): 1956. pp.43. [100.]

DAVID DOW HARVEY, Ford Madox Ford 1873–1939. A bibliography of works and criticism. Princeton 1962. pp.xxiii.633. [2000.]*

Ford, John.

SAMUEL A[ARON] TANNENBAUM, John Ford. (A concise bibliography). Elizabethan bibliographies (no.20): New York 1941. pp.ix.27. [400.]
300 copies printed.

Forman, Justus Miles.

LIST of the works of Justus Miles Forman. Library of Congress: Washington 1916. ff.3. [58.]*

Forster, Edward Morgan.

REX WARNER, E. M. Forster. British council: British book news: Bibliographical series of supplements [no.7]: 1950. pp.32. [50.]

— — New edition. 1960. pp.37. [75.]

Fox, Robert Were.

J. H. COLLINS, A catalogue of the works of Robert Were Fox. Truro 1878. pp.[iv].66. [64.]

Francis, sir Philip.

TONY HAROLD BOWYER, A bibliographical examination of the earliest editions of the letters of Junius. Charlottesville 1957. pp.xxxiv.147. [31.]

Franklin, Benjamin.

HENRY STEVENS, Benjamin Franklin's life and writings. A bibliographical essay on the Stevens' collection of books and manuscripts relating to doctor Franklin. 1881. pp.viii.40. [203.]

LINDSAY SWIFT, Catalogue of works relating to Benjamin Franklin in the Boston public library, including the collection given by doctor Samuel Abbott Green, with the titles of similar works not in the library. Boston public library: Bibliographies of special subjects (no.1): Boston 1883. pp.42. [1000.]

PAUL LEICESTER FORD, Franklin bibliography. A list of books written by, or relating to, Benjamin Franklin. Brooklyn, N.Y. 1889. pp.lxxiii. 467. [1002.]

500 copies printed on one side of the leaf.

[JOHN CLEMENT FITZPATRICK], List of the Benjamin Franklin papers in the Library of Congress. Compiled under the direction of Worthington Chauncey Ford. Washington 1905. pp.322. [2500.]

LIST of works in the New York public library by or relating to Benjamin Franklin. [New York 1906]. pp.55. [700.]

CATALOGUE of an exhibition commemorating the two hundreth [*sic*] anniversary of the birth of Benjamin Franklin. Grolier club: New York 1906. pp.100. [86.]

I[SAAC] MINIS HAYS, Calendar of the papers of Benjamin Franklin in the library of the American philosophical society. American philosophical society: Record of the celebration of the two hundredth anniversary of the birth of Benjamin Franklin (vols.ii–vi): Philadelphia 1908.

i. [Letters to Franklin, 1730–1778]. pp.xx.573. [3500.]

ii. [1779–1782]. pp.ix.526. [3500.]

iii. [1783–1790; letters from Franklin, 1757–1789]. pp.ix.560. [3500.]

iv. [Supplement and miscellaneous, 1642–1810]. pp.ix.510. [3500.]

v. [Index]. pp.x.325.

[A. C. BOGGESS and MRS. LIGHTNER WITMER], Calendar of the papers of Benjamin Franklin in the library of the university of Pennsylvania. University of Pennsylvania: Series in history (no.3): Philadelphia 1908. pp.[ii].vii.399–546. [750.]

LUTHER S[AMUEL] LIVINGSTON, Franklin and his press at Passy. An account of the books, pamphlets, and leaflets printed there, including the long-lost 'Bagatelles'. Grolier club: New York 1914. pp. xiii.217. [32.]

303 copies printed.

WILLIAM J. CAMPBELL, The collection of Franklin imprints in the museum of the Curtis publishing company. With a short-title check list of all the books, pamphlets, broadsides, &c., known to have been printed by Benjamin Franklin. Philadelphia 1918. pp.[ix].333. [790].
475 copies printed.

LIST of works relating to Benjamin Franklin published since the Franklin bicentenary. Library of Congress: [Washington] 1924. ff.6. [44.]*

AN EXHIBITION of books and papers relating to dr. Benjamin Franklin from the collections in this library and the library of William Smith Mason. William L. Clements library: Bulletin (no.12): Ann Arbor 1926. pp.12. [100.]
300 copies printed.

THE ALL-EMBRACING doctor Franklin . . . illustrated by books and manuscripts from the collection of dr. A. S. W. Rosenbach. Free library: Philadelphia 1938. pp.15. [100.]

[AGNES MONGAN and MARY WADSWORTH], Exhibition: Washington, Lafayette, Franklin. Harvard university: Fogg museum of art: [Cambridge] 1944. pp.53. [126.]

BENJAMIN FRANKLIN, Winston Churchill. An exhibition. University of Pennsylvania: University museum: Philadelphia 1951. pp.55. [Franklin: 100.]

L[YMAN] H[ENRY] BUTTERFIELD, B. Franklin's epitaph. [*s.l.* *c.*1951]. pp.31. [12.]

BENJAMIN FRANKLIN et la France. Exposition organisée pour le deux cent cinquantième anniversaire de sa naissance. Bibliothèque nationale: 1956. pp.[v].iv.36. [170.]

BENJAMIN FRANKLIN, 1706–1790. U. S. information agency: Information center service: Subject bibliography (no.9): [Washington] 1955. ff.[i].7. [27.]*

Frazer, sir James George.

THEODORE [DEODATUS NATHANIEL] BESTERMAN, A bibliography of sir James George Frazer. 1934. pp.xxi.100. [266.]

— — Addenda and corrigenda. [By lady Frazer]. 1937. pp.[8]. [17.]

Freneau, Philip.

VICTOR HUGO PALTSITS, A bibliography of the separate and collected works of Philip Freneau, together with an account of his newspapers. New York 1903. pp.xv.96. [75.]

Friedman, Philip.

WRITINGS of Philip Friedman. A bibliography. New York 1955. ff.34. [305.]*

Frost, Robert.

[LAWRANCE ROGER THOMPSON], Robert Frost. A chronological survey. Wesleyan university: Middletown, Conn. 1936. pp.3–59. [100.]

250 copies printed.

W[ILLIAM] B[RANFORD] SHUBRICK CLYMER and CHARLES R. GREEN, Robert Frost. A bibliography. Jones library: Publication (no.3): Amherst, Mass. 1937. pp.159. [750.]

AN EXHIBITION of the work of Robert Frost. Allegheny college: Meadville, Pa. 1938. pp.[14]. [80.]

RAY NASH, *ed.* Fifty years of Robert Frost. A catalogue of the exhibition held in Baker library. Dartmouth college: Hanover 1944. pp.14. [90.]

LOUIS and ESTHER MERTINS, The intervals of Robert Frost. A critical bibliography. Berkeley &c. 1947. pp.[v].91. [200.]

RICHARD H. TEMPLETON, Robert Frost. His poems, portraits & printers 1913–1963. A comprehensive exhibit. Lake Forest-academy: [Lake Forest, Ill. 1963]. pp.[14].

EDNA HANLEY BYERS, Robert Frost at Agnes Scott College. Agnes Scott College: McCain library: Decatur, Ga. 1963. pp.xviii.75. [500.]

Frumkin, Robert Martin.

MIRIAM ZISENWINE FRUMKIN, Robert M. Frumkin: a profile and selected bibliography. Oswego, N.Y. 1962. ff.[i].13. [131.]*

Fuller, Thomas.

THE FULLER collection in the Free reference library. Public libraries: Occasional lists (no.2): Manchester 1891. pp.[ii].10. [100.]

STRICKLAND GIBSON, *ed.* A bibliography of the works of Thomas Fuller. Oxford bibliographical society: Proceedings & papers (vol.iv, part I. ii): Oxford 1936. pp.63–161. [100.]

Gale, Norman.

[GEORGE E. OVER], Alfred Hayes, Richard Le Galienne, Norman Gale. [Rugby 1894]. pp.[ii].11. [Gale: 15.]

Gallichan, Walter M.

BIBLIOGRAPHY of works by Walter M. Gallichan. Library of Congress: Washington 1932. ff.3. [34.]*

Galsworthy, John.

JOHN GALSWORTHY: An appreciation together with a bibliography. 1926. pp.[ii].22. [100.]

H[AROLD] V[INCENT] MARROT, A bibliography of the works of John Galsworthy. 1928. pp.xiii. 252. [750.]

GILBERT H[ENRY] FABES, John Galsworthy. First editions and their values (no.1): 1932. pp.xxiv.64. [100.]

500 copies printed.

R. H. MOTTRAM, John Galsworthy. British council: British book news: Bibliographical series of supplements (no.3): 1953. pp.40. [75.]

I. M. LEVIDOVA, Джон Голсуорси. Био-библиографический указатель. Всесоюзная государственная библиотека иностранной литературы: Москва 1958. pp.60. [494.]

Galt, John.

ROBERT S. CLARK, A selected list of books on John Galt. Corporation public libraries: Glasgow [1951]. pp.12. [50.]

Gardiner, Samuel Rawson.

W[ILLIAM] A. SHAW, A bibliography of the historical works of dr. Creighton . . . dr. Stubbs . . . dr. S. R. Gardiner, and . . . lord Acton. Royal historical society: 1903. pp.63. [Gardiner: 300.]

Gardner, Edmund Garratt.

[CAMILLO PELLIZZI and MONICA GARDNER], Edmund Garratt Gardner. . . . A bibliography of his publications. 1937. pp.[xv].28. [150.]

Garland, Hamlin.

LLOYD A. ARVIDSON, Hamlin Garland. Centennial tributes and a checklist of the Hamlin Garland papers in the . . . library. University of southern California: Library: Library bulletin (no.9): Los Angeles 1962. pp.xvi.159.

Garrick, David.

MARY E[TTA] KNAPP, A checklist of verse by David Garrick. University of Virginia: Bibliographical society: Charlottesville 1955. pp.71. [479.]

Gascoigne, George.

SAMUEL A[ARON] TANNENBAUM, George Gascoigne. (A concise bibliography). Elizabethan bibliographies (no.26): New York 1942. pp.x.22. [387.]

250 copies printed.

Gaskell, Elizabeth and William.

WILLIAM E[DWARD] A[RMYTAGE] AXON and ERNEST AXON, Gaskell bibliography: a list of the writings of mrs. E. C. Gaskell, . . . and of her husband, the rev. William Gaskell. Manchester &c. 1895. pp.22. [225.]

J. A. GREEN, A hand-list of the Gaskell collection in the Public library, Moss Side. Manchester 1903. pp.12. [500.]

JOHN ALBERT GREEN, A bibliographical guide to the Gaskell collection in the Moss Side library. Public libraries: Manchester 1911. pp.[iv].68. [mrs Gaskell: 575.]

BIBLIOGRAPHY of Elizabeth Cleghorn Gaskell. Library of Congress: Washington 1922. ff.4. [40.]*

M. L. PARRISH, Victorian lady novelists. George Eliot, mrs. Gaskell, the Brontë sisters. First editions in the library at Dormy house, Pine Valley, New Jersey. 1933. pp.xii.160. [mrs Gaskell: 70.]

MIRIAM ALLOTT, Elizabeth Gaskell. British council: British book news: Bibliographical series of supplements (no.124): 1960. pp.46. [100.]

Gaster, Moses.

B[RUNO] SCHINDLER, Gaster centenary publication. Royal asiatic society of Great Britain and Ireland: 1958. pp.[viii].40. [281.]

George, Henry.

ROLLIN ALGER SAWYER, Henry George and the single tax. A catalogue of the collection in the New York public library. New York 1926. pp.[iii].90. [2250.]

Gibbings, Robert John.

A. MARY KIRKUS, Robert Gibbings. A bibliography. . . . Edited by Patience Empson and John Harris. 1962. pp.xiii.170. [394.]

Gibbon, Edward.

J[ANE] E[LIZABETH] NORTON, A bibliography of the works of Edward Gibbon. 1940. pp.xvi.256. [300.]

FRANCESCO CORDASCO, Edward Gibbon: a handlist of critical notices & studies. 18th century bibliographical pamphlets (no.10): Brooklyn 1950. pp.8. [59.]

C. V. WEDGWOOD, Edward Gibbon. British council: British book news: Bibliographical series of supplements (no.66): 1955. pp.39. [100.]

Gilbert, sir William Schwenck.

TOWNLEY SEARLE, Sir William Schwenck Gilbert. A topsy-turvy adventure. 1931. pp.[ix]. 105. [350.]

TOWNLEY SEARLE, A bibliography of Sir William Schwenck Gilbert. With bibliographical adventures in the Gilbert & Sullivan operas. [1931]. pp.[viii].107. [600.]
300 copies printed.

REGINALD ALLEN, W. S. Gilbert. An anniversary survey and exhibition checklist. University of Virginia: Bibliographical society: Charlottesville 1963. pp.[vii].84. [1000.]

Gill, Eric.

EVAN R. GILL, Bibliography of Eric Gill. [1953]. pp.xv.235. [664.]

Ginzberg, Louis.

BOAZ COHEN, Bibliography of the writings of Louis Ginzberg. New York 1933. pp.33. [494.]

Gissing, George Robert.

JOHN D[OZIER] GORDAN, George Gissing 1857–1903. An exhibition from the Berg collection. Public library: New York 1954. pp.45. [100.]

A. C. WARD, Gissing. British council: British book news: Bibliographical series of supplements (no.111): 1959. pp.43. [75.]

Gladstone, William Ewart.

WILLIAM EWART GLADSTONE, 1809–1898. A list of books and references to periodicals in the Brooklyn public library. Brooklyn 1909. pp.30. [300.]

Glasgow, Ellen Anderson Gholson.

WILLIAM W. KELLY, Ellen Glasgow. A bibliography. Bibliographical society of Virginia: Charlottesville 1964. pp.xl.330. [1500.]

Godwin, William.

FRANCESCO CORDASCO, William Godwin: a handlist of critical notices & studies. 18th century bibliographical pamphlets (no.9): Brooklyn 1950. pp.8. [30.]

Golding-Bird, Cuthbert Hilton.

GEO[RGE] A. R. WINSTON, Bibliography of the published writings (1876–1924) of Cuthbert Hilton Golding-Bird. Bibliographies of Guy's men (no.10): 1924. pp.11. [125.]

Goldsmith, Oliver.

KATHARINE CANBY BALDERSTON, A census of the manuscripts of Oliver Goldsmith. New York 1926. pp.xii.73. [150.]

TEMPLE SCOTT, Oliver Goldsmith bibliographically and biographically considered. Based on the collection of material in the library of W[illiam, M[cIntire] Elkins, esq. New York 1928. pp. xix.368. [100.]

E[RNEST] R[EGINALD] MCC[LINTOCK] DIX, The works of Oliver Goldsmith. Hand list of Dublin editions before 1801. Bibliographical society of Ireland (vol.iii, no.9): Wexford [printed] 1928. pp.[ii].93–101. [55.]

AN EXHIBITION in the Yale university library of the works of Oliver Goldsmith. New Haven 1928. pp.[ii].8. [56.]

475 copies printed.

A. NORMAN JEFFARES, Oliver Goldsmith. British council: British book news: Bibliographical series of supplements (no.107): 1959. pp.44. [100.]

Goldstein, Kurt.

[JOSEPH I. MEIERS], Kurt Goldstein bibliography. [New York 1958]. ff.[i].14. [190.]*

Goodman, Herman.

BIBLIOGRAPHY of Herman Goodman . . . 1918–1944. New York 1944. pp.39. [1000.]

— Bibliography . . . 1918–1954. [1954]. pp.48. [1250.]

Goodrich, Samuel Griswold.

LIST of writings of Samuel Griswold Goodrich (Peter Parley, *pseud.*). Library of Congress: Washington 1916. ff.4. [121.]*

Gordon, writers named.

JOHN MALCOLM BULLOCH, Bibliography of the Gordons. . . . Section I. University of Aberdeen: University studies (no.94): Aberdeen 1924. pp.xi. 219. [2000.]

on A–Augusta, Charles George (China), and lord George Gordon; 150 copies printed.

Gordon, Alexander.

H. MCLACHLAN, Alexander Gordon. . . . A biography, with a bibliography. University of Manchester: Publications (no.ccxviii): Manchester 1932. pp.xi.197. [1250.]

Gordon, Armistead Churchill.

[A. C. GORDON], A bibliography of the published writings of Armistead C. Gordon. [Staunton, Va.] 1923. pp.8. [100.]

privately printed.

Gordon, Thomas.

J[OHN] M[ALCOLM] BULLOCH, Thomas Gordon, the 'independent whig'. Aberdeen 1918. pp.33. [50.]

25 copies printed.

Gore-Booth, Constance, countess Markievicz.

P[ATRICK] S[ARSFIELD] O'HEGARTY, A bibliography of books by the O'Rahilly, Tom Clarke, Michaél oh-Annracháin, and countess de Markievicz. Dublin 1936. pp.5. [Markievicz: 3.]

25 copies privately printed.

Gosse, sir Edmund William.

A CATALOGUE of the Gosse correspondence in the Brotherton collection. Brotherton library: Leeds 1950. pp.xvi.80. [4000.]

Gould, George Milbry.

[G. M. GOULD], Bibliography of the contributions of George M. Gould . . . to ophthalmology, general medicine, literature, &c. Ithaca, N.Y. 1909. pp.62. [416.]

Graham, Dougal.

JOHN A. FAIRLEY, Dougal Graham and the chapbooks by and attributed to him. With a bibliography. Glasgow 1914. pp.[iii].91. [290.]

25 copies printed.

Graham, Robert Bontine Cunninghame.

LESLIE CHAUNDY, A bibliography of the first editions of the works of Robert Bontine Cunninghame Graham. 1924. pp.16. [44.]

HERBERT FAULKNER WEST, The Herbert Faulkner West collection of R. B. Cunninghame Graham presented . . . to the Dartmouth college library. [Hanover, N.H.] 1938. pp.22. [123.]

85 copies privately printed.

Graves, Robert von Ranke.

MARTIN SEYMOUR-SMITH, Robert Graves. British book news: Bibliographical series of supplements (no.78): 1956. pp.32. [60.]

Gray, John Edward.

[J. E. GRAY and JOHN SAUNDERS], List of the books, memoirs, and miscellaneous papers by dr. John Edward Gray. 1872. pp.58. [1163.]

privately printed; the preface and cover are dated 1875.

Gray, Thomas.

A CATALOGUE, briefly descriptive, of various books, and original manuscripts, of the poet Gray. 1851. pp.[ii].428. [200.]

CLARK SUTHERLAND NORTHUP, A bibliography of Thomas Gray. Cornell studies in english [vol.i]: New Haven 1917. pp.xv.296. [2050.]

— — [supplement]. By Herbert W[illmarth] Starr. Temple university: Philadelphia 1953. pp. xii.152. [1214.]

ROGER MARTIN, Chronologie de la vie et de l'œuvre de Thomas Gray. London &c. 1931. pp.[ii].200. [1000.]

RINTARO FUKUHARA, A bibliographical study of Thomas Gray. [Tokyo] 1933. pp.[ii].viii.69. [100.]

THOMAS GRAY, . . . and William Collins. Winchester college library: [Winchester 1947]. pp.11. [Gray: 24.]

R. W. KETTON-CRAMER, Thomas Gray. British council: British book news: Bibliographical series of supplements (no.104): 1958. pp.31. [60.]

Greeley, Horace.

LIST of references relating to Horace Greeley (exclusive of periodical articles) supplementary to bibliography in J. C. Stockett's Masters of american journalism. Library of Congress: Washington 1921. ff.4. [35.]*

Green, Thomas Hill.

PAUL MONTAGNÉ, Bibliographie relative à un radical religieux en Angleterre au XIXe siècle, ou la philosophie de Thomas Hill Green. Toulouse 1927. pp.67. [65.]

Greene, Graham.

FRANCIS WYNDHAM, Graham Greene. British book news: Bibliographical series of supplements (no.67): 1955. pp.31. [60.]

Greene, Robert.

SAMUEL A[ARON] TANNENBAUM, Robert Greene. (A concise bibliography). Elizabethan bibliographies (no.8): New York 1939. pp.[viii].58. [970.]

300 copies printed.

— — Supplement . . . by S. A. & Dorothy R. Tannenbaum 1945. ff.[i].23. [261.]*

Gregory, Augusta Persse, lady.

ELIZABETH COXHEAD, J. M. Synge and lady Gregory. British council: British book news: Bibliographical series: 1962. pp.35. [50.]

Griffith, Arthur.

P[ATRICK] S[ARSFIELD] O'HEGARTY, A bibliography of the books of Arthur Griffith, Michael Collins and Kevin O'Higgins. Dublin 1937. pp.9. [Griffith: 16.]

30 copies privately printed; interleaved.

Grimaldi, A. B.

ARTICLES, letters, &c., upon our israelitish origin. [*s.l.* 1904]. pp.[7]. [196.]

limited to writings by A. B. Grimaldi.

Grimaldi, Mary Beaufort.

[A. B. GRIMALDI], Writings and translations, &c. by Mary Beaufort Grimaldi. [1904]. pp.7. [90.]

Grosart, Alexander Balloch.

[A. B. GROSART], Hand-list of unique or extremely rare elizabethan-jacobean-carolian books . . . edited . . . by the rev. Alexander B. Grosart. Blackburn 1884–1885. pp.34. [100.]

Grosseteste, Robert.

S[AMUEL] HARRISON THOMSON, The writings of Robert Grosseteste, bishop of Lincoln, 1235–1253. Cambridge 1940. pp.xv.302. [1250.]

Guppy, Henry.

HENRY BUCKLEY CHARLTON, The John Rylands librarian. . . . With a bibliography of the writings of Henry Guppy compiled by Thomas Murgatroyd. Manchester 1941. pp.44. [117.]

Haggard, sir Henry Rider.

GEORGE L[ESLIE] MCKAY, A bibliography of the writings of sir Rider Haggard. 1930. pp.110. [269.]

457 copies printed.

—— Additions and corrections to the Haggard bibliography. By G. L. Mckay and J. E. Scott. 1939. pp.[iv].ii.28. [250.]

100 copies printed.

J. E. SCOTT, A bibliography of the works of sir Henry Rider Haggard. Takeley 1947.

Hall, Granville Stanley.

[LOUIS N. WILSON], Bibliography of the published writings of president G. Stanley Hall. Clark university: Library: Publications (vol.i, no.1): Worcester, Mass. 1903. pp.16. [225.]

Halliwell-Phillipps, James Orchard.

[J. O. HALLIWELL-PHILLIPPS], A list of works illustrative of the life and writings of Shakespeare, the history of Stratford-on-Avon, and the rise and progress of the early english drama, printed for . . . J. O. Halliwell. 1867. pp.71. [82.]

JUSTIN WINSOR, Halliwelliana: a bibliography of the publications of James Orchard Halliwell-Phillipps. Library of Harvard University: Bibliographical contributions (no.10): Cambridge, Mass. 1881. pp.30. [327.]

Hamilton, Alexander.

PAUL LEICESTER FORD, Bibliotheca hamiltoniana. New York 1886. pp.vi.ff.80. [270.]

PAUL LEICESTER FORD, A list of treasury reports and circulars issued by Alexander Hamilton 1789–1795. Brooklyn, N.Y. 1886. ff.23. [129.]
50 copies printed.

PAUL LEICESTER FORD, A list of editions of 'The federalist'. Brooklyn, N.Y. 1886. ff.13. [26.]
50 copies printed.

ALEXANDER HAMILTON: artilleryman. A selective bibliography. Army artillery and guide missile school: Library: Special bibliography (no.12): Fort Sill, Okla. 1957. pp.[i].4. [25.]*

Hamilton, Edith.

FRANKLIN PARKER and JOYCE BRONOUGH, Edith Hamilton at 94; a partial bibliography. [Austin 1961]. pp.7. [100.]*

Hardy, Thomas.

A. P. WEBB, A bibliography of the works of Thomas Hardy. 1916. pp.xiii.128. [750.]

HENRI DANIELSON, The first editions of the writings of Thomas Hardy and their values. 1916. pp.40. [35.]

RICHARD L. PURDY, Thomas Hardy, O.M., 1840–1928. Catalogue of a memorial exhibition of first editions, autograph letters and manuscripts. Yale university library: New Haven 1928. pp.41. [150.]

CARL J[EFFERSON] WEBER, Hardy at Colby. A check-list of the writings by and about Thomas Hardy now in the library of Colby college. Waterville, Me. 1936. pp.152. [1500.]

CARL J[EFFERSON] WEBER, On Thomas Hardy's birthday. Catalogue of an exhibition of first editions, autograph letters, manuscripts and other Hardy material. Colby college: Library: Waterville, Me. 1937. pp.16. [200.]

A DESCRIPTIVE catalogue of the Grolier club centenary exhibition, 1940, of the works of Thomas Hardy. Colby college: Monograph (no.9): Waterville, Me. 1940. pp.[vii].80. [250.]

A CENTURY of Thomas Hardy. Catalogue of a centennial exhibition. Colby college: Library: Waterville, Me. 1940. pp.[16]. [64.]

THE JUBILEE of *Tess*, 1891–1941. Catalogue of an exhibition. Colby college: Library: Waterville, Me. 1941. pp.64. [83.]
200 copies printed.

CARL J[EFFERSON] WEBER, The first hundred years of Thomas Hardy, 1840–1940. A centenary bibliography of Hardiana. Colby college library: Waterville, Me. 1942. pp.276. [4500.]

CARL J[EFFERSON] WEBER, Hardy music at Colby. A check-list. Colby college monograph (no.13): Waterville, Me. 1945. pp.24. [50.]
200 copies printed.

LIST of selected books: Thomas Hardy. Corporation public libraries: Glasgow 1949. pp.12. [125.]

RICHARD LITTLE PURDY, Thomas Hardy. A bibliographical study. 1954. pp.ix.387.

BUNNOSUKE YAMAMOTO, Bibliography of Thomas Hardy in Japan. Tokyo [1957]. pp.ix.294.

Harris, James Rendel.

P[IERRE] L[OUIS] COLLIGNON and E[RIC] F[OULGER] WILLS, An index to the essays dealing with ancient Egypt, the Celts and the Basques by dr.

J. Rendel Harris & miss Helen T. Sherlock. [Winscombe 1953]. pp.70. [65.]

Harris, Joel Chandler.

KATHARINE HINTON WOOTTEN, Bibliography of the works of Joel Chandler Harris. Carnegie library: Monthly bulletin (vol.iv, nos.9–10): Atlanta 1907. pp.6. [250.]

LIST of references on Joel Chandler Harris. Library of Congress: Washington 1915. ff.2. [18.]*

Harrison, Frederic.

FREDERIC HARRISON, Bibliography of Frederic Harrison. Hawkhurst 1908. ff.[ii].22. [300.]
privately printed; a copy revised by the author to 1910 is in the British museum.

Harrisse, Henry.

A[DOLF] GROWOLL, Henry Harrisse. Biographical and bibliographical sketch. Dibdin club: New York 1899. pp.16. [71.]
100 copies printed.

[HENRI CORDIER], Henry Harrisse, 1830–1910. Chartres [printed] 1911. pp.40. [83.]

Harrisse, Henry.

A[DOLF] GROWOLL, Henry Harrisse. Biographical and bibliographical sketch. Dibdin club: New York 1899. pp.16. [71.]

100 copies printed.

[HENRI CORDIER], Henry Harrisse, 1830–1910. Chartres [printed] 1911. pp.40. [83.]

HENRY VIGNAUD, Henry Harrisse. Étude biographique et morale, avec la bibliographie critique de ses écrits. 1912. pp.83. [94.]

NARCISO BINAYÁN, Henry Harrisse. Ensayo biobibliográfico. Publicaciones del Instituto de investigaciones históricas (no.xvi): Buenos Aires 1923. pp.36. [94.]

practically reproduced from Vignaud.

CARLOS [SANZ] LÓPEZ, Henry Harrisse (1829–1910) "principe de los americanistas", su vida — su obra. Con nuevas adiciones a la Bibliotheca americana vetustissima. 1958. pp.5–285. [100.]

this is in part a reprint, in part a facsimile of the Bibliotheca.

Harte, Bret.

GEORGE R[IPPEY] STEWART, A bibliography of the writings of Bret Harte in the magazines and newspapers of California, 1857–1871. University of California: Publications in english (vol.iii, no.3): Berkeley 1933. pp.[iii].119–170. [412.]

BRET HARTE. Bibliography and biographical data. Joseph Gaer, editor. California literary research: Monograph (no.10): [*s.l.* 1935]. ff.189. [1000.]*

THE BRET HARTE library of first editions from the library of bishop G[arfield] Bromley Oxnam given in honor of Raymond Woodburry Pence. DePauw university: Library: Greencastle 1958. pp.20. [150.]

Harting, James Edmund.

TITLES of works by J. E. Harting, 1866–1913. Weybridge 1925. pp.8. [40.]

Hartley, Leslie Poles.

PAUL BLOOMFIELD and BERNARD BERGONZI, L. P. Hartley. . . . Anthony Powell. British council: British book news: Bibliographical series: 1962. pp.40. [Hartley: 20.]

Harvie-Brown, John A.

BIBLIOGRAPHY of the writings of J. A. Harvie-Brown. [Dunipace 1896]. pp.32. [199.]

30 copies privately printed.

Haskins, Charles Homer.

GEORGE W. ROBINSON, Bibliography of Charles Homer Haskins. Cambridge, Mass. [printed] 1929. pp.389–398. [125.]

Haswell, William A.

[W. A. HASWELL], List of papers, etc. by William A. Haswell. Sydney [printed] [1892]. pp.8. [72.]

Hawthorne, Julian.

CHARLES HONCE, A Julian Hawthorne collection. New York 1939. pp.59. [81.]

35 copies privately printed.

Hawthorne, Nathaniel.

VICTOR HUGO PALTSITS, List of books, etc., by and relating to Nathaniel Hawthorne, prepared as an exhibition to commemorate the centenary of his birth. Public library: New York [1904]. pp.11. [250.]

[JACOB CHESTER CHAMBERLAIN], First editions of the works of Nathaniel Hawthorne, together with some manuscripts, letters and portraits, exhibited at the Grolier club. New York 1904. pp.vii.69. [62.]

— — [another edition]. 1904. pp.vii.88. [62.]

— — Second [*sic*] edition. 1905. pp.xi.78. [62.]

40 copies printed.

NINA E[LIZA] BROWNE, A bibliography of Nathaniel Hawthorne. Boston &c. 1905. pp.ix. ff.138.pp.139–216. [1000.]

A CATALOGUE of an exhibition of first editions, association books, autograph letters, and manuscripts of Nathaniel Hawthorne. University of Buffalo: Lockwood memorial library: Buffalo, N.Y. 1937. pp.19. [125.]

JOHN D[OZIER] GORDAN, Nathaniel Hawthorne. The years of fulfilment 1804–1853. An exhibition from the Berg collection, first editions, manuscripts, autograph letters. Public library: New York. 1954. pp.50. [150.]

Hayes, Alfred.

[GEORGE E. OVER], Alfred Hayes, Richard Le Galienne, Norman Gale. [Rugby 1894]. pp.[ii].11. [Hayes: 4.]

Hazlitt, William.

ALEXANDER IRELAND, List of the writings of William Hazlitt and Leigh Hunt, chronologically arranged. 1868. pp.[xxiii].2–233. [Hazlitt: 60.]

200 copies printed.

JULES DOUADY, Liste chronologique des œuvres de William Hazlitt. 1906. pp.ix.54. [750.]

[SIR] GEOFFREY [LANGDON] KEYNES, Bibliography of William Hazlitt. 1931. pp.xix.136. [138.]

J[OHN] B[OYNTON] PRIESTLEY, William Hazlitt. British council: British books news: Bibliographical series of supplements (no.122): 1960. pp.38. [100.]

Hearn, Lafcadio.

MARTHY HOWARD SISSON, Lafcadio Hearn. A bibliography. Bulletin of bibliography pamphlets (no.29): Boston 1933. pp.30. [450.]

Hearn, Lafcadio.

MARTHY HOWARD SISSON, Lafcadio Hearn. A bibliography. Bulletin of bibliography pamphlets (no.29): Boston 1933. pp.30. [450.]

P[ERCIVAL] D[ENSMORE] and IONE PERKINS, Lafcadio Hearn. A bibliography of his writing. Boston &c. 1934. pp.xix.444. [2500.]
200 copies printed.

WILLIAM TARG, Lafcadio Hearn: first editions and values. Chicago 1935. pp.52. [83.]

Heartman, Charles Frederick.

HERRY B. WEISS, The bibliographical, editorial and other activities of Charles F. Heartman. New Orleans [printed] 1938. pp.24. [125.]

399 copies privately printed.

Hemingway, Ernest.

LOUIS HENRY COHN, A bibliography of the works of Ernest Hemingway. New York 1931. pp.116. [200.]

LEE SAMUELS, A Hemingway check list. New York 1951. pp.3–63. [300.]

HANS GÜNTER MUCHAROWSKI, Die werke von Ernest Hemingway. Eine bibliographie der deutschsprachigen Hemingway-literatur und der originalwerke von 1923 bis 1954. Hamburg 1955. ff.[i].48. [500.]*

D. D. ZINK, Ernest Hemingway. Air force academy: Library: Special bibliography series (no.8): [Denver] 1959. pp.[ii].8. [50.]*

HANS W[ILLI] BENTZ, Ernest Hemingway in übersetzungen. Weltliteratur in übersetzungen (8th ser., vol.i): Frankfurt a. M. [1963]. pp.vii. 34.5. [375.]

335 copies printed.

Henry, O. [*pseud.* **William Sidney Porter.**]

PAUL S[TEPHEN] CLARKSON, A bibliography of William Sydney Porter. Caldwell, Idaho 1938. pp.161. [750.]

[INNA MIKHAILOVNA LEVIDOVA], О. Генри. Био-библиографический указатель к 50-летию со дня смерти. Всесоюзная государственная библиотека иностранной литературы: Писатели зарубежных стран: Москва 1960. pp.144. [1207.]

Henty, George Alfred.

[ZEBEDEE MOON], The historical tales of G. A. Henty arranged in chronological order, with a list of books on cognate subjects. [Second edition, revised by J. D. Perr]. Public libraries: Leyton 1915. pp.73. [Henty: 75.]

R[ODERICK] S[TUART] KENNEDY and B[ERNARD] J[AMES] FARMER, Bibliography of G. A. Henty & Hentyana. [1956]. ff.93. [250.]*

the British museum and Library of Congress copies contain manuscript additions.

Herbert, sir Alan Patrick.

GILBERT H. FABES, The first editions of A. E. Coppard, A. P. Herbert and Charles Morgan. 1933. pp.[vi].154. [Herbert: 44.]

Herbert, George.

GEORGE HERBERT PALMER, A Herbert bibliography. Library of Harvard university: Bibliographical contributions (no.59): Cambridge, Mass. 1911. pp.iv.19. [141.]

SAMUEL A[ARON] and DOROTHY A. TANNENBAUM, George Herbert. (A concise bibliography) Elizabethan bibliographies (no.35): New York 1946. ff.[iii].52. [773.]*

Herbert, Henry William.

PAUL S[PENCER] SEYBOLT, The first editions of Henry William Herbert, 'Frank Forester', 1807–1858. Boston 1932. pp.[16]. [62.]

60 copies privately printed.

WILLIAM MITCHELL VAN WINKLE, Henry William Herbert [Frank Forester]. A bibliography of his writings. Portland, Me. 1936. pp.xviii.189. [750.]

Hergesheimer, Joseph.

H[ERBERT] L. R. SWIRE, A bibliography of the works of Joseph Hergesheimer. The Centaur bibliographies of modern american authors [vol.i]: Philadelphia 1922. pp.40. [100.]

300 copies printed.

Herrick, Robert.

SAMUEL A[ARON] TANNENBAUM and DOROTHY R. TANNENBAUM, Robert Herrick. (A concise bibliography). Elizabethan bibliographies (no.45): New York 1949. ff.[iii].iii.58. [860.]*

JOHN PRESS, Robert Herrick. British council: British book news: Bibliographical series of supplements (no.132): 1961. pp.40. [50.]

Hewett, Edgar L.

LESLIE V. MURPHEY, Bibliography of Edgar L. Hewett, 1893–1944. Santa Fé, N.M. 1944. pp.[ii]. 9. [211.]

Hewlett, Maurice Henry.

P[ERCIVAL] H[ORACE] MUIR, A bibliography of the first editions of books by Maurice Henry Hewlett (1861–1923). Bookman's journal: Supplement: 1927. pp.9–36. [58.]

— — Addenda & corrigenda. [*s.l.*1931]. pp.[4]. [4.]

Heywood, John.

KENNETH WALTER CAMERON, The background of John Heywood's 'Witty and witless'. . . . Together with a specialised bibliography of Heywood scholarship. Raleigh, N.C. 1941. pp.46. [75.]

SAMUEL A[ARON] and DOROTHY A. TANNENBAUM, John Heywood. (A concise bibliography). Elizabethan bibliographies (no.36): New York 1946. ff.[iii].31. [426.]*

Heywood, Thomas.

ARTHUR MELVILLE CLARK, A bibliography of Thomas Heywood. Oxford bibliographical society: Proceedings & papers (vol.i, part II): Oxford 1925. pp.97–153. [125.]

SAMUEL A[ARON] TANNENBAUM, Thomas Heywood. [A concise bibliography]. Elizabethan bibliographies (no.6): New York 1939. pp.[viii]. 43. [713.]

300 copies printed.

Higginson, Thomas Wentworth.

A BIBLIOGRAPHY of Thomas Wentworth Higginson. Public library: Cambridge, Mass. 1906. pp.47. [600.]

Higlett, G. A.

FRED. J. MELVILLE, The Higlett booklets. A bijou bibliography. [1925]. pp.9. [15.]

50 copies printed.

Hill, sir George Francis.

A TRIBUTE to sir George Hill on his eightieth birthday. Oxford 1948. pp.43. [400.]

privately printed.

Hirsch, Paul Adolf.

[OLGA HIRSCH], A handlist of some articles & catalogues written or published by Paul Hirsch. With a list of publications of the Paul Hirsch music library. Cambridge [1951]. pp.[v].7. [32.]

100 copies privately printed.

Hirsch, Samuel.

ADOLPH S. OKO, Bibliography of Samuel Hirsch. Cincinnati 1916. pp.15. [111.]

Hobbes, Thomas.

A CATALOGUE of the works of mr. Hobbes. [1675]. pp.[2]. [34.]

HUGH MACDONALD and [JOAN] MARY HARGREAVES, Thomas Hobbes. A bibliography. Bibliographical society: 1952. pp.xvii.84. [109.]

HIROSHI MIZUTA, The list of works of and relating to Thomas Hobbes appended to "The formation and modern concept of human nature", 1954, Tokyo. [Tokyo 1954]. pp.[ii].35. [400.]

T. E. JESSOP, Thomas Hobbes. British council: British book news: Bibliographical series of supplements (no.130): 1960. pp.40. [100.]

Hobbs, William Herbert.

PUBLICATIONS of William Herbert Hobbs. Ann Arbor [printed] [1908]. pp.[8]. [100.]

Hocken, Thomas Morland.

LINDA RODDA, Calendar of dr T. M. Hocken's personal letters and documents preserved in the Hocken library, Otago university. Dunedin 1948. pp.vii.62. [600.]*

Hocking, William Ernest.

RICHARD C. GILMAN, The bibliography of William Ernest Hocking. Colby college: Waterville, Me. 1951. pp.[iv].63. [208.]*

Holcroft, Thomas.

ELBRIDGE COLBY, A bibliography of Thomas Holcroft. Public library: New York 1922. pp.94. [125.]

Holland, Philemon.

[HERBERT SILVETTE], A short-title list of the writings of Philemon Holland. [Charlottesville] 1939. pp.x.18. [52.]

privately printed; the Bodleian library copy contains corrections in ms.

HERBERT SILVETTE, Catalogue of the works of Philemon Holland. Charlottesville, Va. 1940. pp. iii–xvii.29. [71.]

Holmes, Oliver Wendell.

GEORGE B[URNHAM] IVES, A bibliography of Oliver Wendell Holmes. Boston &c. 1907. pp. xv.338. [1000.]

pages 323–337 are blank.

OLIVER WENDELL HOLMES, 1809–1894. A list of books, with references to periodicals, in the Brooklyn public library. Brooklyn 1909. pp.16. [275.]

THOMAS FRANKLIN CURRIER, A bibliography of Oliver Wendell Holmes. . . . Edited by Eleanor M. Tilton. Bibliographical society of America: New York 1953. pp.xiii.708. [5000.]

ANITA RUTMAN, LUCY CLARK and MARJORIE CARVER, The Barrett library. Oliver Wendel Holmes. A checklist of printed and manuscripl works . . . in the library of the university of Virtginia. Charlottesville 1960. pp.[vii].109. [500.]*

Holtby, Winifred.

GEOFFREY HANDLEY-TAYLOR, Winifred Holtby. A concise and selected bibliography. 1955. pp. xvii.76. [500.]

Holyoake, George Jacob.

CHA[RLE]S W[ILLIA]M F. GOSS, A descriptive bibliography of the writings of George Jacob Holyoake. 1908. pp.lxxxii.118. [500.]

Hood, Thomas.

LAURENCE ROBERT MEAN BRANDER, Thomas Hood. British council: British book news: Bibliographical series of supplements: 1963. pp.47. [40.]

Hope, sir Thomas.

A DIARY of the public correspondence of sir Thomas Hope of Craighall, bart., 1633–1645. From the original, in the library at Pinkie house. Bannatyne club: Edinburgh 1843. pp.[vi].vii.234. [1000.]

Hope, sir William St. John.

A. HAMILTON THOMPSON, A bibliography of the published writings of sir William St. John Hope. Leeds 1929. pp.50. [255.]

Hopkins, Gerard Manley.

GERARD MANLEY HOPKINS, 1844–1889. A bibliographical list. Library of Congress: [Washington] 1940. ff.12. [97.]*

Horne, Richard Henry.

ERI J[AY] SHUMAKER, A concise bibliography of the complete works of Richard Henry (Hengist) Horne (1802–1884). Granville, O. 1943. pp.vi.14. [400.]

Houghton, Claude [Claude Houghton Oldfield.]

[SIR] HUGH [SEYMOUR] WALPOLE and CLEMENCE DANE [WINIFRED ASHTON], Claude Houghton. Appreciations . . . with a bibliography. 1935. pp.16. [15.]

Housman, Alfred Edward.

A[NDREW] S[YDENHAM] F[ARRAR] G[OW], A. E. Housman. A list of adversaria, etc. [Cambridge] 1926. pp.12. [195.]
privately printed.

THEODORE G[EORGE] EHRSAM, A bibliography of Alfred Edward Housman. Useful reference series (vol.lxvi): Boston 1941. pp.44. [750.]

JOHN [WAYNFLETE] CARTER and JOHN [HANBURY ANGUS] SPARROW, A. E. Housman. An annotated hand-list. Soho bibliographies (no.2): 1952. pp.54. [50.]

IAN SCOTT-KILVERT, A. E. Housman. British council: British book news: Bibliographical series of supplements (no.69): 1955. pp.40. [35.]

JOHN [WAYNFLETE] CARTER and JOSEPHE W[ILLIAM] SCOTT, A. E. Housman. Catalogue of an exhibition on the centenary of his birth. University college: 1959. pp.36. [50.]

Howard, John.

LEONA BAUMGARTNER, John Howard (1726–1790). . . . A bibliography. Baltimore 1939. pp. [ii].79. [300.]

Howell, James.

WILLIAM HARVEY VANN, Notes on the writings of James Howell. [Waco, Texas (printed) 1924]. pp.[iii].71. [150.]

Howells, William Dean.

WILLIAM M[ERRIAM] GIBSON and GEORGE ARMS, A bibliography of William Dean Howells. Public library: New York 1948. pp.182. [3000.]

FANNIE MAE ELLIOTT and LUCY CLARK, The Barrett library. W. D. Howells. A checklist of printed and manuscript works . . . in the library of the university of Virginia. Charlottesville 1959. pp. [v].68. [300.]*

Howse, sir Henry Greenway.

J. H. E. WINSTON, Bibliography of the published writings (1869–1904) of sir Henry Greenway Howse. Bibliographies of Guy's men (no.4): 1915. pp.6. [50.]

Hubbard, Frank McKinney.

BLANCHE STILLSON and DOROTHY RITTER RUSSO, Abe Martin–Kin Hubbard. A study of a character and his creation intended primarily as a check list of the Abe Martin books. Indianapolis 1939. pp.39. [30.]

350 copies printed.

Hudson, William Henry.

[GEORGE] F[RANCIS] WILSON, A bibliography of the writings of W. H. Hudson. 1922. pp.80. [57.]

Hughes, Lewis.

GEORGE WATSON COLE, Lewis Hughes, the militant minister of the Bermudas and his printed works. American antiquarian society: Worcester, Mass. 1928. pp.67. [14.]

Hughes, Thomas.

M. L. PARRISH and BARBARA KELSEY MAUN, Charles Kingsley and Thomas Hughes. First editions . . . in the library at Dormy house, Pine Valley, New Jersey. 1936. pp.xi.166. [Hughes: 60.]

151 copies printed.

Hulbert, Archer Butler.

BIBLIOGRAPHY of the writings of Archer Butler Hulbert. [Montpelier, Vt. 1929]. pp.10. [102.]

Hume, David.

T[HOMAS] E[DMUND] JESSOP, A bibliography of David Hume and of scottish philosophy from Francis Hutcheson to lord Balfour. 1938. pp.xiv. 201. [Hume: 750.]

Hume, Edgar Erskine.

EDGAR ERSKINE HUME bibliography. [*s.l.* 1941]. ff.19. [250.]*

Hunt, James Henry Leigh.

ALEXANDER IRELAND, List of the writings of William Hazlitt and Leigh Hunt, chronologically arranged. 1868. pp.[xxiii].2–233. [Hunt: 80.]

200 copies printed.

ALEXANDER MITCHELL, A bibliography of the writings of Leigh Hunt. Bookman's journal: [1930]. pp.7–73. [75.]

LUTHER A[LBERTUS] BREWER, My Leigh Hunt library. . . . The first editions. Cedar Rapids 1932. pp.xlv.391. [200.]

125 copies privately printed.

LUTHER A[LBERTOS] BREWER, My Leigh Hunt library. The holograph letters. Iowa City [1938]. pp.vi.421. [500.]

Hutchinson, Thomas.

CHARLES DEANE, A bibliographical essay on governor Hutchinson's historical publications. Boston 1857. pp.39. [10.]

50 copies privately printed.

Hutton, Edward.

DENNIS E[VERARD] RHODES, The writings of Edward Hutton. A bibliographical tribute. 1955. pp.64. [225.]

250 copies printed.

Huxley, Aldous Leonard.

P[ERCIVAL] H[ORACE] MUIR and B[ERTIE] VAN THAL, Bibliographies of the first editions of books by Aldous Huxley and T. F. Powys. 1927. pp.61. [Huxley: 500.]

not limited to books.

HANSON R[AWLINGS] DUVAL, Aldous Huxley. A bibliography. New York 1939. pp.205. [1000.]

ALDOUS HUXLEY. The writings of Aldous Huxley, 1916–1943. An exhibition of the collection of Jacob I[srael] Zeitlin at the library of the university of California. [Los Angeles 1943]. pp.[16].

500 copies printed.

JOCELYN BROOKE, Aldous Huxley. British council: British book news: Bibliographical series of supplements (no.55): 1954. pp.31. [75.]

CLAIRE JOHN ESCHELBACH and JOYCE LEE SHOBER, Aldous Huxley. A bibliography 1916–1959. University of California bibliographic guides: Berkeley 1961. pp.x.150. [1281.]*

Huxley, Thomas Henry.

WARREN R[OYAL] DAWSON, The Huxley papers. A descriptive catalogue of the correspondence, manuscripts and miscellaneous papers of . . . Thomas Henry Huxley. Imperial college of science and technology: 1946. pp.xii.201. [3000.]

WILLIAM IRVINE, Thomas Henry Huxley. British council: British book news: Bibliographical series of supplements (no.119): 1960. pp.40. [75.]

Hyde, Charles Gilman.

GERARD J. GIEFER, CYNTHIA BARNES and MORRILL G. FOLSON, Publications and reports of Charles Gilman Hyde. University of California: Water resources center archives: Report (no.4): Berkeley 1959. pp.iii.38. [232.]*

Hyde, Douglas.

P[ATRICK] S[ARSFIELD] O'HEGARTY, A bibliography of dr. Douglas Hyde. Dublin 1939. pp.19. [50.]

40 copies privately printed; interleaved.

Imagists.

AN EXHIBITION. The Glenn Hughes drama and imagist poetry collection. University of Texas: Humanities research center: [Austin] 1959. pp.14. [95.]

500 copies printed.

Ingram, John Kells.

[T. W. LYSTER], Bibliography of the writings of John Kells Ingram, 1823–1907. Cumann na Leabharlann: Dublin [1909]. pp.46. [125.]

Irving, Washington.

THE SELIGMAN COLLECTION of Irvingiana. A catalogue of manuscripts and other material by or about Washington Irving given to the New York public library by mrs. Isaac N. Seligman and mr. George S[idney] Hellman. New York 1926. pp.31. [200.]

R[OBERT] W[ILLIAM] G[LENROIE] VAIL, The Hellman collection of Irvingiana. A catalogue of manuscripts and other material by or about Washington Irving given to the New York public library by mr. George S. Hellman. New York 1929. pp.15. [60.]

STANLEY T[HOMAS] WILLIAMS and MARY ALLEN EDGE, A bibliography of the writings of Washington Irving. A check list. New York 1936. pp.xxi.200. [3000.]

WILLIAM R[OBERT] LANGFELD and PHILIP C[ONKLIN] BLACKBURN, Washington Irving. A bibliography. Public library: New York 1933. pp.ix.91. [1000.]

Jacobson, Walter Hamilton Acland.

GEO[RGE] A. R. WINSTON, Bibliography of the published writings (1877–1923) of Walter Hamilton Acland Jacobson. Bibliographies of Guy's men (no.9): 1924. pp.8. [75.]

Jakobson, Roman.

A BIBLIOGRAPHY of the publications of Roman Jakobson on language, literature and culture. [Cambridge, Mass. 1951]. pp.17. [263.]*

James V.

ROBERT KERR HANNAY, The letters of James V. Edited by Denys Hay. Edinburgh 1954. pp.xvi. 468. [1250.]

James, Henry.

LE ROY PHILLIPS, A bibliography of the writings of Henry James. Boston &c. 1906. pp.xi.200. [900.]

250 copies printed; pp.188–199 are blank.

— — [second edition]. New York 1930. pp. xviii.285. [1250.]

MICHAEL SWAN, Henry James. British council: British book news: Bibliographical series of supplements: 1950. pp.43. [200.]

LEON EDEL and DAN H. LAURENCE, A bibliography of Henry James. Soho bibliographies (vol.viii): 1957. pp.411. [1100.]

— — Second edition. 1961. pp.427. [1200.]

James, Montague Rhodes.

[A. E. SCHOLFIELD], Elenchys scriptorvm Montacvtii Rhodes Iames qvae typis impressa vsqve ad annvm M.DCCCC.XXXV in lvcem prodiervnt. Cantabrigiae 1935. pp.35. [450.]

100 copies privately printed.

S. G. LUBBOCK, A memoir of Montague Rhodes James. . . . with a list of his writings by A. F. Scholfield. Cambridge 1939. pp.[vii].87. [500.]

James, William.

RALPH BARTON PERRY, Annotated bibliography of the writings of William James. 1920. pp.[v].69. [300.]

additions by Pedro S. Zulen appear in The journal of philosophy ([*Lancaster. Pa.*] *1921*), *xviii.615–616.*

Jarrell, Randall.

CHARLES M. ADAMS, Randall Jarrell. A bibliography. Chapel Hill 1958. pp.72. [500.]

Jefferies, John Richard.

HAROLD JOLLIFFE, A catalogue of the books in the Richard Jefferies collection of the Swindon public libraries. Swindon 1948. pp.16. [125.]

Jeffers, John Robinson.

S[YDNEY] S[EYMOUR] ALBERTS, A bibliography of the works of Robinson Jeffers. New York 1933. pp.xvii.264. [500.]

487 copies printed.

ROBINSON JEFFERS, 1905–1935. An exhibition. [Occidental college: Los Angeles 1935]. pp.[191]. [25.]

200 copies printed.

[ALICE GAY], Robinson Jeffers at Occidental college. A check list of the Jeffers collection in the Mary Norton Clapp library. Los Angeles 1955. pp.23. [100.]

ANITA RUTMAN, LUCY [TRIMBLE] CLARK and MARJORIE CARVER, Robinson Jeffers. A checklist of printed and manuscript works . . . in the library. University of Virginia: Barrett library: Charlottesville 1960. pp.[vii].41. [700.]*

Jefferson, Thomas.

HAMILTON BULLOCK TOMPKINS, Bibliotheca jeffersoniana. A list of books written by or relating to Thomas Jefferson. New York &c. 1887. pp.187. [301.]

350 copies printed, on one side of the leaf.

CALENDAR of the correspondence of Thomas Jefferson. Bulletin of the Bureau of rolls and library of the Department of state (nos.6, 8, 10): Washington 1894–1903. pp.viii.541+iii.593+iii. 270. [20,000.]

RICHARD HOLLAND JOHNSTON, A contribution to a bibliography of Thomas Jefferson. Washington 1905. pp.iv.73. [1500.]

30 copies printed.

FRANK E. WOODWARD, Reference list of works relating to Thomas Jefferson. Malden, Mass. 1906. ff.[2]. [25.]

SELECT list of references on Thomas Jefferson. Library of Congress: Washington 1919. ff.8. [71.]*
— Additional references. 1931. ff.2. [19.]*

W. HARVEY WISE and JOHN W[ILLIAM] CRONIN, A bibliography of Thomas Jefferson. Presidential bibliographical series (no.3): Washington 1935. pp.72. [1166.]

THE JEFFERSON bicentennial, 1743–1943. A catalogue of the exhibition at the Library of Congress. Washington 1943. pp.iii.171. [500.]

THOMAS JEFFERSON, 1743–1943. A guide to the rare books, maps & manuscripts exhibited at the university of Michigan. William L. Clements library: Bulletin (no.xxxviii): Ann Arbor 1943. pp.32. [50.]

EVERETT E[UGENE] EDWARDS, Selected references on Thomas Jefferson and his contributions to agriculture. Department of agriculture: Library: list (no.8): Washington 1944. pp.7. [90.]*

CONSTANCE E. THURLOW and FRANCIS L[EWIS] BERKELEY, The Jefferson papers of the university of

Virginia. A calendar. University of Virginia bibliographical series (no.8): Charlottesville 1950. pp.xii.345. [2341.]

COOLIE VERNER, A further checklist of the separate editions of Jefferson's Notes on the state of Virginia. Bibliographical society of the university of Virginia: Charlottesville 1950. ff.3–26. [30.]*

THOMAS JEFFERSON and architecture. A list of books and articles in the library of Virginia. Alderman library: Charlottesville 1953. ff.3. [30.]*

WILLIAM B[AINTER] O'NEAL, A checklist of writings on Thomas Jefferson as an architect. American association of architectural bibliographers: Publication (no.15): [Charlottesville] 1959. pp.18. [150.]

Jewett, Sarah Orne.

CLARA CARTER WEBER and CARL J[EFFERSON] WEBER, A bibliography of the published writings of Sarah Orne Jewett. Colby college monograph (no.18): Waterville, Me. 1949. pp.xi.107. [650.]

300 copies printed.

Jillson, Willard Rouse.

[W. R. JILLSON], A bibliography of the several

books, reports, papers and maps principally relating to geology written and prepared by Williard [*sic*] Rouse Jillson. Kentucky geological survey (6th ser., no.1 &c.): Frankfort, Ky.

1920 . . . (6th ser., no.1). pp.7. [32.]
1921 . . . (6th ser., no.2). pp.11. [52.]
1922 . . . (6th ser., no.3). pp.14. [71.]
1924 . . . (6th ser., no.4). pp.17. [108.]
1926 . . . (6th ser., no.11). pp.22. [147.]

these are successive editions.

PAULINE NORRIS, Collected writings of Willard Rouse Jillson. Frankfort, Ky. 1933. pp.15. [276.]

ANNE E. OVERSTREET, The books, pamphlets and reprints of Willard Rouse Jillson. A bibliography (1917–1953). Dearborn, Mich. 1954. pp.33. [252.]

CHARLES MANNING, A selective bibliography of the historical writings of Willard Rouse Jillson (1919–1959). Frankfort, Ky. 1961. pp.16. [121.]

John of Gaddesden.

GEORGE DOCK, Printed editions of the Rosa anglica of John of Gaddesden. [*s.l.* 1907]. pp.11. [23.]

Johnson, Charles.

PHILIP GOSSE, A bibliography of the works of captain Charles Johnson. 1927. pp.82. [68.]

150 copies printed.

Johnson, Charles Spurgeon.

CHARLES SPURGEON JOHNSON. A bibliography. Fisk university library: [Nashville 1947]. pp.16. [100.]

Johnson, Robert Livingston.

RICHARD H. WISSLER, Challenge to action. . . . A biographical-bibliography. [1963]. pp.[ii].xxv. 377. [3113.]*

Johnson, Samuel.

LIST of books and articles relating to Samuel Johnson, 1709–1784, compiled on the occasion of the exhibition held at the Yale university library, November 1–6, 1909. [New Haven 1909]. pp.24. [375.]

SAMUEL JOHNSON, 1709–1784. A list of books, with references to periodicals, in the Brooklyn public library. Brooklyn 1909. pp.20. [300.]

CHAUNCEY BREWSTER TINKER, Catalogue of an exhibition of manuscripts, first editions, early engravings, and various literature relating to Samuel Johnson, 1709–1784. Yale university library: New Haven 1909. pp.12. [96.]

CATALOGUE of an exhibition commemorative of the bicentenary of the birth of Samuel Johnson. Grolier club: New York 1909. pp.viii.107. [70.]

WILLIAM PRIDEAUX COURTNEY, A bibliography of Samuel Johnson. . . . Revised . . . by David Nichol Smith. Oxford historical and literary studies (vol.iv): Oxford 1915. pp.iii–viii.186. [1000.]

—— A reissue . . . illustrated with facsimiles. 1925. pp.viii.186. [1000.]

350 copies printed.

W[ILLIAM] J[AMES] COUPER, Dr. Johnson in the Hebrides: a bibliographical paper. Glasgow 1916. pp.23. [13.]

privately printed.

[ROBERT WILLIAM CHAPMAN], Johnson, d^r^. Samuel. Hand-list (roughly chronological) of all known editions, up to 1785, of the principal works published in Johnson's lifetime. [Oxford 1921] ff.[i].10. [125.]*

Clinton. Oxford 1936. pp.xxvii.258. [1607.]

R[OBERT] W[ILLIAM] CHAPMAN, Johnson's letters. [1937]. pp.39. [1250.]

JAMES L[OWRY] CLIFFORD, Johnsonian studies, 1887–1950. A survey and bibliography. Minneapolis [1951]. pp.ix.140. [2078.]

S. C. ROBERTS, Samuel Johnson. British council: British book news: Bibliographical series of supplements (no.47): 1954. pp.44. [100.]

AN EXHIBITION in honor of the 200th anniversary of the publication of Johnson's Dictionary. Columbia university: Libraries: [New York 1955]. pp.16. [55.]

DR. SAMUEL JOHNSON. . . . Celebrations in Birmingham of the 250th anniversary of his birth. An exhibition of books, manuscripts . . . arranged jointly by the Reference library and the Museum and art gallery. [Birmingham 1959]. pp.28. [188.]

[HERBERT CAHOON], Samuel Johnson. . . . An exhibition of first editions, manuscripts, letters, and portraits to commemorate the 250th anniversary of his birth, and the 200th anniversary of the publication of his *Rasselas*. Pierpont Morgan library: New York 1959. pp.[46]. [125.]

the Bodleian press-marks are added in ms. to a copy in that library.

[RALPH BORTHWICK ADAM], Catalogue of the Johnsonian collection of R. B. Adam. Buffalo 1921. pp.[437]. [2500.]

privately printed.

— — [another edition]. The R. B. Adam library relating to dr. Samuel Johnson and his era. 1929. pp.[564]+[411]+[485]. [3000.]

500 copies printed; the pagination is erratic throughout and has been ignored.

NOTES on a loan collection of Johnsonian books & mss. shown at Amen house. 1925. pp.8. [40.]

AN EXHIBITION of original manuscripts . . . and books of and relating to dr. Samuel Johnson . . . from the collection of dr. A. S. W. Rosenbach. Free library: Philadelphia 1934. pp.[7]. [35.]

ALLEN T[RACY] HAZEN and EDWARD L[IPPINCOTT] MCADAM, A catalogue of an exhibition of first editions of the works of Samuel Johnson. Yale university: New Haven 1935. pp.32. [150.]

CLAUDE COLLEER ABBOTT, A catalogue of papers relating to Boswell, Johnson & sir William Forbes found at Fettercairn house, a residence of . . . lord

CATALOGUE of an exhibition of books in the Birmingham library to celebrate the 250th anniversary of the birth of dr. Samuel Johnson. [Birmingham 1959]. pp.[iv].13. [50.]

100 copies printed.

Johnson, Treat Baldwin.

LIST of more important scientific publications. [*s.l.* 1916]. pp.11. [200.]

Johnston, Arthur.

WILLIAM JOHNSTON, The bibliography and extant portraits of Arthur Johnston. Aberdeen 1895. pp.33. [100.]

36 copies privately printed.

— — [another edition]. The bibliography and portraits of Arthur Johnston. Aberdeen 1896. pp. 28. [100.]

16 copies privately printed.

Johnston, Richard Malcolm.

EDMUND CLARENCE STEDTMAN and STEPHEN B[EAUREGARD] WEEKS, Literary estimate and bibliography of Richard Malcolm Johnston. Harrisburg, Pa. 1898. pp.15. [50.]

— — Supplement. List of references on Richard

Malcolm Johnston. Library of Congress: Washington 1922. ff.3. [28.]*

Johnston-Lavis, Henry James.

[H. J. JOHNSTON-LAVIS], List of books, memoirs, articles, letters, etc. of H. J. Johnston-Lavis. 1912. pp.ii.24. [161.]

Jollie, Thomas.

THOMAS JOLLIE's papers. A list of the papers in Dr. Williams's library, manuscript no.12.78. Dr Williams's library: Occasional paper (no.3): 1956. pp.[12]. [58.]*

Jones, John Beauchamp.

LIST of works of John Beauchamp Jones. Library of Congress: Washington 1916. ff.2. [20.]*

Jones, Rufus Matthew.

NIXON ORWIN RUSH, A bibliography of the published writings of Rufus M. Jones. Colby college monograph (no.12): Waterville, Me. 1944. pp.vi.57. [650.]

200 copies printed.

Jones, Thomas Gwynn.

OWEN WILLIAMS, A bibliography of Thomas Gwynn Jones. Denbighshire county libraries: Wrexham 1938. pp.53. [496.]

55 copies printed.

Jones, sir William.

GARLAND H[AMPTON] CANNON, Sir William Jones, orientalist. An annotated bibliography of his works. Honolulu [1952]. pp.xvi.88. [46.]

Jonson, Ben.

H[ERBERT] L. FORD, Collation of the Ben Jonson folios, 1616–1631 — 1640. Oxford [printed] 1932. pp.30.

SAMUEL A[ARON] TANNENBAUM, Ben Jonson. (A concise bibliography). Elizabethan bibliographies (no.2): New York 1938. pp.viii.151. [2651.]

300 copies printed.

— — Supplement . . . by S. A. Tannenbaum and Dorothy R. Tannenbaum. [1947]. ff.[ii].ii.85. [1280.]*

J. B. BAMBOROUGH, Ben Jonson. British council: British book news: Bibliographical series of supplements (no.112): 1959. pp.43. [100.]

Jordan, David Starr.

FOR international peace. A list of books, reviews . . . in the interests of peace, friendship, and understanding between nations, by David Starr Jordan, 1898–1925. Stanford university: 1925. pp.30. [400.]

ALICE N[EWMAN] HAYS, David Starr Jordan. A bibliography of his writings, 1871–1931. Stanford university publications: University series: Library studies (vol.i): Stanford 1952. pp.195. [2017.]

Joyce, James Augustine Aloysius.

P[ATRICK] S[ARSFIELD] O'HEGARTY, A bibliography of James Joyce. Dublin 1946. pp.12. [23.]
40 copies privately printed.

JAMES FULLER SPOERRI, Catalog of a collection of the works of James Joyce exhibited at the Newberry library. Chicago 1948. pp.[71]. [143.]
privately printed; the British museum copy contains a typewritten supplement.

ALAN [DEAN] PARKER, James Joyce: a bibliography of his writings, critical material and miscellanea. Useful reference series (no.76): Boston 1948. pp.[v].259. [500.]*
a fragment of this work was issued, under the same title, in 1946.

JAMES JOYCE, Sa vie, son œuvre, son rayonnement. Paris [1949]. pp.[126]. [600.]
in the main an exhibition catalogue.

JOHN J. SLOCUM and HERBERT CAHOON, A bibliography of James Joyce, 1882–1941. Soho bibliographies (no.5): 1953. pp.ix.195. [373.]

JAMES FULLER SPOERRI, Finnegans wake. . . . A check list, including publications of portions under the title Work in progress. Northwestern university: Library: Evanston, Ill. 1953. pp.18. [75.]

JAMES F[ULLER] SPOERRI, James Joyce. Books and pamphlets relating to the author and his works. University of Virginia: Bibliographical society: Secretary's news sheet (no.34): Charlottesville 1955. pp.16. [60.]*
—— Supplement. . . . (no.42): 1959. pp.[8]. [25.]*
a supplement also forms part of nos.37 and 48.

J. I. M. STEWART, James Joyce. British council: British book news: Bibliographical series of supplements (no.91): 1957. pp.43. [60.]

ALAN M. COHN, James Joyce. An exhibition from the collection of dr. Harley K. Croessmann.

Southern Illinois university: Library: [Carbondale 1957]. pp.iii.13. [34.]

ROBERT E[DWARD] SCHOLES, The Cornell Joyce collection. A catalogue. Ithaca [1961]. pp.xvii.225. [1450.]

PETER SPIELBERG, James Joyce's manuscripts & letters at the university of Buffalo. A catalogue. [Buffalo] 1962 [1963]. pp.xxii.241. [500.]

ROBERT H. DEMING, A bibliography of James Joyce studies. University of Kansas: Library series (no.18): [Lawrence] 1964. pp.[viii].180. [1434.]

Kaiser, John Boynton.

[GERTRUDE OELLIRCH *and others*], An annotated bibliography of the writings of John Boynton Kaiser published 1911 to 1958. Public library: NPL news supplement: Newark 1958. pp.32. [146.]

Keats, John.

[HARRY NELSON GAY], List of the first thousand works acquired by the Keats-Shelley memorial, Rome. 1910. pp.115. [Keats: 75.]

[—] — List of the second thousand works. . . . 1913. pp.99. [125.]

SHORT bibliographies of Wordsworth, Coleridge, Byron, Shelley, Keats. English association: Leaflet (no.23): 1912. pp.13. [250.]

CATALOGUE of a loan exhibition commemorating the anniversary of the death of John Keats. Public library: Boston 1921. pp.[iii].63. [200.]

J[AMES] R[OBERTSON] MAC GILLIVRAY, Keats. A bibliography and reference guide. University of Toronto: Department of english: Studies and texts (no.3): [Toronto] 1949. pp.lxxxi.210. [1250.]

EDMUND [CHARLES] BLUNDEN, John Keats. British council: British book news. Bibliographical series of supplements: 1950. pp.37. [45.]

Kennedy, John Fitzgerald.

JOHN F. KENNEDY 1917–1963. A chronological list of references. Library of Congress: Washington 1964. pp.iii.68. [220.]

limited to the president's own writings.

Kenyon, John Samuel.

ANNOTATED bibliography of the publications of John S. Kenyon. [*s.l.*] 1954. ff.[ii].23. [75.]

privately reproduced from typewriting.

Ker, William Paton.

J[OHN] H[ENRY] P[YLE] PAFFORD, W. P. Ker, 1855–1923. A bibliography. 1950. pp.72. [350.]

Keyes, Charles Rollins.

LIST of the scientific writings of Charles Rollins Keyes. Baltimore 1909. pp.23. [415.]

Keynes, sir Geoffrey Langdon.

[W. R. LE FANU], Geoffrey Keynes. Tributes . . . with a bibliographical check list of his publications. Osler club: 1961. pp.64. [400.]

Kimball, Sidney Fiske.

MARY KANE, A bibliography of the works of Fiske Kimball. Edited by Frederick Doveton Nichols. Charlottesville 1959. pp.[vii].67. [500.]*

King, Charles.

C[HARLES] E[MIL] DORNBUSCH, Charles King, american army novelist. A bibliography from the collection of the National library of Australia. Cornwallville, N.Y. 1963. pp.vi.20. [100.]

King, Charles.

C[HARLES] E[MIL] DORNBUSCH, Charles King, american army novelist. A bibliography from the collection of the National library of Australia. Cornwallville, N.Y. 1963. pp.vi.20. [100.]

Kingsley, Charles.

M. L. PARRISH and BARBARA KELSEY MAUN, Charles Kingsley and Thomas Hughes. First editions . . . in the library at Dormy house, Pine Valley, New Jersey. 1936. pp.xi.166. [Kingsley: 150.]

151 copies printed.

Kipling, Rudyard.

[MILBURG FRANCISCO MANSFIELD], Kiplingiana. Biographical and bibliographical notes anent Rudyard Kipling. New York 1899[–1900]. pp. [iv].188.[iv]. [250.]

originally issued as a periodical entitled A Kipling note book, *twelve numbers of which were issued in February 1899–January 1900.*

FREDERIC LAWRENCE KNOWLES, A Kipling primer, including biographical and critical chapters, an index to mr. Kipling's principal writings, and bibliographies. 1900. pp.219. [500.]

[LUTHER SAMUEL LIVINGSTON], The works of Rudyard Kipling. The description of a set of the first editions . . . in the library of a New York collector [Tracy Dows]. New York 1901. pp. viii.92. [46.]

77 copies printed.

THE KIPLING index, being a guide to the . . . editions of Rudyard Kipling's works and the verses. 1914. pp.40. [750.]

G. F. MONKSHOOD [*pseud.* WILLIAM JAMES CLARKE], The less familiar Kipling, and Kiplingana. 1917. pp.168. [100.]

— — Third . . . edition. 1936. pp.256. [300.]

E[RNEST] W[ALTER] MARTINDELL, A bibliography of the works of Rudyard Kipling. 1922. pp.xiii. 112. [219.]

450 copies printed.

— — New edition. 1923. pp.xviii.222. [800.]

FLORA [VIRGINIA] LIVINGSTON, Bibliography of the works of Rudyard Kipling. New York 1927. pp.xviii.523. [525.]

— — Supplement. Cambridge [Mass.] 1938. pp.xv.333. [2000.]

CATALOGUE of the works of Rudyard Kipling exhibited at the Grolier club . . . 1929. Grolier club: New York 1930. pp.xi.203. [648.]
325 copies printed.

ELLIS AMES BALLARD, Catalogue, intimate and descriptive, of my Kipling collection. Philadelphia 1935. pp.254. [750.]
120 copies privately printed.

M[ARGARET] SHIRLEY GRINLINTON, A selected list of the more important books by Rudyard Kipling in the Alexander Turnbull library, Wellington. Alexander Turnbull library: Bibliographical list (no.4): Wellington 1941. ff.[i].6. [60.]*

JAMES MCG[REGOR] STEWART, Rudyard Kipling. A bibliographical catalogue. Edited by A. W. Yeats. Toronto 1959. pp.xviii.674. [1000.]

[HELMUT E. GERBER and EDWARD LAUTERBACH], Rudyard Kipling: an annotated bibliography of writings about him. Purdue university: English fiction in transition (vol.iii, nos.3–5): Lafayette, Ind. 1960. pp.iii.74 + v.75–148 + iii.149–235. [1500.]*

ALVICE WHITEHURST YEATS, Kipling collections in the James McG. Stewart and the university of Texas libraries. Austin 1961. ff.viii.183. [3000.]*
20 copies reproduced from typewriting.

Kirkman, Francis.

STRICKLAND GIBSON, A bibliography of Francis Kirkman. Oxford bibliographical society: Publications (new ser., vol.i, fasc.2): Oxford 1949. pp.47–152. [125.]

Kittredge, George Lyman.

JAMES THORPE, A bibliography of the writings of George Lyman Kittredge. Cambridge, Mass. 1948. pp.xiv.125. [400.]

Knapp, Charles.

C. KNAPP, Bibliography of Charles Knapp, 1893–1923. Geneva, N.Y. 1923. pp.[v].77. [519.]

Koch, C.

[C. KOCH], List of publications. Transvaal museum: Pretoria 1955. ff.9. [100.]*

Kroeber, Alfred L.

LIST of more important scientific publications. [*s.l.* 1918]. pp.[7]. [125.]

Kropotkin, prince Petr Aleksieevich.

LIST of writings in english by prince Petr Aleksieevich Kropotkin. Library of Congress: Washington 1919. ff.5. [62.]*

Kyd, Thomas.

SAMUEL A[ARON] TANNENBAUM, Thomas Kyd. (A concise bibliography). Elizabethan bibliographies (no.18): New York 1941. pp.ix.34. [576.]

300 copies printed.

Laing, David.

THOMAS GEORGE STEVENSON, Notices of David Laing, . . . to which is added a chronological list of the various publications which were issued under his editorial superintendence from the year 1815 to the year 1878 inclusive. Edinburgh 1878. pp.vii.104. [200.]

GILBERT GOUDIE, David Laing, LL.D. A memoir of his life and literary work. Edinburgh 1913. pp. xliii.319. [214.]

250 copies privately printed.

Lamb, Charles and Mary.

ALEXANDER IRELAND, List of the writings of William Hazlitt and Leigh Hunt, chronologically arranged; with . . . a chronological list of the works of Charles Lamb. 1868. pp.[xxiii].2–233. [Lamb: 26.]

LUTHER S[AMUEL] LIVINGSTON, A bibliography of the first editions in book form of the writings of Charles and Mary Lamb published prior to Charles Lamb's death in 1834. New York 1903. pp.xv.209. [75.]

100 copies printed.

J[OSEPH] C[HARLES] THOMSON, Bibliography of the writings of Charles and Mary Lamb. Hull 1908. pp.xiv.142. [300.]

[REGINALD HARVEY GRIFFITH], Charles Lamb. . . . An exhibition of books and manuscripts in the library of the university of Texas. Austin 1935. pp.7. [50.]

EDMUND BLUNDEN, Charles Lamb. British council: British book news: Bibliographical series of supplements (no.56): 1954. pp.40. [100.]

Lambert, Asael Carlyle.

[A. C. LAMBERT], A bibliography of some of the productive work of A. C. Lambert. A second edition. . . . [and] supplement. [Huntington Park 1962]. ff.26.6. [150.]*

Landor, Walter Savage.

THOMAS JAMES WISE and STEPHEN WHEELER, A bibliography of the writings in prose and verse of Walter Savage Landor. Bibliographical society: 1919. pp.xxiii.426. [350.]

[T. J. WISE], A Landor library. A catalogue of printed books, manuscripts, and autograph letters by Walter Savage Landor collected by Thomas James Wise. 1928. pp.xxiv.104. [200.]
25 copies privately printed.

G. ROSTREVOR HAMILTON, Walter Savage Landor. British council: British book news: Bibliographical series of supplement (no.126): 1960. pp.40. [100.]

Lande, sir William Arbuthnot.

WILLIAM WALE, Bibliography of the published writings (1883–1912) of sir William Arbuthnot Lane, bart. Bibliographies of Guy's men (no.3): 1914. pp.19. [325.]

[SIR W. A. LANE], Bibliography of the published writings (1883–1938) of sir William Arbuthnot Lane. [1938]. pp.24. [400.]
privately printed.

Lang, Andrew.

[CHARLES M. FALCONER], Specimens of a bibliography of the works of Andrew Lang. Dundee 1889. pp.65. [40.]

25 copies privately printed.

C. M. FALCONER, The writings of Andrew Lang . . . arranged in the form of a bibliography. Dundee [printed] 1894. pp.[ii].24. [35.]

described on the cover as 'Specimen pages for private distribution'; 100 copies printed.

[C. M. FALCONER], Catalogue of a library, chiefly the writings of Andrew Lang. Dundee 1898. pp. viii.32. [495.]

25 copies privately printed.

Laprade, William Thomas.

WILLIAM B[ASKERVILLE] HAMILTON, A preliminary list of the printed writings of William Thomas Laprade. Durham 1952. pp.32. [250.]

Lawrence, David Herbert.

EDWARD D[AVID] MCDONALD, A bibliography of the writings of D. H. Lawrence. The centaur bibliographies [of modern american authors] (no.6): Philadelphia 1925. pp.146. [300.]

500 copies printed.

KENNETH YOUNG, D. H. Lawrence. British council: British book news: Supplement (no.31): 1952. pp.56. [150.]

— — [third edition]. 1960. pp.56. [250.]

EARL TANNENBAUM, *ed.* D. H. Lawrence. An exhibition of first editions, manuscripts, paintings, letters and miscellany at Southern Illinois university library. Carbondale 1958. pp.xiii.63. [212.]

V[IVIAN] DE S[OLA] PINTO, *ed.* D. H. Lawrence after thirty years, 1930–1960. Catalogue of an exhibition held in the art gallery of the university. Nottingham 1960. pp.56. [306.]

[FRANCIS] WARREN ROBERTS, A bibliography of D. H. Lawrence. Soho bibliographies (vol.xii [*sic*, xiii]): 1963. pp.399. [1200.]

Lawrence, George Newbold.

LYMAN SPALDING FOSTER, The published writings of George Newbold Lawrence. Smithsonian institution: United States national museum: Bulletin (no.40 = Bibliographies of american naturalists, vol.iv): Washington 1892. pp.xi.124. [121.]

— — The writings of D. H. Lawrence, 1925–1930. A bibliographical supplement. . . . (no.10): 1931. pp.134. [400.]

350 copies printed.

GILBERT H. FABES, D. H. Lawrence. First editions and their values (no.2): 1933. pp.xvi.112. [100.]
500 copies printed.

E[RNEST] W[ARNOCK] TEDLOCK, The Frieda Lawrence collection of D. H. Lawrence manuscripts. A descriptive bibliography. Albuquerque 1948. pp.xxxix.333. [200.]

WILLIAM WHITE, D. H. Lawrence. A checklist, 1931–1950. Detroit 1950. pp.3–46. [600.]
350 copies printed.

Lawrence, Thomas Edward.

T. GERMAN-REED, Bibliographical notes on T. E. Lawrence's Seven pillars of wisdom and Revolt in the desert. 1928. pp.[v].16. [5.]
375 copies printed.

G., Annotations on some minor writings of 'T. E. Lawrence'. 1935. pp.28. [60.]
500 copies printed.

ELIZABETH W. DUVAL, T. E. Lawrence. A bibliography. New York 1938. pp.[ii].96. [159.]
500 copies printed.

THOMAS EDWARD LAWRENCE. A list of references

by and on col. T. E. Lawrence in the Imperial war museum library. [1952]. pp.3. [30.]*

T. E. LAWRENCE. Fifty letters, 1920–35. An exhibition. University of Texas: Humanities research center: [Austin 1962]. pp.36. [50.]

Lawson, Henry Archibald Hertzberg.

GEORGE MACKANESS, An annotated bibliography of Henry Lawson. Sydney 1951. pp.[vii].101. [100.]

WALTER W. STONE, A chronological checklist of Henry Lawson's contributions to "The bulletin" (1887–1924). Cremorne 1954. ff.[i].21. [500.]
70 copies reproduced from typewriting.

Leacock, Stephen Butler.

MARIO VILLIERS HIGGINS, *ed.* A bibliography of Stephen Butler Leacock. Montreal 1935. pp.36. [400.]

GERHARD R[ICHARD] LOMER, Stephen Leacock. A check-list and index of his writings. National library of Canada: Ottawa 1954. pp.3–153. [1600.]

Lear, Edward.

[WILLIAM B. OSGOOD FIELD], Edward Lear on my shelves. Munich [printed] 1933. pp.3–456. [75.]
155 copies privately printed.

Lee, Frederick George.

LIST of works by the rev. Frederick George Lee. 1876. pp.16. [100.]

12 copies privately printed.

Le Gallienne, Richard.

[GEORGE E. OVER], Alfred Hayes, Richard Le Gallienne, Norman Gale. [Rugby 1894]. pp.[ii].11. [Le Gallienne: 11.]

R[OBERT] J. C. LINGEL, A bibliographical checklist of the writings of Richard Le Gallienne. Metuchen, N.J. 1926. pp.95. [92.]

151 copies printed.

Lewis, Cecil Day.

CLIFFOR DYMENT, C. Day Lewis. British council: British book news: Bibliographical series of supplements (no.62): 1955. pp.48. [50.]

Lewis, Sinclair.

B. A. GILENSON and I. M. LEVIDOVA, Синклер Льюис. Всесоюзная государственная библиотека иностранной литературы: Писатели зарубежных стран: Москва 1959. pp.88. [914.]

SINCLAIR LEWIS. An exhibition from the Grace Hegger Lewis-Sinclair Lewis collection. University of Texas: Humanities research center: [Austin] 1960. pp.28. [100.]

Lewis, Wyndham.

E. W. F. TOMLIN, Wyndham Lewis. British council: British book news: Bibliographical series of supplements (no.64): 1955. pp.40. [60.]

Liddel, Duncan.

[PETER JOHN ANDERSON], Duncan Liddel . . . professor in the university of Helmstedt, 1591–1607. Aberdeen [printed] 1910. pp.20. [122.]

P. J. ANDERSON, Notes on academic theses, with bibliography of Duncan Liddel. Aberdeen university: Studies (no.58): Aberdeen 1912. pp. [iii].52. [Liddel: 125.]

Lindsay, Nicholas Vachel.

HERBERT F[AULKNER] WEST, The George Matthew Adams Vachel Lindsay collection. A note and descriptive list. Dartmouth college: Library: Hanover, N.H. 1945. pp.11. [29.]

Little, Andrew George.

AN ADDRESS presented to Andrew George Little with a bibliography of his writings. Oxford 1938. pp.36. [250.]

privately printed.

Lloyd, Edward.

JOHN MEDCRAFT, Bibliography of the penny bloods of Edward Lloyd. Dundee 1945. pp.[14]. [200.]

privately printed.

Locke, John.

H. O. CHRISTOPHERSEN, A bibliographical introduction to the study of John Locke. Skrifter utgitt av det Norske videnskaps-akademi: Historisk-filosofisk klasse (1930, no.8): Oslo 1930. pp.134. [500.]

PHILIP LONG, A summary catalogue of the Lovelace collection of the papers of John Locke in the Bodleian library. Oxford bibliographical society: Publications (n.s., vol.viii): Oxford 1959. pp.iii–xii.64. [2000.]

MAURICE CRANSTON, Locke. British council: British book news: Bibliographical series of supplements (no.135): 1961. pp.38. [100.]

Lodge, sir Oliver Joseph.

THEODORE [DEODATUS NATHANIEL] BESTERMAN, A bibliography of sir Oliver Lodge. 1935. pp.xiv. 220. [1216.]

Lodge, Thomas.

SAMUEL A. TANNENBAUM, Thomas Lodge. (A concise bibliography). Elizabethan bibliographies (no.11): New York 1940. pp.[ix].30. [500.]

300 copies printed.

London, Jack.

JACK LONDON, Bibliography and biographical data. California literary research: Monograph (no.1): [*s.l.* 1934]. ff.[i].37. [200.]*

Longfellow, Henry Wadsworth.

[WILLIAM EVARTS BENJAMIN], The Longfellow collectors' hand-book. A bibliography of first editions. New York 1885. pp.59. [44.]

250 copies printed.

LUTHER S[AMUEL] LIVINGSTON, A bibliography of the first editions in book form of the writings of Henry Wadsworth Longfellow. Compiled largely from the collection formed by the late

Jacob Chester Chamberlain. The Chamberlain bibliographies: New York 1908. pp.[ii].xiv.132. [100.]
privately printed.

Lowell, James Russell.

GEORGE WILLIS COOKE, A bibliography of James Russell Lowell. Boston &c. 1906. pp.ix.ff.2–208. [1000.]

LUTHER S. LIVINGSTON, A bibliography of the first editions in book form of the writings of James Russell Lowell. Compiled largely from the collection formed by the late Jacob Chester Chamberlain. The Chamberlain bibliographies: New York 1914. pp.xvii.136. [225.]
privately printed.

Lowell, Robert.

JEROME MAZZARO, The achievement of Robert Lowell: 1939–1959. Detroit 1960. pp.[vii].41. [350.]

Lowry, Henry Dawson.

[A. J. A. SYMONS], H. D. Lowry 1869–1906. pp.8. [9.]
30 copies privately printed.

Lydgate, John.

ELEANOR PRESCOTT HAMMOND, Two British museum manuscripts (Harley 2251 and Adds. 34360). A contribution to the bibliography of John Lydgate. [*s.l.* 1904]. pp.28. [100.]

HENRI NOBLE MAC CRACKEN, The Lydgate canon. Philological society: Transactions (1907–1909: appendix): 1908. pp.[ii].xlvi. [200.]

Lyly, John.

SAMUEL A[ARON] TANNENBAUM, John Lyly. (A concise bibliography). Elizabethan bibliographies (no.12): New York 1940. pp.ix.38. [675.]
300 copies printed.

Lytle, Andrew Nelson.

JACK DE BELLIS, An Andrew Nelson Lytle check list. University of Virginia: Bibliographical society: Secretary's news sheet (no.46): Charlottesville 1960. pp.15. [100.]*

Maas, Paul.

[P. MAAS], A select list of the writings of Paul Maas, 1901–1950. Oxford 1951. pp.27. [400.]

Macaulay, Thomas Babington Macaulay, baron.

G. R. POTTER, Macaulay. British council: British book news: Bibliographical series of supplements (no.116): 1959. pp.40. [75.]

McCosh, James.

JOSEPH H. DULLES, McCosh bibliography. A list of the published writings of the rev. James McCosh. [Princeton 1895]. ff.[i].9. [225.]

MacDonagh, Thomas.

P[ATRICK] S[ARSFIELD] O'HEGARTY, A bibliography of books written by Thomas MacDonagh and Joseph Mary Plunkett. Dublin 1931. pp.[ii].5. [MacDonagh: 11.]

30 copies privately printed; interleaved.

MacDonald, George.

JOHN MALCOLM BULLOCH, A centennial bibliography of George MacDonald. Aberdeen 1925. pp.72. [400.]

50 copies printed.

McFee, William.

JAMES T[INKHAM] BABB, A bibliography of the writings of William McFee. Garden City, N.Y. 1931. pp.xxv.126. [650.]

360 copies printed.

McGee, Thomas d'Arcy.

JAMES COLEMAN, Bibliography of Thomas D'Arcy McGee. Bibliographical society of Ireland (vol.ii, no.7): Dublin 1925. pp.[ii].135–139. [75.]

Machen, Arthur.

HENRY DANIELSON, Arthur Machen. A bibliography. 1923. pp.x.59. [25.]

500 copies printed.

NATHAN VAN PATTEN, Arthur Machen. A bibliographical note. Kingston [Ont.] 1926. pp.[ii].4. [40.]

Mackenzie, sir George.

F. S. FERGUSON, A bibliography of the works of sir George Mackenzie. Edinburgh bibliographical society: Edinburgh 1937. pp.60. [75.]

30 copies printed.

McKenzie, William Patrick.

[JESSICA M. EATON], List of articles, poems, and addresses by William P. McKenzie in the christian science periodicals. Cambridge, Mass. [printed] 1944. pp.15. [400.]

MacLeish, Archibald.

ARTHUR MIZENER, A catalogue of the first editions of Archibald MacLeish. Yale university: Library: [New Haven] 1938. pp.30. [350.]

— — [supplement]. Writings of Archibald MacLeish. Library of Congress: Washington 1942. ff.18. [203.]*

— — [supplement]. 1944. ff.11. [109.]*

— — Additional references. 1946. pp.12–14. [22.]*

ARCHIBALD MACLEISH, writings in anthologies. Library of Congress: Washington 1944. ff.10. [82.]*

McNabb, Vincent Joseph.

CHARLES R[OBERT] AUTH, A bibliography of the published writings of . . . Vincent McNabb.

Dominican house of studies: Washington 1955. ff.[ii].25. [500.]*

— — Third edition. 1963. ff.72. [1500.]*

McNeill, John Thomas.

HOLLEY M. SHEPHERD, A bio-bibliography of John Thomas McNeill. Andover-Harvard theological library: Cambridge 1960. pp.46. [424.]

Macpherson, James.

RUDOLF TOMBO, Ossian in Germany. Bibliography, general survey. Columbia university: Germanic studies (vol.i, no.2): New York 1901. pp.vi.157. [400.]

P. VAN TIEGHEM, Ossian et l'Ossianisme dans la littérature européenne au XVIIIe siècle. Neophilologiese bibliotheek [vol.iv]: Groningen &c. 1920. pp.[iii].60. [50.]

GEORGE F[RASER] BLACK, Macpherson's Ossian and the ossianic controversy. A contribution towards a bibliography. Public library: New York 1926. pp.41. [700.]

V[ASILY] I[VANOVICH] MASLOV, Оссиан в России. (Библиография). Ленинград 1928. pp.65. [188.]

MacSwiney, Terence.

P[ATRICK] S[ARSFIELD] O'HEGARTY, A bibliography of the books of Terence MacSwiney and F. Sheehy Skeffington. Dublin [printed] 1936. pp.[ii].7. [MacSwiney: 7.]
30 copies privately printed.

Madariaga, Salvador de.

SALVADOR DE MADARIAGA: a bibliographical list. Library of Congress: Washington 1936. ff.12. [85.]*

Mahan, Alfred Thayer.

[GEORGE K. KIRKHAM and THOMAS R. BASKERVILLE], Publications by rear admiral A. T. Mahan. [New York 1930]. ff.12. [350.]
100 copies privately printed, on one side of the leaf.

Maidment, James.

THOMAS GEORGE STEVENSON, Bibliographical list of the various publications by James Maidment, equire. Edinburgh 1859. pp.20. [63.]
100 copies privately printed.

THOMAS GEORGE STEVENSON, The bibliography of James Maidment, from the year M.DCC.XVII to M.DCCC.LXXVIII. Edinburgh 1883. pp.xi.55. [80.]

100 copies privately printed.

Mangan, James Clarence.

P[ATRICK] S[ARSFIELD] O'HEGARTY, A bibliography of James Clarence Mangan. Dublin 1941. pp.8. [25.]

35 copies privately printed.

Mansfield, Katherine, *pseud.*

RUTH ELVISH MANTZ, The critical bibliography of Katherine Mansfield. 1931. pp.xx.204. [750.]

MANSFIELDIANA. A brief Katherine Mansfield bibliography. N.Z. collectors' monographs (no. 3): Wellington 1948. pp.vi.9. [50.]

IAN A. GORDON, Katherine Mansfield. British council: British book news: Bibliographical series of supplements (no.49): 1954. pp.36. [100.]

Markham, sir Clements Robert.

ANTONIO OLIVAS, Contribución a la bibliografía de sir Clements Robert Markham. Universidad mayor de San Marcos: Biblioteca: Lima 1924 [*sic*, 1942]. pp.[ii].25. [225.]

Markham, Gervase.

F[REDERICK] N[OËL] L[AWRENCE] POYNTER, A bibliography of Gervase Markham. Oxford bibliographical society: Publications (n.s. vol.xi): Oxford 1962. pp.vii.219. [500.]

Marlowe, Christopher.

WILLIAM HEINEMANN, An essay towards a bibliography of Marlowe's 'Tragical history of dr. Faustus'. 1884. pp.30. [71.]

one of the British museum copies has a note in the author's hand.

SAMUEL A[ARON] TANNENBAUM, Christopher Marlowe. (A concise bibliography). Elizabethan bibliographies (no.1): New York 1937. pp.96. [1500.]

— — Additions . . . (supplement 1). 1937. pp.[7]. [100.]

— — Supplement. 1947. ff.[ii].ii.99. [1497.]*

PHILIP HENDERSON, Christopher Marlowe. British council: British book news: Bibliographical series of supplements (no.81): 1956. pp.47. [100.]

— — Revised edition. 1962. pp.47. [100.]

Marsh, George Perkins.

H[ARRY] L[YMAN] KOOPMAN, Bibliography of George Perkins Marsh. University of Vermont: Library: Burlington 1892. pp.24. [150.]

Marshall, John.

WRITINGS of John Marshall. Library of Congress: Washington 1905. ff.5. [24.]*

LIST of references relating to John Marshall. Library of Congress: Washington 1907. ff.13. [88.]*

JAMES A. SERVIES, A bibliography of John Marshall. United States commission for the celebration of the two hundredth anniversary of the birth of John Marshall: Washington 1956. pp. xix.182. [1822.]

Marston, John.

SAMUEL A[ARON] TANNENBAUM, John Marston. (A concise bibliography). Elizabethan bibliographies (no.14): New York 1940. pp.ix.34. [538.]

300 copies printed.

Martineau, Harriet.

JOSEPH B[ARRY] RIVLIN, Harriet Martineau. A bibliography of the separately printed books. Public library: New York 1947. pp.150. [628.]

R[OBERT] K[IEFER] WEBB, A handlist of contributions to the *Daily news* by Harriet Martineau, 1852–1866. [New York? 1960]. ff.[iv].51. [1500.]*

Marvell, Andrew.

JOHN PRESS, Andrew Marvell. British council: British book news: Bibliographical series of supplements (no.98): 1958. pp.42. [50.]

Masefield, John Edward.

I[OLO] A[NEURIN] WILLIAMS, John Masefield. Bibliographies of modern authors (no.2): 1921. pp.iii.12. [75.]

CHARLES H[ERBERT] SIMMONS, A bibliography of John Masefield. New York 1930. pp.xi.171. [400.]

HENRY W[OOD] NEVINSON, John Masefield. An appreciation . . . together with a bibliography. 1931. pp.[ii].17. [100.]

GEOFFREY HANDLEY-TAYLOR, John Masefield. . . . A bibliography. [1960]. pp.96. [200.]

EDDA BARBER, Masers. California institute of technology: jet propulsion laboratory: Astronautics information literature search (no.57): Pasadena 1960. pp.iv.32. [214.]*

Massinger, Philip.

SAMUEL A[ARON] TANNENBAUM, Philip Massinger. (A concise bibliography). Elizabethan bibliographies (no.4): New York 1938. pp.viii.39. [676.]

Masson, Arthur.

ROBERT MURDOCH LAWRANCE, Burns's school reading-book. Aberdeen 1931. pp.22. [8.]

a bibliography of Masson's Collection of english prose and verse; *100 copies printed.*

Mather, family of.

THOMAS JAMES HOLMES, The minor Mathers. A list of their works. Cambridge, Mass. 1940. pp.xxx.218. [750.]

200 copies printed.

Mather, Cotton.

GEORGE LYMAN KITTREDGE, Cotton Mather's scientific communications to the Royal society. American antiquarian society: Worcester, Mass. 1916. pp.42. [100.]

THOMAS JAMES HOLMES, Cotton Mather. A bibliography of his works. Cambridge, Mass. 1940. pp.xxxvi.461 + [vii].463–910 + vii.911–1395. [600.]

500 copies printed.

Mather, Increase.

THOMAS J. HOLMES, Increase Mather, his works. Being a short-title catalogue of the published writings that can be ascribed to him. Cleveland 1930. pp.[v].59. [600.]

250 copies privately printed.

THOMAS JAMES HOLMES, Increase Mather: a bibliography of his works. Cleveland 1931. pp. xxxii.352+[vii].353–711. [250.]

500 copies printed.

Matthews, James Brander.

THE BOOKSHELF of Brander Matthews. New York 1931. pp.[x].115. [595.]

— — [another edition]. 1913. pp.76. [600.]
— — — [supplement]. 1919. pp.43. [300.]
— — — [supplement]. 1920. pp.16. [60.]

Maugham, William Somerset.

FREDERICK T. BASON, A bibliography of the writings of William Somerset Maugham. 1931. pp.80. [95.]

RAYMOND TOOLE STOTT, Maughamiana. The writings of W. Somerset Maugham. 1950. pp. xiii.73. [500.]
includes writings on Somerset Maugham.

KLAUS W. JONAS, A bibliography of the writings of W. Somerset Maugham. [South Hadley, Mass.] 1950. pp.xvii.97. [750.]*

JOHN BROPHY, Somerset Maugham. British council: British book news: Bibliographical series of supplements (no.22): 1952. pp.48. [100.]

REYMOND TOOLE STOTT, The writings of William Somerset Maugham. 1956. pp.136. [322.]
— — Supplement. 1961. pp.20. [100.]

[JOHN TERRY BENDER], A comprehensive exhibition of the writings of W. Somerset Maugham drawn from various private collections and libraries. Stanford university: Library: [Stanford 1958]. pp.[47]. [101.]

Melville, Herman.

MEADE MINNIGERODE, Some personal letters of Herman Melville and a bibliography. New York &c. 1922. pp.xii.195. [75.]

BOOKS about Herman Melville, 1819–1891. Library of Congress: Washington 1931. single leaf. [6.]*

HERBERT CAHOON, Herman Melville. A check list of books and manuscripts in the collections of the New York public library. Public library: Gordon Lester Ford memorial study (no.4): New York 1951. pp.28. [350.]

ANNUAL Melville bibliography. Public library: Providence, R.I.*
1951. ff.[i].6. [75.]
[*continued as:*]
Melville bibliography.
1952–1957. ff.[iii].28. [350.]

Mencken, Henry Louis.

H. L. MENCKEN. . . . Bibliography. By F. C. Henderson. New York 1920. pp.32. [60.]

CARROLL FREY, A bibliography of the writings of H. L. Mencken. Centaur bibliographies (no.4): Philadelphia 1924. pp.[iv].70.[x]. [125.]

JANE WILHELM, Henri Louis Mencken checklist. Enoch Pratt free library: Baltimore 1957. pp.8.

BERNARD H. PORTER, H. L. Mencken. A bibliography. Denver [1958]. pp.12. [175.]

BETTY ADLER and JANE WILHELM, H. L. M. The Mencken bibliography. Enoch Pratt library: Baltimore [1961]. pp.xiii.367. [7500.]

Meredith, George.

JOHN LANE, George Meredith and his reviewers. . . . A bibliography. [1890]. pp.iii–xxii[*sic*, lxxii]. [150.]

forms an appendix to Richard Le Gallienne, George Meredith, *1890.*

—— [fifth edition]. [1900]. pp.lxxxiv. [300.]

forms an appendix to R. Le Gallienne, George Meredith[5], *1900.*

ARUNDELL [JAMES KENNEDY] ESDAILE, Bibliography of the writings in prose and verse of George Meredith. 1907. pp.70. [350.]

ARUNDELL ESDAILE, A chronological list of

George Meredith's publications. 1914. pp.[ii].66. [225.]

MAURICE BUXTON FORMAN, A bibliography of the writings in prose and verse of George Meredith. Bibliographical society: 1922. pp.xxxii.325. [400.]

— — Supplement. Meredithiana. 1924. pp.vii. 319. [1500.]

BERTHA COOLIDGE, A catalogue of the Altschul collection of George Meredith in the Yale university library. Boston [printed] 1931. pp.xvii.197. [600.]

500 copies privately printed.

PHYLLIS BARTLETT, George Meredith. British council: British book news: Bibliographical series: 1963. pp.44. [75.]

Merton, Thomas.

FRANK DELL'ISOLA, Thomas Merton. A bibliography. New York 1956. pp.x.116. [520.]

an earlier edition appears in Thought (*Fordham university: 1954–1955*), *xxix.575–596.*

Meyerstein, Edward H. W.

EDWARD H. W. MEYERSTEIN. Poet and novelist.

Morgan, John.

HARRY SIRR, J. Morgan, his Phœnix britannicus, with notes about his other works. Margate [printed] 1906. pp.10. [6.]

Morison, Stanley.

JOHN [WAYNFLETE] CARTER, A handlist of the writings of Stanley Morison. Cambridge 1950. pp.ix.47. [176.]
privately printed.

Morley, Christopher Darlington.

ALFRED P[YLE] LEE, A bibliography of Christopher Morley. Garden City, N.Y. 1935. pp.ix.277. [250.]
printed on buff paper.

GUY R[EDVERS] LYLE and H[ENRY] TATNALL BROWN, A bibliography of Christopher Morley. Washington 1952. pp.xi.198. [750.]*

AN EXHIBITION of C. D. M. manuscripts & first editions at the Humanities research center, the university of Texas. [Austin 1961]. pp.48. [170.]

Morris, William.

H[ARRY] BUXTON FORMAN, The books of William Morris described, with some account of his doings in literature and in the allied crafts. 1897. pp.xv.224. [750.]

TEMPLE SCOTT [*pseud.* J. H. ISAACS], A bibliography of the works of William Morris. 1897. pp.vii.120. [350.]

WILLIAM MORRIS. Some books and periodicals in the Cleveland public library. [Cleveland] 1910. pp.16. [300.]

C[HARLES] E[DWYN] VAUGHAN, Bibliographies of Swinburne, Morris and Rossetti. English association: Leaflet (no.29): 1914. pp.12. [Morris: 100.]

[R. C. H. BRIGGS], A handlist of the public addresses of William Morris to be found in generally accessible publications. William Morris society: Dublin 1961. pp.16. [75.]

Mossom, Robert.

JOHN INGLE DREDGE, Dr. Robert Mossom . . . with a bibliography of his works. Manchester [printed] 1882. pp.12. [10.]
privately printed.

Mottram, Ralph Hale.

GILBERT H[ENRY] FABES, The first editions of Ralph Hale Mottram. 1934. pp.128. [50.]

300 copies printed.

Mountford, Charles Pearcy.

HAROLD L. SHEARD, Charles Pearcy Mountford. An annotated bibliography, chronology and checklist of books, papers, manuscripts and sundries from the library of Harold L. Sheard. Studies in australian bibliography (no.8): Cremorne 1958. pp.[ii].vii.81. [250.]*

Mügge, M. A.

[M. A. MÜGGE], An annotated list of books written and published by M. A. Mügge. [*s.l.* 1932]. pp.3. [16.]

the British museum copy contains an addition in ms. by the author.

Muir, Edwin.

J. C. HALL, Edwin Muir. British council: British book news: Bibliographical series of supplements (no.71): 1956. pp.36. [30.]

Mundy, Anthony.

SAMUEL A[ARON] TANNENBAUM, Anthony Mundy, including the play of 'Sir Thomas More'. (A concise bibliography). Elizabethan bibliographies (no.27): New York 1942. pp.x.36. [556.]

Murray, David.

SYLVIA W. MURRAY, David Murray: a bibliographical memoir. Dumbarton 1933. pp.52. [250.]

Murry, John Middleton.

PHILIPPE MAIRET, John Middleton Murry. British book news: Bibliographical series of supplements (no.102): 1958. pp.40. [75.]

Nashe, Thomas.

SAMUEL A[ARON] TANNENBAUM, Thomas Nashe. (A concise bibliography). Elizabethan bibliographies (no.21): 1941. pp.ix.31. [525.]

Nathan, Robert.

DAN H. LAURENCE, Robert Nathan. A bibliography. Yale university: Library: New Haven 1960. pp.xi.97. [331.]

Neville, Henry.

WORTHINGTON CHAUNCEY FORD, The Isle of pines, 1668. An essay in bibliography. Club of odd volumes: Boston 1920. pp.xii.117. [30.]

Newman, John Henry.

LIST of works written and edited by . . . cardinal Newman, in the library of sir William H. Cope, bart., at Bramshill. Portsmouth [printed] [1888]. [130.]

privately printed.

LIST of references on John Henry Newman. Library of Congress: Washington 1921. ff.17. [239.]*

CLARENCE E. SLOANE, John Henry Newman. An illustrated brochure of his first editions. Holy cross college: [Worcester, Mass. 1953]. pp.[viii]. 54. [100.]

J. M. CAMERON, John Henry Newman. British council: British book news: Bibliographical series of supplements (no.72): 1956. pp.44. [200.]

Newton, Alfred Edward.

GEORGE H[ENRY] SARGENT, The writings of A. Edward Newton. Philadelphia 1927. pp.xx.52. [65.]

100 copies printed.

Newton, sir Isaac.

A CATALOGUE of the Portsmouth collection of books and papers written by or belonging to sir Isaac Newton, the scientific portion of which has been presented by the earl of Portsmouth to the university of Cambridge. Cambridge 1888. pp. xxx.56. [1000.]

GEORGE J[OHN] GRAY, Bibliography of the works of sir Isaac Newton: together with a list of books illustrating his life and works. Cambridge 1888. pp.40. [231.]

120 copies printed.

— — Second edition. 1907. pp.[viii].80. [412.]

A DESCRIPTIVE catalogue of the Grace K[night] Babson collection of the works of sir Isaac Newton and the material relating to him in the Babson institute library, Babson park, Mass. New York 1950. pp.xiv.229. [606.]

— — A supplement . . . by Henry P. Macomber. Babson institute: [Babson Park, Mss.] 1955. pp. viii.93. [250.]

450 copies printed.

FREDERICK E[DWARD] BRASCH, Sir Isaac Newton. An essay on sir Isaac Newton and newtonian thought as exemplified in the Stanford collection. [Stanford, Cal. 1962]. pp.[iii].28. [75.]

Noah, Mordecai Manuel.

MORDECAI MANUEL NOAH (1785–1851): a bibliographical list. Library of Congress: Washington 1930. ff.6. [53.]*

Norlie, Olaf Morgan.

O. M. NORLIE, After supper. A list of the published writings of Olaf Morgan Norlie . . . 1894–1944. Saint Olaf college: Northfield, Minn. 1944. ff.315+[i].316–634. [3777.]*

Norris, Benjamin Franklin.

JOSEPH GAER, *ed*. Frank Norris. . . . Bibliography and bibliographical data. California literary research: Monograph (no.3): [*s.l.* 1934]. ff.[i].50. [250.]*

KENNETH A. LOHF and EUGENE P[AUL] SHEEHY, Frank Norris. A bibliography. Los Gatos, Cal. 1959. pp.109. [525.]

Nyvall, David.

E. GUSTAV JOHNSON, Bibliography of the published works of professor David Nyvall. Covenant historical commission: Chicago 1937. pp.14. [32.]

O'Curry, Eugene.

CENTENARY exhibition. John O'Donovan 1806–1861, Eugene O'Curry 1794–1862. Royal irish academy: [Dublin 1961]. pp.[12]. [62.]

O'Grady, Standish.

P[ATRICK] S[ARSFIELD] O'HEGARTY, A bibliography of books written by Standish O'Grady. Dublin 1930. pp.8. [18.]

25 copies printed; interleaved.

O'Hannracháin, Michael.

P[ATRICK] S[ARSFIELD] O'HEGARTY, A bibliography of books by the O'Rahilly, Tom Clarke, Michaél O'h-Annracháin and countess de Markievicz. Dublin 1936. pp.5. [O'Hannracháin: 3.]

25 copies privately printed.

O'Higgins, Kevin.

P[ATRICK] S[ARSFIELD] O'HEGARTY, A bibliography of the books of Arthur Griffith, Michael Collins and Kevin O'Higgins. Dublin 1937. pp.9. [O'Higgins: 2.]

30 copies privately printed; interleaved.

A bibliography. Public libraries: Bristol [1936]. pp.[4]. [40.]

printed on grey paper.

Meynell, Alice Christiana.

[SIR FRANCIS MEYNELL], Alice Meynell, 1847–1922. Catalogue of the centenary exhibition of books, manuscripts, letters and portraits. National book league: 1947. pp.[ii].45. [133.]

TERENCE L[EO] CONNOLLY, Alice Meynell centenary tribute, 1847–1947. Boston [1948]. pp.72. [146.]

Middleton, Thomas.

SAMUEL A[ARON] TANNENBAUM, Thomas Middleton. (A concise bibliography). Elizabethan bibliographies (no.13): New York 1940. pp.ix.35. [563.]

300 copies printed.

Mill, John Stuart.

JOHN STUART MILL, Bibliography of the published writings of John Stuart Mill. Edited from his manuscript . . . by Ney MacMinn . . . , J[ohn] R. Hainds... James McNab McCrimmon. Northwestern university studies in the humanities (no. 12): Evanston, Ill. 1945. pp.xiv.101. [750.]

MAURICE CRANSTON, John Stuart Mill. British council: British book news: Bibliographical series of supplements (no.99): 1958. pp.34. [75.]

Millay, Edna St. Vincent.

KARL YOST, A bibliography of the works of Edna St. Vincent Millay. New York &c. 1937. pp.vii.248. [600.]

Miller, Arthur.

I[NNA] M[IKHAILOVNA] LEVIDOVA, Артур Миллер. Всесоюзная государственная библиотека иностранной литературы: Писатели зарубежных стран: Москва 1961. pp.56. [337.]

Miller, Henry Valentine.

BERN PORTER, Henry Miller. A chronology and bibliography. Berkeley, Cal. 1945. pp.36. [350.]
500 copies printed.

THOMAS H[AMILTON] MOORE, Bibliography Henry Miller. Henry Miller literary society: Minneapolis 1961. pp.32. [500.]

ESTA LOU RILEY, Henry Miller: an informal bibliography 1924–1960. Fort Hays Kansas state college: Fort Hays studies: Bibliography series (no.1): [Hays] 1961. pp.vi.54. [452.]

MAXIME RENKEN, A bibliography of Henry Miller, 1945–1961. Swallow pamphlets (no.12): Denver [1962]. pp.14. [400.]

Millin, Sarah Gertrude.

MORAG WHYTE, Bibliography of the works of Sarah Gertrude Millin. University of Cape Town: School of librarianship: Bibliographical series: [Rondebosch] 1952. ff.[ii].vi.21. [151.]*

Milton, John.

WORKS of Milton, etc. Lenox library: Contributions to a catalogue (no.vi): New York 1881. pp. 46. [191.]

MILTON [JOHN]. British museum: Catalogue of printed books: 1892. coll.56. [1000.]

[GEORGE CHARLES WILLIAMSON and CHARLES EDWARD SAYLE], Milton tercentenary. The portraits, prints and writings of John Milton.

[Edited by John Peile]. Christ's college: Cambridge 1908. pp.vi.168. [611.]

—— Second edition. 1908. pp.vi.168. [611.]

MILTON tercentenary. Catalogue of exhibits. Public library: Stoke Newington 1908. pp.55. [250.]

CATALOGUE of an exhibition commemorative of the tercentenary of the birth of John Milton. Grolier club: [New York] 1908. pp.vi.116. [119.]

CATALOGUE of an exhibition of original editions of the principal works of John Milton. John Rylands library: Manchester 1908. pp.24. [40.]

ELBERT N[EVIUS] S[EBRING] THOMPSON, John Milton. Topical bibliography. New Haven 1916. pp.xi.104. [1000.]

[S. W. G.], Early editions of Milton's works in Christ's college library. [Cambridge] 1921. pp.8. [117.]

DAVID HARRISON STEVENS, Reference guide to Milton from 1800 to the present day. Chicago 1930. pp.x.302. [2850.]

—— Addenda. Contributions to a Milton bibliography, 1800–1930. . . . By Harris Francis Fletcher. University of Illinois: Studies in language and literature (vol.xvi, no.1): Urgana 1931. pp.166. [1250.]

THE JOHN MILTON collection formed by Henry Austin Whitney. [*s.l.* 1935]. pp.[ii].21. [250.]

HARRIS F[RANCIS] FLETCHER, Collection of first editions of Milton's works. . . . An exhibition. University of Illinois: Library: Adah Patterson memorial fund publication (no.2). Urbana 1953. pp.[viii].24. [62.]

F[RANCIS] F[ALCONER] MADAN, A revised bibliography of Salmasius's *Defensio regia* and Milton's *Pro populo anglicano defensio*. 1954. pp.[iii].101–121. [Milton: 23.]

the British museum copy contains manuscript notes by the author.

CALVIN HUCKABAY, John Milton. A bibliographical supplement 1929–1957. Duquesne university: Philological studies (no.1): Pittsburgh &c. 1960. pp.xi.211. [1964.]

a supplement to the works of Stevens and Fletcher.

Mingana, Alphonse.

D[AVID] S[AMUEL] MARGOLIOUTH and G[EOFFREY] WOLEDGE, A. Mingana. A biography and bibliography. Aberdeen [printed] 1939. pp.16. [90.]

Mitchel, William.

GEORGE P. JOHNSTON, William Mitchel, the tincklarian doctor. A bibliography: 1711–39. Edinburgh 1921. pp.[ii].25. [100.]

privately printed.

Mitchell, Silas Weir.

[S. W. MITCHELL], A catalogue of the scientific and literary work of S. Weir Mitchell. [Philadelphia 1894]. pp.40. [136.]

NOLIE MUMEY, Silar Weir Mitchell. . . . A sketch of his life and his literary contributions. Denver 1934. pp.201. [750.]

Mood, Fulmer.

A BIBLIOGRAPHY of the publications of Fulmer Mood, 1929–1942. Berkeley &c. 1943. pp.8. [60.]

Moore, George.

I[OLO] A[NEURIN] WILLIAMS, George Moore. Bibliographies of modern authors (no.3): 1921. pp.[v].13. [45.]

[HELMUT E. GERBER], George Moore: an annotated bibliography of writings about him. English fiction in transition (vol.ii, no.2): West Lafayette, Ind. 1959. ff.vii.44+iv.45–91. [500.]*

Moore, Marianne.

EUGENE P[AUL] SHEEHY and KENNETH A. LOHF, The achievement of Marianne Moore. A bibliography 1907–1957. Public library: New York 1958. pp.43. [750.]

Moore, Thomas.

ANDREW GIBSON, Thomas Moore and his first editions. Belfast [printed] 1904. pp.[ii].28. [75.]

FLORENCE S[ELMA] HELLMAN, List of references in the Library of Congress relating to Thomas Moore, 1779–1852 (exclusive of music). Library of Congress: [Washington] 1932. [308.]*

M. J. MAC MANUS, A bibliographical hand-list of the first editions of Thomas Moore. Dublin 1934. pp.24. [70.]
25 copies privately printed.

More, Paul Elmer.

MALCOLM YOUNG, Paul Elmer More. A bibliography. Princeton university: Library publication: Princeton 1941. pp.[vii].40. [400.]

More, sir Thomas.

THE ALFRED COCK memorial. Catalogue of books, portraits, &c., of or relating to sir Thomas More, collected by the late Alfred Cock, . . .

presented to the ... Guildhall library. 1903. pp.28. [250.]

FRANK SULLIVAN and MAJIE PADBERG SULLIVAN, Moreana, 1478–1945. A preliminary check list of material by and about saint Thomas More. Rockhurst college: Kansas City 1946. pp.[175]. [1500.]*

FRANK SULLIVAN, Syr Thomas More, a first bibliographical notebook. Loyola university: Los Angeles 1953. pp.111. [25.]

MAJIE PADBERG SULLIVAN, Moreana. Materials for the study of st. Thomas More. Los Angeles 1958. pp.[ii].12. [100.]*
a only; no more published.

R[EGINALD] W[ALTER] GIBSON, St. Thomas More: a preliminary bibliography of his works and of Moreana to the year 1750.... With a bibliography of Utopiana compiled by R. W. Gibson and J[ohn] Max Patrick. New Haven &c. 1961. pp. xxi.499. [925.]

Morgan, Charles.

GILBERT H. FABES, The first editions of A. E. Coppard, A. P. Herbert and Charles Morgan. 1933. pp.[vi].154. [Morgan: 11.]

O'Kelly, Seumas.

P[ATRICK] S[ARSFIELD] O'HEGARTY, A bibliography of books by Seumas O'Kelly. Dublin 1934. pp.7. [13.]

25 copies privately printed; interleaved.

Oldham, John.

HAROLD F[LETCHER] BROOKS, A bibliography of John Oldham, the restoration satirist. Oxford bibliographical society: Proceedings & papers (vol.v, part 1): Oxford 1936. pp.38. [42.]

Oldmixon, John.

[JOHN] OLDMIXON, Memoirs of the press, historical and political, for thirty years past. 1742. pp.[xii].64. [25.]

this is actually an account of his own work.

Oliver, George.

T[HOMAS] N[ADAULD] BRUSHFIELD, The Bibliography of the rev. George Oliver. [1885]. pp.11. [40.]

a copy in the Bodleian library contains voluminous ms. notes by the author.

O'Neill, Eugene Gladstone.

LIST of references on Eugene Gladstone O'Neill. Library of Congress: Washington 1922. ff.4. [29.]*

RALPH SANBORN and BARRETT H[ARPER] CLARK, A bibliography of the works of Eugene O'Neill. New York 1931. pp.xiv.173. [250.]

500 copies printed.

ANN DUNCAN BROWN, Eugene O'Neill. A list of recent references. Compiled . . . under the direction of Florence S[elma] Hellman. Library of Congress: [Washington] 1940. ff.15. [121.]*

JORDAN Y[ALE] MILLER, Eugene O'Neill and the american critic. A summary and bibliographical checklist. Hamden [Conn.] &c. 1962. pp.iii–ix. 517. [1818.]

Onions, Charles Talbut.

A LIST of the published writings of Charles Talbut Onions. Oxford 1948. pp.19. [100.]

Opie, Amelia.

AMELIA OPIE, 1769–1853. Public library: [Norwich 1953]. pp.[6]. [50.]

Orwell, George. [*pseud.* **Eric Blair.**]

I[AN] R[OY] WILLISON, George Orwell. Some materials for a bibliography. [1953]. ff.[ii].xii.227. [1000.]*

TOM HOPKINSON, George Orwell. British council: British book news: Bibliographical series of supplements (no.39): 1953. pp.40. [50.]

Osborn, Henry Fairfield.

H. ERNESTINE RIPLEY, Bibliography of the published writings of Henry Fairfield Osborn for the years 1877–1915.... Second edition. [New York] 1916. pp.[ii].74. [422.]

— — Supplement. 1917. pp.[2]. [19.]
— — Supplement. 1918. pp.4. [45.]
— — Supplement two. 1919. pp.2. [31.]
— — Supplement three. 1921. single leaf. [19.]
— — Supplement four. 1922. pp.2. [20.]

FLORENCE MILLIGAN, Fifty-two years of research, observation and publication, 1877–1929. . . . by Henry Fairfield Osborn. [Third edition]. New York 1930. pp.xii.160. [180.]

Osler, sir William.

MINNIE WRIGHT BLOGG, Bibliography [of sir William Osler]. [*s.l.* 1919]. pp.46. [730.]

— — Bibliography of the writings of sir William Osler. . . . Revised. Baltimore 1921. pp.96. [1195.]

MAUDE E[LIZABETH SEYMOUR] ABBOTT, Classified and annotated bibliography of sir William Osler's publications. . . . Second edition. McGill university: Medical museum: Montreal 1939. pp.xvi.163. [2000.]

the first edition was published in the Journal *of the Canadian medical association (1920), pp.103–123.*

Owen, Robert.

RENA REESE, List of books and pamphlets in a special collection in the library of the Workingmen's institute, New Harmony, Ind. [*s.l.*] 1909. pp.21. [300.]

[ARTHUR JOHN HAWKES], A bibliography of Robert Owen, the socialist, 1771–1858. National library of Wales: Aberystwyth 1914. pp.54. [400.]

a copy with ms. corrections and additions is in the British museum; also issued, with a different title-page, by the Welsh bibliographical society.

—— Second edition. [Edited by William Williams]. 1925. pp.viii.92. [629.]

SHIGERU GOTÔ, Robert Owen, 1771–1858: a new bibliographical study.

—— Vol.II. A supplement to volume one, with special reference to the various Robert Owen collections in England, Wales and Scotland. Osaka university of commerce: Studies (no.3): [Osaka] 1934. pp.[vi].x.220.19. [611.]

[MARGARET BÉRENGÈRE CAMPBELL CANNEY], Robert Owen 1771–1858. Catalogue of an exhibition of books held in the library of the university of London. 1959. pp.[iv].40. [121.]

Paine, Thomas.

RICHARD GIMBEL, Thomas Paine. A bibliographical check list of Common sense with an account of its publication. New Haven 1956. pp.124. [300.]

RICHARD GIMBEL, The resurgence of Thomas Paine. With the catalogue of an exhibition Thomas Paine fights for freedom in three worlds. American antiquarian society: Worcester, Mass. 1961. pp.[ii].97–111.397–492. [427.]

Patchen, Kenneth.

GAIL EATON, Kenneth Patchen. A first bibliography. Denver [1948]. pp.[4]. [14.]

Payen-Payne, J. Bertrand.

WORKS written or edited by J. Bertrand Payen-Payne. [*s.l.* 1899]. pp.46. [20.]

Pearse, Padraic H.

P[ATRICK] S[ARSFIELD] O'HEGARTY, A bibliography of books written by P. H. Pearse. Dublin 1931. pp.[ii].6. [25.]

30 copies privately printed; interleaved.

Pearson, Karl.

G[EOFFREY] M[CKAY] MORANT and B[ERNARD] L[EWIS] WELCH, A bibliography of the statistical and other writings of Karl Pearson. University college: Biometrika: 1939. pp.viii.119. [670.]

Peele, George.

SAMUEL A[ARON] TANNENBAUM, George Peele. (A concise bibliography). Elizabethan bibliographies (no.15): 1940. pp.x.36. [587.]

300 copies printed.

Pepys, Samuel.

[EDWARD KELLY PURNELL], Report on the Pepys manuscripts, preserved at Magdalene college, Cambridge. Royal commission on historical manuscripts: 1911. pp.xxxii.377. [750.]

LIST of references on Samuel Pepys. Library of Congress: Washington 1916. ff.9. [93.]*

[E. CHAPPELL], Catalogue of Pepysiana belonging to mr. Edwin Chappell exhibited . . . at the Royal naval college. 1931. pp.[8]. [62.]

[EDWIN CHAPPELL], Bibliographia pepysiana. 1933. pp.[28]. [225.]

EDWIN CHAPPELL, A short-title Pepys bibliography. 1933. pp.[4]. [60.]

Pettigrew, James Bell.

LIST of works published by J. Bell Pettigrew. [Edinburgh 1873]. pp.30. [12.]

—[another edition]. [1874]. pp.51. [12.]

Philips, Ambrose.

LIST of references on the life and works of Ambrose Philips (1675–1749). Library of Congress: Washington 1921. ff.4. [36.]*

Phillip, John.

[SIR W[ALTER] W[ILSON] GREG, John Phillip. Notes for a bibliography. 1911. pp.[iv].56. [24.]

Phillips, Henry.

[H. PHILLIPS], Published writings of Henry Phillips. [Philadelphia *c.*1883]. pp.[2]. [45.]

Phillips, Philip Lee.

LIST of publications of Philip Lee Phillips. Library of Congress: Washington 1924. ff.5. [49.]*

Phillips, William Battle.

[W. B. PHILLIPS], Contribution to scientific and technical publications, 1883–1913. [Austin, Tex. 1913]. pp.19. [200.]

Pickford, John.

[J. PICKFORD], A list of the contributions to "Notes and queries" . . . written by the rev. John Pickford. 1885. pp.18. [550.]

during 1856–1868 Pickford used the pseudonym Oxoniensis.

—— Second impression revised. 1887. pp.21. [750.]

Pike, Albert.

WILLIAM L[LEWELLYN] BOYDEN, Bibliography of the writings of Albert Pike. Washington 1921. pp.[iv].71. [1000.]

WILLIAM LLEWELLYN, Bibliography of the writings of Albert Pike. Edited by Ray Baker Harris. Washington 1957. pp.[ii].109. [500.]

Plunkett, Joseph Mary.

P[ATRICK] S[ARSFIELD] O'HEGARTY, A bibliography of books written by Thomas MacDonagh and Joseph Mary Plunkett. Dublin 1931. pp.[ii].5. [Plunkett: 2.]

30 copies privately printed; interleaved.

Pocock, Guy Noel.

GUY N. POCOCK. . . . A bibliography. Public libraries: Bristol [1939]. pp.[6]. [75.]

Poe, Edgar Allan.

CLARA W. BRAGG, Material by and about Edgar Allan Poe to be found in the library of Columbia university. New York 1909. pp.18. [135.]

Individual Authors

LIST of references on Edgar Allan Poe. Library of Congress: Washington 1916. ff.3. [26.]*
— Additional references. 1925. ff.2. [12.]*

CHARLES F[REDERICK] HEARTMAN and KENNETH REDE, A census of first editions and source materials by Edgar Allan Poe in american collections. Metuchen, N.J. 1932. pp.67+91+36. [700.]
240, 202, 100 copies printed.

JOHN W[OOSTER] ROBERTSON, Bibliography of the writings of Edgar A. Poe. San Francisco 1934. pp.[xi].235+[vii].300.[xi]. [600.]
vol.ii is entitled Commentary on the bibliography of Edgar A. Poe*; 350 copies printed.*

CHARLES F[REDERICK] HEARTMAN and JAMES R. CANNY, A bibliography of the first printing of the writings of Edgar Allan Poe. Together with a record of . . . contributions to . . . periodicals and newspapers. Also some spurious Poeiana and fakes. Heartman's historical series (no.53): Hattiesburg, Miss. 1940. pp.264. [750.]
'less than' 350 copies printed.
— — Revised edition. 1943. pp.295. [750.]

INDEX to early american periodical literature, 1728–1870. Part 2. Edgar Allan Poe. New York 1941. pp.20. [400.]

JOHN WARD OSTROM, Check list of letters to and from Poe. University of Virginia: Bibliographical series (no.4): Charlottesville 1941. pp.[v].57. [733.]*

GEŌRGIOS KŌNSTANTINOV KATSIMPALĒS, 'Ελληνική βιβλιογραφία Έδγαρ Πόε. Α'. Τα πουματα. 'Αθηνα 1955. pp.15. [138.]

JOHN CARL MILLER, John Henry Ingram's Poe collection at the university of Virginia. Charlottesville 1960. pp.xlix.397. [1044.]*

Pollard, Alfred William.

[GWENDOLEN MURPHY], A select bibliography of the writings of Alfred W. Pollard. Oxford [printed] 1938. pp.ix.69. [300.]

260 copies privately printed.

Pope, Alexander.

POPE commemoration, 1888. Loan museum. Catalogue of the books, autographs, paintings . . . exhibited in the Town hall Twickenham. 1888. pp.58. [149.]

AN EXHIBITION of the first editions of the works of Alexander Pope. Grolier club: [New York] 1911. pp.vii.80. [101.]

— — [another edition]. A catalogue of the first editions [&c.]. 1911. pp.[ii].vii.86. [101.]
200 copies printed.

G[EORGE] A[THERTON] AITKEN, Notes on the bibliography of Pope. 1914. pp.3–36. [50.]

REGINALD HARVEY GRIFFITH, Alexander Pope. A bibliography. . . . Volume I . . . Pope's own writings. University of Texas: Studies [in english]: Austin 1922–1927. pp.xxxv.297+[viii].xxxvii–lvii.267–593.xxii. [700.]
no more published.

[T. J. WISE], A Pope library. A catalogue of plays, poems, and prose writings by Alexander Pope collected by Thomas James Wise. 1931. pp.xxiv. 116. [200.]
160 copies privately printed.

É[MILE] AUDRA, Les traductions françaises de Pope (1717–1825). Étude de bibliographie. 1931. pp.xviii.137. [240.]

WILLIAM DARNALL MAC CLINTOCK, Joseph Warton's Essay on Pope. A history of the five editions. Chapel Hill 1933. pp.xii.74. [6.]

JAMES EDWARD TOBIN, Alexander Pope. A list of critical studies published from 1895 to 1944. New York 1945. pp.30. [414.]

IAN JACK, Pope. British council: British book news: Bibliographical series of supplements (no. 48): 1954. pp.36. [100.]

Porter, Arthur Kingsley.

LUCY KINGSLEY PORTER, *ed.* The writings of A. Kingsley Porter, 1883–1933. A bibliography. Fogg art museum: Cambridge [Mass.] 1934. pp. iv.16. [100.]

Porter, Katherine Anne.

EDWARD SCHWARTZ, Katherine Anne Porter. A critical bibliography. Public library: New York 1953. pp.42. [300.]

Potocki, Geoffrey Wladislas Vaile, count de Montalk.

RICHARD ALDINGTON, A letter . . . and a summary bibliography of count Potocki's published works. Draguignan [1963]. pp.[6]. [15.]

Potter, Beatrix.

JANE QUINBY, Beatrix Potter. A bibliographical check list. New York 1954. pp.121. [90.]
250 copies printed.

Pound, Ezra Loomis.

JOHN [HAMILTON] EDWARDS, A preliminary checklist of the writings of Ezra Pound, especially his contributions to periodicals. New Haven 1953. pp.viii.73. [717.]

DONALD [CLIFFORD] GALLUP, A bibliography of Ezra Pound. Soho bibliographies (vol.xviii): 1963. pp.454. [2300.]

Pound, Roscoe.

FRANKLYN C[HRISTOPHER] SETARO, A bibliography of the writings of Roscoe Pound. Harvard series of legal bibliographies (vol.iii): Cambridge 1942. pp.vii.193. [773.]

[—] — [supplement]. A bibliography . . . 1940–1960. By George A. Strait. 1960. pp.52.

Powell, Anthony Dymoke.

PAUL BLOOMFIELD and BERNARD BERGONZI, L. P. Hartley. . . . Anthony Powell. British council: British book news: Bibliographical series: 1962. pp.40. [Powell: 20.]

Powell, Thomas Reed.

BIBLIOGRAPHY of Thomas Reed Powell. Cambridge, Mass. [1949]. pp.41. [425.]

privately printed.

Power, sir D'Arcy.

LIFE history and abstract of work of sir D'Arcy Power. [1924]. ff.31. [250.]*

Powys, John Cowper, *and* Theodore Francis.

P[ERCY] H. MUIR and B. VAN THAL, Bibliographies of the first editions of books by Aldous Huxley and T. F. Powys. 1927. pp.61. [Powys: 31].

LLOYD EMERSON SIBERELL, A bibliography of the first editions of John Cowper Powys. Cincinnati 1934. pp.53. [70.]

350 copies printed.

R[EGINALD] C[HARLES] CHURCHILL, The Powys brothers. British book news: Bibliographical series of supplements: 1962. pp.40. [100.]

Prescott, William Hickling.

CLINTON HARVEY GARDINER, William Hickling Prescott. An annotated bibliography of published works. Library of Congress: Hispanic foundation: Bibliographical series (no.4): Washington 1958. [1959]. pp.[ii].xvi.275. [721.]*

Price, Joseph Charles.

LOUISE M. ROUNTREE, An annotated bibliography on Joseph Charles Price (1882–1893). Livingstone college: [Salisbury, N.C. 1960]. ff. [ii].10. [50.]*

— — [another edition]. 1963. ff.[10]. [50.]

Priest, Josiah.

WINTHROP HILLYER DUNCAN, Josiah Priest. . . . A study and bibliography. American antiquarian society: Worcester, Mass. 1935. pp.60. [65.]

Priestley, John Boynton.

IVOR JOHN CARNEGIE BROWN, J. B. Priestley. British book news: Bibliographical series of supplements (no.84): 1957. pp.39. [100.]

J. B. PRIESTLEY: an exhibition of manuscripts and books. University of Texas: Humanities research center: Austin 1963. pp.32. [156.]

Priestley, Joseph.

A CATALOGUE of books, written by dr. Priestley, and printed for J. Johnson. [1794]. pp.[8]. [90.]

— [another edition]. 1804. pp.[15]. [97.]

JOHN F[ARQUHAR] FULTON and CHARLOTTE H[ODGE] PETERS, Works of Joseph Priestley, 1733–1804. Preliminary short title list. Yale university: School of medicine: Laboratory of physiology: New Haven 1937. pp.[ii].20. [400.]*

typewritten additions were issued in 1938.

Puckle, James.

G. STEINMAN STEINMAN, The author of 'The Club' identified. 1872. pp.20. [12.]

privately printed.

[GEORGE WILIAM KOHLMETZ], Bibliographical notes on a collection of editions of the book known as 'Puckle's club'. Rowfant club: Cleveland 1899. pp.70. [31.]

150 copies privately printed.

Pullen, Henry William.

F[ALCONER] MADAN, 'The fight at dame Europa's school' and the literature connected with it. 1882 [*on cover:* 1881]. pp.35. [170.]

50 copies printed; also attributed to Junius Lawrence; the British museum and Bodleian library copies contain ms. notes by the author.

Pusey, Edward Bouverie.

WORKS, sermons, &c. by the rev. E. B. Pusey. [*s.l.*] 1883. pp.16. [50.]

Pye-Smith, Philip Henry.

J. H. E. WINSTON, Bibliography of the published writings (1866–1910) of Philip Henry Pye-Smith. Bibliographies of Guy's men (no.5): 1915. pp.12. [80.]

Quaife, Milo Milton.

M. M. QUAIFE, Forty-six years: the published writings of Milo M. Quaife. . . . Edited by Joe L. Norris. Algonquin club: Detroit 1956. pp.[ii].52. [350.]

Quarles, Francis.

JOHN R[OBERT BACKHOUSE] HORDEN, Francis Quarles, 1592–1644. A bibliography of his works to the year 1800. Oxford bibliographical society: Publications (n.s. ii): [Oxford 1953]. pp.x.83. [200.]

Queen Ellery [*pseud.* **Frederic Dannay** *and* **Manfred Bennington Lee.**]

[ELLERY QUEEN], An exhibition on the occasion of the opening of the Ellery Queen collection. University of Texas: Humanities research center: Austin 1959. pp.[ii].30. [200.]

500 copies printed.

Raleigh, sir Walter.

[WILBERFORCE EAMES], A bibliography of sir Walter Raleigh. New York 1886. pp.35. [125.]

34 copies privately printed.

T[HOMAS] N[ADAULD] BRUSHFIELD, The bibliography of the 'History of the world' and of the 'Remains' of sir Walter Ralegh. 1886. pp.8. [30.]

not limited to the works mentioned in the title.

Raleigh, sir Walter.

[WILBERFORCE EAMES], A bibliography of sir Walter Raleigh. New York 1886. pp.35. [125.]

34 copies privately printed.

T[HOMAS] N[ADAULD] BRUSHFIELD, The bibliography of the 'History of the world' and of the 'Remains' of sir Walter Ralegh. 1886. pp.8. [30.]

not limited to the works mentioned in the title.

T[HOMAS] N[ADAULD] BRUSHFIELD, The bibliography of sir Walter Raleigh. Plymouth &c. 1886. pp.[ii].36. [250.]

— — Second edition. Exeter 1908. pp.[xi].181. [330.]

a copy with ms. notes, cuttings &c. is in the Bodleian library.

Raleigh, sir Walter Alexander.

SIR WALTER RALEIGH. A bibliography. [Oxford 1922]. pp.7. [100.]

Ramsay, Allan.

ANDREW GIBSON, New light on Allan Ramsay. Edinburgh 1927. pp.xi.152. [41.]

500 copies printed.

BURNS MARTIN, A bibliography of the writings of Allan Ramsay. Glasgow bibliographical society: Records (vol.x): Glasgow 1931. pp.x.114. [411.]

Randolph, John.

JOHN RANDOLPH of Roanoke, 1773–1833. A bibliographical list. Library of Congress: [Washington] 1929. ff.10. [100.]*

WILLIAM E. STOKES and FRANCIS L[EWIS] BERKELEY, The papers of Randolph of Roanoke. A preliminary checklist of his surviving texts in manuscript and in print. University of Virginia: Library: Charlottesville 1950. pp.171. [2762.]

Randolph, Thomas.

SAMUEL A[ARON] and DOROTHY R. TANNENBAUM, Thomas Randolph. (A concise bibliography). Elizabethan bibliographies (no.38): New York 1947. ff.[ii].i.24. [347.]*

Read, sir Herbert.

FRANCIS BERRY, Herbert Read. British council: British book news: Bibliographical series of supplements (no.45): 1953. pp.40. [50.]

— — Revised edition. 1961. pp.43. [75.]

Reade, Charles.

M. L. PARRISH and ELIZABETH V. MILLER, Wilkie Collins and Charles Reade. First editions (with a few exceptions) in the library at Dormy house. 1940. pp.x.356. [Reade: 150.]

150 copies printed.

FRANCESCO CORDASCO and KENNETH W. SCOTT, Wilkie Collins and Charles Reade: a bibliography of critical notice and studies. Brooklyn 1949. pp.vi.7. [104.]

Reese, Lizette Woodworth.

[ALEXANDER C. WIRTH], Complete bibliography of Lizette Woodworth Reese. Baltimore 1937. pp.20. [14.]

Reeve, John.

[JOSEPH and ISAAC FROST], A list of books and general index to John Reeve & Lodowicke Muggleton's works: being the third and last testament of the only god our lord Jesus Christ. 1846. pp.24. [17.]

Reid, Forrest.

FORREST REID. An exhibition. Libraries, museums and art committee: Belfast 1954.pp.xxxvi. [183.]

Reneau, Isaac Tipton.

A LISTING of the contents and indexes of the papers of Isaac Tipton Reneau. College of the Bible: Bosworth memorial library: Bibliographical contributions (no.4): Lexington, Ky. 1956. ff.[ii].39. [500.]*

Rhodes, Eugene Manlove.

W. H. HUTCHINSON, A bar cross liar. Bibliography of Eugene Manlove Rhodes. Stillwater, Okla. 1959. pp.iii–xiv.95. [500.]

Richardson, Samuel.

WILLIAM MERRITT SALE, Samuel Richardson. A bibliographical record of his literary career, with historical notes. New Haven 1936. pp.xxiv.141. [90.]

FRANCESCO [G. M.] CORDASCO, Richardson. A list of critical studies published from 1896 to 1946. Long Island university: Eighteenth century bibliographical pamphlets (no.3): Brooklyn 1948. pp.12. [131.]

R. F. BRISSENDEN, Samuel Richardson. British council: British book news: Bibliographical series of supplements (no.101): 1958. pp.42. [50.]

Riley, James Whitcomb.

LIST of references on James Whitcomb Riley (supplementing bibliography contained in E. H. Eitel's biographical ed. of the complete works. Indianapolis, 1913, v.6). Library of Congress: Washington 1917. ff.3. [37.]*

ANTHONY J. and DOROTHY R[ITTER] RUSSO, A bibliography of James Whitcomb Riley. Indiana historical society: Indianapolis 1944. pp.xxi.251. [200.]

Robertson, Thomas William.

THOMAS WILLIAM ROBERTSON, 1829–1871: a bibliographical list. Library of Congress: Washington 1928. ff.9. [102.]*

Robinson, Edwin Arlington.

LUCIUS [MORRIS] BEEBE and ROBERT J. BULKLEY, A bibliography of the writings of Edwin Arlington Robinson. Cambridge, Mass. 1931. pp.61. [50.]

300 copies printed.

[BACON COLLAMORE and LAWRANCE ROGER THOMPSON], Edwin Arlington Robinson. A collection of his works from the library of Bacon Collamore. Hartford 1936. pp.x.66. [125.]

privately printed.

CHARLES BEECHER HOGAN, A bibliography of Edwin Arlington Robinson. New Haven 1936. pp.xiii.221. [750.]

a supplement by the author appears in the Papers *of the American bibliographical society (1941), xxxv.*

LILLIAN LIPPINCOTT, A bibliography of the writings and criticisms of Edwin Arlington Robinson. Useful reference series (no.59): Boston 1937. pp.86. [1000.]

EDWIN ARLINGTON ROBINSON at Colby college. Waterville, Me. 1944. pp.[4].

[KARL BROWN and M. C. WEAKS], Edward Arlington Robinson. A descriptive list of the Lewis M[ontefiore] Isaacs collection of Robinsoniana. Public library: New York 1948. pp.25. [300.]

the collection is now in the New York public library.

Robinson, George W.

[G. W. ROBINSON], A list of the chief printed works of George W. Robinson. Cambridge [printed] 1927. pp.21. [50.]

[G. W. ROBINSON], A select bibliography of George W. Robinson. 1928. pp.10. [21.]

Robinson, Henry Crabb.

INEZ ELLIOTT, Index to the Henry Crabb Robinson letters in Dr. Williams's library. Dr. Williams's library: Occasional paper (no.10): 1960. pp.36. [1000.]

Rogers, John. *see* **Rogerenes.**

Rogers, Samuel.

[CHARLES T. TALLENT-BATEMAN], Samuel Rogers. List of the poet's illustrated editions in the probably unique) collection of mr. Tallent-Bateman. Manchester &c. [1926]. pp.[4]. [23.]

Rohmer, Sax [*pseud.* **Arthur Sarsfield Ward.**]

BRADFORD M. DAY, Sax Rohmer. A bibliography. Denver &c. [1963]. pp.35. [250.]*

Rolfe, Frederick William Serafino Austin Lewis Mary.

CECIL WOOLF, A bibliography of Frederick Rolfe, baron Corvo. Soho bibliographies (vol. vii): 1957. pp.136. [200.]

[CECIL WOOLF and TIMOTHY D'ARCH SMITH], Frederick William Rolfe, baron Corvo. A catalogue . . . of a loan exhibition. Central public library: St Marylebone [1960]. pp.[ii].11. [125.]*

Rolfe, William James.

A BIBLIOGRAPHY of William James Rolfe. Public library: Cambridge, Mass. 1907. pp.40. [1000.]

Rolle, Richard.

HOPE EMILY ALLEN, Writings ascribed to Richard Rolle. Modern language association of America: Monograph series (vol.iii): New York 1927. pp. iii–xvi.568. [200.]

Rollins, Hyder Edward.

HERSCHEL [CLAY] BAKER, Hyder Edward Rollins. A bibliography. Cambridge, Mass. 1960. pp. [vii].51. [154.]

Roosevelt, Eleanor.

MRS ELEANOR (ROOSEVELT) ROOSEVELT (Mrs Franklin D. Roosevelt): a list of references, writings of Mrs. Roosevelt, books and essays. Library of Congress: Washington 1948. ff.4. [48.]*

Roosevelt, Franklin Delano.

A BRIEF list of references on Franklin Delano Roosevelt, president of the United States, 1933– . Library of Congress: Washington 1933. ff.6. [79.]*

SELECTED list of biographies of president Roosevelt, annotated from notices in the Book review digest. Library of Congress: Washington 1941. ff.4. [19.]*

AN EXHIBITION of materials from the Franklin D. Roosevelt library at Hyde Park, N.Y. National archives: Washington [1943]. pp.12.*

ERNEST J. HALTER, Collecting first editions of Franklin Roosevelt. Contributions to an FDR bibliography. Chicago [1949]. pp.xx.195. [950.]

77 copies privately printed.

DIARIES and other personal narratives of persons associated with the White house during the Roosevelt administration. Library of Congress: Washington 1951. ff.5. [43.]*

ROBERT L. JACOBY, Calendar of the speeches and other published statements of Franklin D. Roosevelt, 1910–1920. Franklin D. Roosevelt library: Hyde Park, N.Y. 1952. pp.vii.160. [918.]

Roosevelt, Theodore.

LIST of the writings of Theodore Roosevelt, chronologically arranged. Library of Congress: Washington 1905. ff.8. [57.]*

SELECT list of references on president Theodore Roosevelt. Library of Congress: Washington 1905. ff.3. [23.]*

— [another edition]. 1917. ff.3. [30.]*

— — Additional references. 1931. ff.5. [49.]*

LIST of writings of Theodore Roosevelt (exclusive of articles in periodicals). Library of Congress: Washington 1920. ff.8. [94.]*

JOHN HALL WHEELOCK, A bibliography of Theodore Roosevelt. New York 1920. pp.32. [750.]

official papers are excluded; 500 copies printed.

THEODORE ROOSEVELT, man of letters. A centennial exhibition. American academy of arts and letters [&c.]: [New York 1957]. pp.[23]. [125.]

Rosenbach, Abraham Simon Wolf.

JOHN FLEMING, A bibliography of the books, contributions and articles written by A. J. W. Rosenbach. Philadelphia 1946. pp.9. [100.]

Rosenberger, Francis Coleman.

FRANCIS COLEMAN ROSENBERGER, A list of published writings. Pennsylvania historical junto: Washington 1959. pp.48. [500.]

Rosenberger, Homer Tope.

MILTON RUBINCAM, Homer Tope Rosenberger. A bibliographical record. Pennsylvania historical junto: Washington 1958. pp.58. [177.]

Rosse, Irving C.

CONTRIBUTIONS of Irving C. Rosse. Washington [1901]. pp.8. [105.]

Rossetti, Dante Gabriel.

WILLIAM MICHAEL ROSSETTI, Bibliography of the works of Dante Gabriel Rossetti. 1905. pp.54. [80.]

250 copies printed.

WILLIAM M. ROSSETTI, Dante Gabriel Rossetti. Classified lists of his writings. 1906. pp.[iii].48. [375.]

100 copies privately printed.

C[HARLES] E[DWYN] VAUGHAN, Bibliographies of Swinburne, Morris and Rossetti. English association: Leaflet (no.29): 1914. pp.12. [Rossetti: 25.]

DANTE GABRIEL ROSSETTI centenary. Public library: Chelsea [1928]. pp.[4]. [75.]

PAULL FRANKLIN BAUM, Dante Gabriel Rossetti. An analytical list of manuscripts in the Duke university library. Durham, N.C. 1931. pp.ix.122. [100.]

400 copies printed.

OSWALD DOUGHTY, Dante Gabriel Rossetti. British council: British book news: Bibliographical series of supplements (no.85): 1957. pp.32. [75.]

Rowson, Susanna Haswell.

R[OBERT] W[ILLIAM] G[LENROIE] VAIL, Susanna Haswell Rowson, the author of Charlotte Temple. A bibliographical study. American antiquarian society: Worcester, Mass. 1933. pp.116. [275.]

Royden, Agnes Maude.

A. MAUDE ROYDEN, A reading list. Oakland, Cal. 1928. pp.[4]. [75.]

Ruffin, Edmund.

EARL G. SWEM, An analysis of Ruffin's Farmer's register, with a bibliography of Edmund Ruffin. Virginia state library: Bulletin (vol.xi, nos.3–4): Richmond 1919. pp.[ii].39–144. [2151.]

Rugg, Harold Ordway.

FRANKLIN PARKER, Harold Ordway Rugg, 1886–1960; a partial bibliography. Austin [1961]. pp.24. [300.]

Ruskin, John.

[RICHARD HERNE SHEPHERD], The bibliography of Ruskin. [1878]. pp.viii.48. [131.]

the preface is dated October 1878.

[—] — [another edition]. [1878]. pp.viii.59. [158.]

the preface is signed January 1879, but a presentation copy in the British museum is dated December 1878.

— — Fifth edition. [1882]. pp.[iii].75. [250.]

WILLIAM E[DWARD] A[RMYTAGE] AXON, John Ruskin: a bibliographical biography. [*s.l.*] 1879. pp.22. [60.]

— — Second edition. 1881. pp.27. [60.]

[H. C. WIGG], Catalogue of the books of Henry C. Wigg. . . . Section IV. The Turner-Ruskin series. Carlton, Melbourne 1882. pp.xl.24. [Ruskin: 250.]

many of the books have only a remote connexion with Ruskin.

THOMAS J[AMES] WISE and JAMES P. SMART, A complete bibliography of the writings in prose and verse of John Ruskin . . . with a list of the more important Ruskiniana. [1889–]1893. pp. xxviii.329+xi.263. [1154.]

250 copies privately printed; 100 of these contain illustrations, which were issued in [1893] with a separate titlepage, Illustrations to the Bibliography of John Ruskin; *pp.41–44 of vol.i were cancelled and reprinted.*

M[ARY] ETHEL JAMESON, A bibliographical contribution to the study of John Ruskin. Cambridge [Mass.] 1901. pp.xi.156. [3000.]

[SIR EDWARD TYAS COOK and ALEXANDER WEDDERBURN], Bibliography. The works of John Ruskin (vol.xxxviii): 1912. pp.xxvii.391. [5000.]

PETER QUENNELL, John Ruskin. British council: British book news: Bibliographical series of supplements (no.76): 1956. pp.36. [125.]

Russell, Bertrand, earl.

ALAND DORWARD, Bertrand Russell. British council: British book news: Bibliographical series of supplements: 1950. pp.44. [150.]

Russell, George William.

ALAN DENSON, Printed writings by George W. Russell (AE). A bibliography. 1961. pp.255. [650.]

Russell, Thomas O'Neill.

JAMES COLEMAN, Bibliography of Thomas O'Neill Russell [and Oliver Joseph Burke]. Bibliographical society of Ireland: Bibliographies of irish writers series: Dublin [printed] 1919. pp.4. [Russell: 15.]

Rutherford, Mark, *pseud.*

SIMON NOWELL SMITH, Mark Rutherford: a short bibliography of the first editions. Bookman's journal: Supplement: 1930. pp.23. [24.]

Rye, Walter.

BIBLIOGRAPHY of the works of Walter Rye, all of which are in the local collection of the Norwich public library. [*s.l.*] 1916. pp.7. [110.]

GEO[RGE] A[RTHUR] STEPHEN, Walter Rye. Memoir, bibliography, and catalogue of his Norfolk manuscripts in the Norwich public libraries. Norwich 1929. pp.32. [Rye: 350.]

Ryle, John Charles.

CATALOGUE of publications written by the right rev. bishop Ryle. Stirling [1900]. pp.8. [425.]

Sacheverell, Henry.

F[ALCONER] MADAN, A bibliography of dr. Henry Sacheverell. Oxford 1884. pp.73. [300.]
100 copies privately printed.

Sandburg, Carl.

CARL SANDBURG: a bibliography. Library of Congress: Washington 1948. ff.62. [646.]*

[LESLIE W. DUNLAP], The Sandburg range. An exhibit of materials from Carl Sandburg's library. University of Illinois: Adah Patton memorial fund: Publication (no.6): [Urbana 1958]. pp.47. [73.]

Sandys, George.

FREDSON [THAYER] BOWERS and RICHARD BEALE DAVIS, George Sandys. A bibliographical catalogue of printed editions in England to 1700. Public library: New York 1950. pp.53. [40.]

Sassoon, Siegfried.

[SIR] GEOFFREY [LANGDON] KEYNES, A bibliography of Siegfried Sassoon. Soho bibliographies (vol.x): 1962. pp.199. [408.]

Sawyer, Paul.

WILLARD ROUSE JILLSON, A bibliography of Paul Sawyer. Frankfort, Ky. 1939. pp.16. [48.]

Schreiner, Olive Emilie Albertina.

EVELYN VERSTER, Olive Emilie Albertina Schreiner, 1855–1920. Bibliography. University of Cape Town: School of librarianship: Bibliographical series: [Capetown] 1946 [1950]. ff.iii.26. [274.]*

Scott, sir Walter.

CATALOGUE of the loan exhibition in commemoration of sir Walter Scott. Edinburgh 1871. pp.60. [125.]

Individual Authors

[SIR WILLIAM STIRLING MAXWELL, DAVID LAING and JAMES DRUMMOND], The Scott exhibition, MDCCCLXXI. Catalogue. Edinburgh 1872. pp. xiv.206. [200.]

reissued in 1874 with the compilers' names on the titlepage.

[JAMES DUNCAN and ALEXANDER BALHARRIE], Catalogue of the Burns, Scott and Shakespeare exhibition, . . . from the collection of A[lexander] C[rawford] Lamb. Victoria galleries: Dundee [1896]. pp.115. [5000.]

JOHN THOMSON, Descriptive catalogue of the writings of sir Walter Scott. Free library: Bulletin (no.1): Philadelphia 1898. pp.106. [350.]

LIST of editions of sir Walter Scott's novels in the Library of Congress: Washington 1916. ff.6. [68.]*

A LIST of the american editions of the writings of Sir Walter Scott in the Library of Congress. Washington 1916. ff.12. [314.]*

— [supplement]. 1931. ff.6. [63.]*

ALBERT CAPLAN, The bibliography of sir Walter Scott, bart. Philadelphia [1928]. pp.45. [122.]

150 copies printed.

GREVILLE WORTHINGTON, A bibliography of the Waverley novels. Bibliographia (vol.iv): 1931. pp.xvi.144. [23.]
500 copies printed.

W[ILLIA]M C[LARKSON] VAN ANTWERP, A collector's comment on his first editions of the works of sir Walter Scott. San Francisco 1932. pp.[vii]. 157. [100.]
400 copies printed.

[WILLIAM K. DICKSON], Catalogue of the sir Walter Scott exhibition. Edinburgh 1932. pp. vii.70. [80.]

SIR WALTER SCOTT, author of the Waverly novels. List of the autograph manuscripts and the editions of his works in a commemorative exhibition. Columbia university library: [New York] 1932. pp.19. [85.]

SHORT-TITLE catalogue of first editions of sir Walter Scott in the library of William C[larkson] Van Antwerp. [San Francisco] 1933. pp.[ii].27.
200 copies privately printed.

ALLSTON BURR, Sir Walter Scott, an index placing the short poems in his novels and in his long poems and dramas. Cambridge [Mass.] 1936. pp.iv.130. [750.]

WILLIAM RUFF, A bibliography of the poetical works of sir Walter Scott, 1796–1832. Edinburgh bibliographical society: Transactions (vol.i, part 2): Edinburgh 1937. pp.99–239. [192.]

corrections and additions appear at i.277–281; reissued separately in 1938.

JAMES CLARKSON CORSON, A bibliography of sir Walter Scott. A classified and annotated list of books and articles relating to his life and works, 1797–1940. Edinburgh &c. 1943. pp.xv.428. [3000.]

[I. M. LEVIDOVA], Вальтер Скотт. Био-библиографический указатель к 125-летию со дня смерти. Всесоюзная государственная библиотека иностранной литературы: Писатели зарубежных стран: Москва 1958. pp.84. [500.]

IAN JACK, Sir Walter Scott. British council: British book news: Bibliographical series of supplements (no.103): 1958. pp.40. [75.]

Sealsfield, Charles.

OTTO HELLER and THEODORE H[ERZL] LEON, Charles Sealsfield. Bibliography of his writings . . . and an annotated catalogue of literature relating to his works and his life. Washington university: Studies (new series): Language and literature (no.8): St. Louis 1939. pp.x.88. [445.]

Shapiro, Karl.

WILLIAM WHITE, Karl Shapiro. A bibliography. Detroit 1960. pp.115. [500.]

350 copies printed.

Shatzky, Jacob.

M. KOSOVER and M. UNGER, A bibliography of the writings of Jacob Shatzky. New York 1939. pp.[ii].81. [579.]

Shaw, George Bernard.

SELECT list of references on George Bernard Shaw (periodical literature of continental Europe). Library of Congress: Washington 1907. ff.8. [49.]*

GEOFFREY H[ARRY] WELLS, A bibliography of the books and pamphlets of George Bernard Shaw. Bookman's journal: Supplement: 1925. pp.16. [43.]

— — [another edition]. 1928. pp.46. [122.]

MAURICE HOLMES, Some bibliographical notes on the novels of George Bernard Shaw. [1928]. pp.20. [5].

500 copies printed.

ALTHA ELIZABETH TERRY, Jeanne d'Arc in periodical literature, 1894–1929, with special reference to Bernard Shaw's 'Saint Joan'. Institute of french studies: New York 1930. pp.xiii.127. [Shaw: 200.]

X[AVIER] HEYDET, Shaw kompendium. Verzeichnis und analyse seiner werke, Shaw-bibliographie, verzeichnis der literatur über Shaw, verzeichnis der aufführungen seiner werke in England und Deutschland. Paris 1936. pp.3–228. [1500.]

BERNARD SHAW. Catalogue of an exhibition. National book league: [1946]. pp.254. [300.]

F[RITZ] E[RWIN] LOEWENSTEIN, The rehearsal copies of Bernard Shaw's plays. 1950. pp.36. [30.]

A[LFRED] C[HARLES] WARD, Bernard Shaw. British council: British book news: Bibliographical series of supplements [no.1]: 1950. pp.56. [250.]

— — Fourth edition. 1960. pp.56. [250.]

SHAW. A select handlist of books by and about him. Public libraries: Bethnal Green: [1950]. pp. [6(folder)]. [60.]

[I. M. LEVIDOVA *and others*], Бернард Шоу. Био-библиографический указатель к 100 летию со дня рождения. Всесоюзная государственная библиотека иностранной литературы: Писатели зарубежных стран: Москва 1956. pp.84. [694.]

[JOHN DOZIER GORDAN], Bernard Shaw 1856–1950. An exhibition from the Berg collection. Manuscripts, autograph letters, first editions. Public library: New York 1956. pp.51. [150.]

A[RNOLD] M[ATVEEVICH] GORBUNOV, Бернарда Шоу 1856–1950. Памятка читателю. Государственная . . . библиотека СССР имени В. И. Ленина: Москва 1956. pp.52. [50.]

Shea, John Gilmary.

EDWARD [PETER] SPILLANE, Bibliography of John Gilmary Shea. [*s.l.* 1913]. pp.26. [250.]

Shelley, Percy Bysshe.

H[ARRY] BUXTON FORMAN, The Shelley library. . . . I. Shelley's books, pamphlets, and broadsides; posthumous separate issues; and posthumous books wholly or mainly by him. 1886. pp.127. [83.]

no more published.

FREDERICK S. ELLIS, An alphabetical table of contents to Shelley's poetical works. Shelley Society: 1888. pp.21. [325.]

500 copies printed.

[CHARLES WELCH], Hand-list of manuscripts, letters, printed books, & personal relics of Percy Bysshe Shelley and his circle. Exhibited in the Guildhall library. 1893. pp.27. [300.]

50 copies printed.

THOMAS R[OBERTS] SLICER, Percy Bysshe Shelley. An appreciation . . . with an illustrated bibliography. New York 1903. pp.83. [20.]

165 copies printed; limited to the early writings.

PERCY VAUGHAN, Early Shelley pamphlets. 1905. pp.32. [7.]

[HARRY NELSON GAY], List of the first thousand works acquired by the Keats-Shelley memorial, Rome. 1910. pp.115. [Shelley: 200.]

[—] — List of the second thousand works. . . . 1913. pp.99. [200.]

SHORT bibliographies of Wordsworth, Coleridge, Byron, Shelley, Keats. English association: Leaflet (no.23): 1912. pp.13. [250.]

RUTH S[HEPARD] GRANNRISS, A descriptive catalogue of the first editions in book form of the writings of Percy Bysshe Shelley, based on a memorial exhibition held at the Grolier club. New York 1923. pp.xx.134. [150.]

350 copies printed.

THOMAS J[AMES] WISE, A Shelley library. A catalogue of printed books, manuscripts and autograph letters by Percy Bysshe Shelley, Harriet Shelley, and Mary Wollstonecraft Shelley. 1924. pp.xvii.166. [600.]

20 copies privately printed.

SEYMOUR [MONTEFIORE ROBERT ROSSO] DE RICCI, A bibliography of Shelley's letters, published and unpublished. Bois-Colombes [printed] 1927. pp. 296. [1000.]

privately printed.

AN ACCOUNT of an exhibition of books and manuscripts of Percy Bysshe Shelley. University of Texas: Library: Austin 1935. pp.[iv].40. [100.]

Sherborn, Charles Davies.

A LIST of contributions to various subjects by Charles Davies Sherborn. [1906]. pp.9. [110.]

Sheridan, Philip Henry.

PHILIP HENRY SHERIDAN, 1831–1888: a bibliographical list. Library of Congress: Washington 1935. ff.11. [108.]*

Sheridan, Richard Brinsley Butler.

W[ILLIAM] A[UBREY CECIL] DARLINGTON, Sheridan, 1751–1816. British council: British book news: Bibliographical series of supplements: 1951. pp.29. [30.]

Shirley, James.

SAMUEL A[ARON] and DOROTHY R. TANNENBAUM, James Shirley. (A concise bibliography). Elizabethan bibliographies (no.34): New York 1946. ff.[iv].42. [591.]*

Shorter, Dora Sigerson.

[THOMAS JAMES WISE], The books of Dora Sigerson Shorter. [Ashley Library]: Edinburgh [printed] 1924. pp.8. [39.]

Shotwell, James Thomson.

BIBLIOGRAPHY, 1904–1941, James Thomson Shotwell. [*s.l.* 1942]. ff.22. [600.]

Shufeldt, Robert Wilson.

R. W. SHUFELDT, 1881–1887. Contributions to science and bibliographical resumé of the writings of R. W. Shufeldt. New York 1887. pp.20. [127.]

Sidney, sir Philip.

SAMUEL A[ARON] TANNENBAUM, Sir Philip Sidney. (A concise bibliography). Elizabethan bibliographies (no.23): New York 1941. pp.x.70. [1500.]

300 copies printed.

JAMES O[RCHARD] HALLIWELL[-PHILLIPPS], Descriptive notices of works in a small collection of sydneian literature in the library of James O. Halliwell. Brixton hill 1854. pp.8. [9.]

KENNETH MUIR, Sir Philip Sidney. British council: British book news: Bibliographical series of supplements (no.120): 1960. pp.40. [100.]

Sill, Edward Rowland.

EDWARD ROWLAND SILL (1841–1887). A bibliographical list. Library of Congress: [Washington] 1933. ff.6. [110.]*

Simcoe, H. A.

PENHEALE PRESS. A catalogue of works published by the rev. H. A. Simcoe, Penheale, near Launceston, Cornwall. Launceston 1854. pp.10. [225.]

Simms, William Gilmore.

OSCAR WEGELIN, A bibliography of the separate

writings of William Gilmore Simms of South Carolina, 1806–1870. . . . Third edition. Heartman's historical series (no.58): Hattiesburg 1941. pp.24. [87.]

149 copies printed.

[ALEXANDER SAMUEL SALLEY], Catalogue of the Salley collection of the works of Wm. Gilmore Simms. Columbia, S.C. 1943. pp.121. [400.]

Simpson, Percy.

A LIST of the published writings of Percy Simpson. Oxford 1950. pp.30. [110.]

Sinclair, Upton Beall.

BOOKS of Upton Sinclair in translations and foreign editions. Pasadena, Cal. 1930. pp.34. [525.]

— — Second edition. 1938. pp.48. [772.]

BOOKS of Upton Sinclair. [Pasadena, Cal. 1931]. pp.[4]. [40.]

JOSEPH GAER, *ed.* Upton Sinclair. Bibliography and biographical data. California literary research: Monograph (no.6): [*s.l.* 1934]. ff.54. [250.]*

A CATALOGUE of books, manuscripts and other materials from the Upton Sinclair archives. University of Indiana: Lilly library: Bloomington [1963]. pp.56.

Sitwell, Edith, sir Osbert, and Sacheverell.

THOMAS BALSTON, Sitwelliana, 1915–1927. Being a handlist of works by Edith, Osbert, and Sacheverell Sitwell and of their contributions to certain selected periodicals. 1928. pp.x.24. [70.]

ROGER [THOMAS BALDWIN] FULFORD, Osbert Sitwell. British council: British book news: Bibliographic series of supplements: 1951. pp.44. [100.]

RICHARD FIFOOT, A bibliography of Edith, Osbert and Sacheverell Sitwell. Soho bibliographies (vol.xi): 1963. pp.394. [1000.]

Skeffington, F. Sheehy.

P. S. O'HEGARTY, A bibliography of the books of Terence MacSwiney and F. Sheehy Skeffington. Dublin [printed] 1936. pp.[ii].7. [Skeffington: 8.]

30 copies privately printed.

Skelton, John.

PETER [MORRIS] GREEN, John Skelton. British council: British book news: Bibliographical series of supplements (no.128): 1960. pp.46. [50.]

Slezer, John.

JAMES CAMERON, A bibliography of Slezer's Theatrum Scotiæ. . . . With an analytical table of the plates by . . . W. Johnston. Edinburgh bibliographical society: Papers (vol.iii, no.7): Edinburgh [1897]. pp.141–147. [8.]

Slingerland, Mark Vernon.

M. D. LEONARD, A bibliography of the writings of professor Mark Vernon Slingerland. Cornell university: Agricultural experiment station: Bulletin (no.348): Ithaca, N.Y. 1914. pp.621–652. [750.]

Slosson, Edwin Emery.

BIBLIOGRAPHY of the writings of Edwin E. Slosson. Science service: Washington 1929. ff.45. [1850.]*

Small, John Kunkel.

[JOHN HENDLEY BARNHART], Bibliography of John Kunkel Small. [*s.l.*] 1935. pp.15. [350.]

Smart, Christoph.

G[EORGE] J[OHN] GRAY, A bibliography of the writings of Christopher Smart. 1903. pp.41. [30.]

GEOFFREY GRIGSON, Christopher Smart. British council: British book news: Bibliographical series of supplements (no.136): 1961. pp.44. [50.]

Smith, Adam.

DAVID MURRAY, French translations of the Wealth of nations. Glasgow 1905. pp.15. [12.]

CHARLES J[ESSE] BULLOCK, The [Homer Bews] Vanderblue memorial collection of Smithiana . . . deposited in the Kress library. Harvard graduate school of business administration: Baker library (= Kress library of business and economics, Publication no.2): Boston 1939. pp.xiv.68. [500.]

BURT FRANKLIN and FRANCESCO [G. M.] CORDASCO, Adam Smith. A bibliographical checklist. An international record of critical writings . . . 1876–1950. Burt Franklin bibliographical series (no.iii): New York 1950. pp.63. [446.]

Smith, Goldwin.

JNO. JAS. [JOHN JAMES] COOPER, Goldwin Smith, D.C.L. A brief account of his life and writings. Reading [printed] [1912]. pp.14. [75.]

Smith, James.

WILLARD ROUSE JILLSON, A bibliography of the

life and writings of col. James Smith of Bourbon county, Kentucky, 1737–1812. Kentucky historical society: Frankfort 1947. pp.3–51. [75.]

Smith, sir James Edward.

WARREN R. DAWSON, Catalogue of the manuscripts in the library of the Linnean society of London. Part I. — The Smith papers. (The correspondence and miscellaneous papers of sir James Edward Smith . . .). 1934. pp.114. [3500.]

Smith, John.

WILBERFORCE EAMES, A bibliography of captain John Smith. New York 1927. pp.48. [52.]

Smith, Sydney Ure.

SYDNEY URE SMITH memorial exhibition. Michell library of N.S.W.: [Sydney] 1950. pp.41. [200.]

Smith, Thomas.

EDWARD G[LOVER] MARTIN, The papers of Thomas Smith. A bibliography. [Winchester, Mass.] 1961. pp.[iii].18. [141.]*

— Revised edition. 1962. pp.[v].35. [164.]*

Smith, William Benjamin.

HENRY ORMAL SEVERANCE, William Benjamin Smith. University of Missouri bulletin (vol. xxxvii, no.3 = Library series, no.17): Columbia 1936. pp.23. [250.]

Smithies, T. B.

CATALOGUE of illustrated temperance publications originated by the late T. B. Smithies. National temperance publication depot: [1887]. pp.[12]. [250.]

Smollett, Tobias.

FRANCESCO [G. M.] GORDASCO, Smollett criticism, 1925–1945. Long Island university: Brooklyn 1947. pp.[vi].9. [73.]*

FRANCESCO [G. M.] CORDASCO, Smollett criticism, 1770–1924. Long Island university: Brooklyn 1948. pp.vii.28. [305.]*

LAURENCE BRANDER, Tobias Smollett. British council: British book news: Bibliographical series of supplements: 1951. pp.36. [75.]

Smyth, W. H.

[W. H. SMYTH], Synopsis of the published and privately-printed works by admiral W. H. Smyth. 1864. pp.60. [175.]

privately printed.

Solis-Cohen, Solomon.

EDWARD D[AVIDSON] COLEMAN, Bibliography of the writings and addresses of Solomon Solis-Cohen. [Philadelphia 1940]. pp.84. [1000.]

Somerville, Edith Œnone, *and* **Martin Ross** [*pseud.* **Violet Florence Martin.**]

ELIZABETH HUDSON, A bibliography of the first editions of the works of E. Œ. Somerville and Martin Ross . . . with explanatory notes by E. Œ. Somerville. New York 1942. pp.x.80. [50.]
300 copies printed.

Southey, Robert.

ROBERT SOUTHEY, 1774–1843, poet and man of letters. Lecture and exhibition. Public libraries: Bristol 1943. pp.12. [125.]

Southwell, Robert.

JAMES G. MCDONALD, The poems and prose writings of Robert Southwell, S.J. A bibliographical study. Roxburghe club: Oxford [printed] 1937. pp.[ii].xix.162. [109.]

Spenser, Edmund.

FREDERIC IVES CARPENTER, An outline guide to the study of Spenser. Chicago 1894. pp.24. [400.]

CATALOGUE of an exhibition of the original editions of the works of Edmund Spenser. Grolier club: New York 1899. pp.19. [23.]

FREDERIC IVES CARPENTER, A reference guide to Edmund Spenser. Chicago 1923. pp.vi.333. [3000.]

— — Edmund Spenser. A bibliographical supplement. By Dorothy F. Atkinson. Baltimore 1937. pp.xv.242. [2000.]

FRANCIS R[ARICK] JOHNSON, A critical bibliography of the works of Edmund Spenser printed before 1700. Johns Hopkins university: Tudor and Stuart club: Baltimore 1933. pp.xiv.61. [29.]

ROSEMARY FREEMAN, Edmund Spenser. British council: British book news: Bibliographical series of supplements (no.89): 1957. pp.39. [75.]

WALDO F. MCNEIR and [GEORG] FOSTER PROVOST, Annotated bibliography of Edmund Spenser, 1937–1960. Duquesne studies: Philological series (vol.3): Pittsburgh 1962. pp.xxi.255. [1185.]

Spurgeon, Charles Haddon.

A GLANCE at the Spurgeon library. By an old comrade. [1897]. pp.32. [150.]

— — [another edition]. [*c*.1905]. pp.32. [150.]

Squier, Ephraim George.

A LIST of books, pamphlets, and more important contributions to periodicals, etc., by hon. E. George Squier. New York 1876. pp.8. [91.]

FRANK SQUIER, A collection of books by Ephraim George Squier. New York 1939. ff.[ii].44. [150.]
100 copies reproduced from typewriting.

Squire, sir John Collings.

I[OLO] A[NEURIN] WILLIAMS, John Collings Squire and James Stephens. Bibliographies of modern authors (no.4): 1922. pp.[v].13. [Squire: 30.]

Starrett, Vincent.

CHARLES HONCE, A Vincent Starrett library. Mount Vernon [N.Y.] 1941. pp.5–85. [129.]
100 copies printed.

Stead, William Force.

WILLIAM FORCE STEAD. Biographical sketch and bibliography of his works. Enoch Pratt free library: [Baltimore] 1944. ff.[9].*

Steele, sir Richard.

A. R. HUMPHREYS, Steele, Addison and their periodical essays. British council: British book news: Bibliographical series of supplements (no.109): 1959. pp.46. [100.]

Steffens, Lincoln.

BIBLIOGRAPHY of Lincoln Steffens. Library of Congress: Washington 1926. ff.6. [89.]*

Stein, Gertrude.

ROBERT BARTLETT HAAS and DONALD CLIFFORD GALLUP, A catalogue of the published and unpublished writings of Gertrude Stein exhibited in the Yale university library. New Haven 1941. pp.64. [533.]

JULIAN SAWYER, Gertrude Stein. A bibliography. New York [1941]. pp.164. [500.]

GEORGE JAMES FIRMAGE, A check-list of the published writings of Gertrude Stein. University of Massachusetts: Amherst 1954. pp.8. [186.]

Steinbeck, John.

JOHN STEINBECK: an exhibition of american and foreign editions. University of Texas: Humanities research center: [Austin 1963]. pp.32. [100.]

Stephens, James.

I[OLO] A[NEURIN] WILLIAMS, John Collings Squire and James Stephens. Bibliographies of modern authors (no.4): 1922. pp.[v].13. [Stephens: 15.]

BIRGIT BRAMSBÄCK, James Stephens. A literary and bibliographical study. Upsala irish studies (vol.iv): Upsala &c. 1959. pp.209. [835.]

Sterling, George.

CECIL JOHNSON, A bibliography of the writings of George Sterling. San Francisco 1931. pp.[ii]. viii.64. [200.]

300 copies printed.

Sterne, Laurence.

FRANCESCO CORDASCO, Laurence Sterne. A list of critical studies published from 1896 yo 1946. Eighteenth century bibliographical pamphlets (no.4): Brooklyn 1948. pp.[x].13. [154.]

D. W. JEFFERSON, Laurence Sterne. British council: British book news: Bibliographical series of supplements (no.52): 1954. pp.35. [50.]

Stevens, Henry.

CATALOGUE of the historical and bibliographical works of mr. Henry Stevens of Vermont. [1895]. pp.12. [27.]

the cover is included in the pagination.

Stevens, Wallace.

SAMUEL FRENCH MORSE, Wallace Stevens. A preliminary checklist of his published writings: 1898–1954. Yale university: Library: New Haven 1954. pp.66. [350.]

SAMUEL FRENCH MORSE, JACKSON R. BRYER and JOSEPH N. RIDDEL, Wallace Stevens checklist and bibliography of Stevens criticism. Denver [1963]. pp.98. [650.]

Stevenson, Edward Luther.

PUBLICATIONS of Edward Luther Stevenson. [*s.l. c.*1915]. pp.15. [58.]

Stevenson, Robert Louis.

[GEORGE MILLER WILLIAMSON], Catalogue of a collection of the books of Robert Louis Stevenson in the library of George M. Williamson. Jamaica, N.Y. [printed] 1901. pp.[95]. [115.]

150 copies printed.

W[ILLIAM] F[RANCIS] PRIDEAUX, A bibliography of the works of Robert Louis Stevenson. 1903. pp.xvi.301. [400.]

— — New . . . edition. Edited . . . by mrs. Luther S[amuel] Livingston. 1917. pp.viii.401. [600.]

A[BRAHAM] S. W[OLF] ROSENBACH, A catalogue of the books and manuscripts of Robert Louis Stevenson in the library of the late Harry Elkins Widener. Philadelphia 1913. pp.xi.266. [226.]

150 copies privately printed; the collection forms part of Harvard university library.

FIRST editions of the works of Robert Louis Stevenson . . . with other Stevensoniana exhibited at the Grolier club. New York 1914. pp.viii.74. [235.]

J[OHN] HERBERT SLATER, Robert Louis Stevenson. A bibliography of his complete works. Bibliographers' handbooks: 1914. pp.vii.46. [100.]

ANNOTATED list of the dr. Wm. Gemmell collection of the works of Robert Louis Stevenson. [Mitchell library: Glasgow] 1919. ff.[iv].27.[iii]. [148.]*

ROBERT LOUIS STEVENSON. Catalogue of the Stevenson exhibition under the auspices of the Literary anniversary club . . . displayed in the San Francisco public library. [San Francisco] 1932. pp.22. [100.]

ROBERT LOUIS STEVENSON, 1850–1894. Catalogue of the Stevenson collection . . . in the central library. Public libraries committee: Edinburgh 1950. pp.38. [400.]

LIST of selected books on Robert Louis Stevenson. Corporation public libraries: Glasgow 1950. pp.16. [150.]

GEORGE L[ESLIE] MCKAY, A Stevenson library. Catalogue of a collection . . . formed by Edwin J[ohn] Beinecke. Yale university: Library: New Haven.

- i–ii. Printed books, pamphlets, broadsides, etc. 1951. pp.xix.372 + xiii.373–860. [2628.]
- iii. Autograph letters by Robert Louis Stevenson and his wife. 1956. pp.xvii.861–1195. [1232.]
- iv. Letters to and about Robert Louis Stevenson. 1958. pp.xxi.1197–1705. [2028.]
- v. Manuscripts by Robert Louis Stevenson and others. 1961. pp.xix.1707–2219. [1464.]

500 copies printed.

I. M. LEVIDOVA, Роберт Луи Стивенсон. Всесоюзная государственная библиотека иностранной литературы: Писатели зарубежных стран: Москва 1958. pp.52. [386.]

Stockton-Hough, John.

LIST of papers and reprints written by John Stockton-Hough. [*s.l.* 1886]. pp.[2]. [27.]

Stowe, Harriet Elizabeth Beecher.

GRACE EDITH MAC LEAN, "Uncle Tom's cabin" in Germany. University of Pennsylvania: Americana germanica (vol.x): New York 1910. pp.101. [300.]

LIST of references relating to Harriet Beecher Stowe (exclusive of periodical articles). Library of Congress: Washington 1921. ff.4. [38.]*

CHESTER E[UGENE] JORGENSON, Uncle Tom's cabin as book and legend. A guide to an exhibition. Friends of the Detroit public library: Detroit 1952. pp.51. [142.]

Strachey, Giles Lytton.

R. A. SCOTT-JAMES, Lytton Strachey. British council: British book news: Bibliographical series of supplements (no.65): 1955. pp.39. [100.]

MARTIN KALLICH, Lytton Strachey: an annotated bibliography of writings about him. Purdue university: English fiction in transition (vol.v, no.3): Lafayette, Ind. 1962. ff.v.79. [600.]*

Stuart, Jesse.

HENSLEY C[HARLES] WOODBRIDGE, Jesse Stuart: a bibliography. Harrogate, Tenn. 1960. pp.iii–xxviii.74. [1500.]

Stubbs, William.

W. A. SHAW, A bibliography of the historical works of dr. Creighton . . . dr. Stubbs . . . dr. S. R. Gardiner, and . . . lord Acton. Royal historical society: 1903. pp.63. [Stubbs: 750.]

Sullivan, sir Arthur Seymour.

TOWNLEY SEARLE, A bibliography of sir William Schwenk Gilbert. With bibliographical adventures in the Gilbert & Sullivan operas. [1931]. pp.[viii].l.107. [600.]

SIRVART POLADIAN, Sir Arthur Sullivan: an index to the texts of his vocal works. Detroit studies in music bibliography (no.2): Detroit 1961. pp.xviii.91. [2000.]

Sullivan, T. D., A. M., D. B.., R. and D.

JAMES COLEMAN, Bibliography of the brothers Sullivan. Bibliographical society of Ireland (vol. iii, no.3): Wexford [printed] 1926. pp.[7]. [50.]

Summerall, Charles Pelot.

CHARLES PELOT SUMMERALL. A register of his papers in the Library of Congress: Washington 1958. ff.9.*

Summers, Montague.

TIMOTHY DIARCH SMITH, A bibliography of the works of Montague Summers. New Hyde Park, N.Y. [1964]. pp.164. [345.]

Swemm, Earl Gregg.

JAMES ALBERT SERVIES, Earl Gregg Swemm. A bibliography. College of William and Mary in Virginia: Library contributions (no.1): [Williamsburg] 1960. pp.60.

500 copies printed.

Swift, Jonathan.

STANLEY LANE-POOLE, Notes for a bibliography of Swift. 1884. pp.36. [250.]

25 copies printed.

LUCIUS L[EE] HUBBARD, Contributions towards a bibliography of Gulliver's travels. Chicago 1922. pp.191. [250.]

200 copies printed.

H[ERMAN] TEERINK, A bibliography of the writings in prose and verse of Jonathan Swift. The Hague 1937. pp.iii–xii.434. [1575.]

— — Second edition. A bibliography of the writings of Jonathan Swift. Edited by Arthur H[awley] Scouten. Philadelphia [1963]. pp.xviii. 453. [1643.]

315 copies printed.

LOUIS A. LANDA and JAMES EDWARD TOBIN, Jonathan Swift. A list of critical studies published from 1895 to 1945.... To which is added Remarks on some Swift manuscripts in the United States by Herbert Davis. Eighteenth century bibliographical pamphlets: New York 1945. pp.62. [600.]

CATALOGUE of the exhibition held in the library ... to commemorate the bicentenary of the death of Jonathan Swift. Friends of the library of Trinity college: Dublin 1945. pp.16. [90.]

[JOHN DAVY HAYWARD], A catalogue of printed books and manuscripts by Jonathan Swift, D.D., exhibited in the Old schools in the university of Cambridge. Cambridge 1945. pp.46. [85.]

AUTREY NELL WILEY, Jonathan Swift. An exhibition of printed books. University of Texas: [Austin 1945]. pp.48. [100.]

[JOHN] MIDDLETON MURRY, Swift. British council: British book news: Bibliographical series of supplements (no.61): 1955. pp.44. [150.]

Swinburne, Algernon Charles.

[RICHARD HERNE SHEPHERD], The bibliography of Swinburne. [1883]. pp.viii.40. [175.]

250 copies privately printed.

[—] — New [fourth] edition. 1887. pp.40. [210.]

250 copies privately printed.

THOMAS J[AMES] WISE, A bibliographical list of the scarcer works and uncollected writings of Algernon Charles Swinburne. 1897. pp.117. [150.]

50 copies privately printed.

J[OSEPH] C[HARLES] THOMSON, Bibliographical list of the writings of Algernon Charles Swinburne. Wimbledon 1905. pp.48. [275.]

C[HARLES] E[DWYN] VAUGHAN, Bibliographies of Swinburne, Morris and Rossetti. English association: Leaflet (no.29): 1914. pp.12. [Swinburne: 100.]

[SIR EDMUND WILLIAM GOSSE], A catalogue of the works of Algernon Charles Swinburne in the library of mr. Edmund Gosse. 1919. pp.34. [150.]

50 copies privately printed.

THOMAS J[AMES] WISE, A bibliography of the writings in prose and verse of Algernon Charles Swinburne. 1919–1920. pp.xvi.511 + xvi.411. [450.]

125 copies privately printed.

— — [another edition]. Complete works of Algernon Charles Swinburne (vol.xx): 1927. pp.iii–xii.575. [674.]

FLORA V[IRGINIA] LIVINGSTON, Swinburne's proof sheets and american first editions. Bibliographical data relating to a few of the publications of Algernon Charles Swinburne. Cambridge, Mass. 1920. pp.32. [20.]

privately printed.

A CATALOGUE of first editions of the works of Algernon Charles Swinburne in the library of Edward K. Butler. Boston 1921. pp.25. [70.]

65 copies privately printed.

[T. J. WISE], A Swinburne library. A catalogue of printed books, manuscripts and autograph letters by Algernon Charles Swinburne collected by Thomas James Wise. 1925. pp.xv.298. [500.]

30 copies privately printed.

H. J. C. GRIERSON, Swinburne. British council:

British book news: Bibliographical series of supplements (no.44): 1953. pp.31. [75.]

Symonds, John Addington.

PERCY L[ANCELOT] BABINGTON, Bibliography of the writings of John Addington Symonds. 1925. pp.xi.244. [560.]

500 copies printed.

Synge, John Millington.

M. J. MAC MANUS, A bibliography of books written by John Millington Synge. Dublin [printed] 1930. pp.7. [12.]

25 copies privately printed; interleaved; with an addendum slip.

[IAN SHAW MAC PHAIL and MARY POLLARD], John Millington Synge, 1871–1909: a catalogue of an exhibition held . . . on the occasion of the fiftieth anniversary of his death. Trinity college: Library: Dublin 1959. pp.40. [146.]

ELIZABETH COXHEAD, J. M. Synge and lady Gregory. British council: British book news: Bibliographical series: 1962. pp.35. [50.]

Talmage, Thomas De Witt.

LIST of books in the Library of Congress by Thomas De Witt Talmage. Library of Congress: Washington 1925. ff.5. [66.]*

Targett, James Henry.

WILLIAM WALE, Bibliography of the published writings of James Henry Targett. [Bibliographies of Guy's men (no.2)]: 1913. pp.8. [85.]

Tarkington, Booth.

BARTON CURRIE, Booth Tarkington. A bibliography. New York 1932. pp.vi.154. [100.]

DOROTHY RITTER RUSSO and THELMA L[OIS] SULLIVAN, A bibliography of Booth Tarkington, 1869–1946. Historical society: Indianapolis 1949. pp.xix.303. [1000.]

Taylor, John.

WILLIAM JOHNSTON, A bibliography of the thumb Bibles of John Taylor. Aberdeen 1910. pp.[ii].13. [17.]

40 copies printed.

BOOKS and pamphlets by, and attributed to, John Taylor, the water-poet. [*s.l.* 1955]. ff.[44]. [44.]*

Taylor, Thomas.

RUTH BALCH, Thomas Taylor the Platonist,

1758–1835. List of original works and translations. Newberry library: Chicago 1917. pp.34. [150.]

150 copies reproduced from typewriting.

Tennyson, Alfred, lord.

[RICHARD HERNE SHEPHERD], Tennysoniana. Notes bibliographical and critical. 1866. pp.xii [*sic*, x].170. [100.]

the pagination is erratic, there being no pages 30–41, 62–63, 88–89, 102–105, 128–139, and unnumbered pages appearing between pp. 163 and 164 and between pp. 164 and 165.

— — The lover's tale; a supplementary chapter to Tennysoniana. [*c*.1870]. pp.8.

50 copies printed of the supplement.

— — Second edition. 1879. pp.viii.208. [250.]

[RICHARD HERNE SHEPHERD], The bibliography of Tennyson. . . . By the author of "Tennysoniana". 1896. pp.vii.88. [125.]

A CHRONOLOGICAL list of the works of Alfred lord Tennyson, with some few items of Tennysoniana . . . exhibited at the Grolier club. [New York] 1897. pp.24. [75.]

[LUTHER SAMUEL LIVINGSTON], Bibliography of the first editions in book form of Alfred, lord Tennyson. New York 1901. pp.x.96. [90.]

306 copies printed; this is the catalogue of a collection which is now in the Pierpont Morgan library, New York.

— — Supplement. 1903. pp.16. [20.]

J[OSEPH] C[HARLES] THOMSON, Bibliography of the writings of Alfred, lord Tennyson. Wimbledon 1905. pp.72. [124.]

[THOMAS JAMES WISE], A bibliography of the writings of Alfred, lord Tennyson. 1908. pp.xv. 365+vii.211. [400.]

100 copies privately printed.

ALFRED TENNYSON. . . . A list of books, with references to periodicals, in the Brooklyn public library. Brooklyn 1909. pp.20. [350.]

TENNYSON centenary exhibition. Catalogue. Fine art society: 1909. pp.43. [125.]

[FANNIE ELIZABETH RATCHFORD], An exhibition of manuscripts and printed books . . . : Alfred, lord Tennyson. [University of Texas: Austin 1942]. pp.20.

THE POET laureate, Alfred, lord Tennyson. . . . 150th anniversary of the poet's birth at Somersby, Lincolnshire. List of items shown in an exhibition. Usher art gallery: [Lincoln 1959]. pp.[21]. [200.]*

THE TENNYSON collection presented to the university of Virginia in honor of Edgar Finley Shannon, jr. Charlottesville [1961]. pp.5–53. [250.]*

the collection was that of Templeton Crocker.

SIR CHARLES [BRUCE LOCKER] TENNYSON, Tennyson collection, Usher gallery. Lincoln 1963. pp.34. [394.]

Thackeray, William Makepeace.

[RICHARD HERNE SHEPHERD], The bibliography of Thackeray. [1880]. pp.viii.62. [225.]

a second edition appears in W. M. Thackeray, Sultan stork *(1887), pp.219–260.*

CHARLES PLUMPTRE JOHNSON, Hints to collectors of original editions of the works of William Makepeace Thackeray. 1885. pp.48. [37.]

CHARLES PLUMPTRE JOHNSON, The early writings of William Makepeace Thackeray. 1888. pp. xiv.64. [100.]

WILLIAM MAKEPEACE THACKERAY. . . . A list of books and of references to periodicals in the Brooklyn public library. Brooklyn 1911. pp.52. [500.]

CATALOGUE of an exhibition commemorating the hundredth anniversary of the birth of William Makepeace Thackeray. Grolier club: New York 1912. pp.viii.106. [150.]

— [another edition]. 1912. pp.xii.142. [150.]

260 copies printed.

[H. S. VAN DUZER and EDWARD TURNBULL], A Thackeray library. First editions and first publications . . . collected by Henry Sayre Van Duzer. New York 1919. pp.xiii.199. [750.]

175 copies privately printed.

JOHN D[OZIER] GORDAN, William Makepeace Thackeray. An exhibition from the Berg collection. First editions, manuscripts, autograph letters and drawings. Public library: New York 1947. pp.[ii].39. [200.]

LAURENCE BRANDER, Thackeray. British council: British book news: Bibliographical series of supplements (no.110): 1959. pp.46. [100.]

Thomas, Dylan.

WILLIAM HOWARD HUFF, Dylan Thomas. A bibliography. Northwestern university: Library: Reference department: Evanston, Ill. 1953. pp.26.*

J[OHN] ALEXANDER ROLPH, Dylan Thomas. A bibliography. 1956. pp.xix.108. [370.]

G. S. FRASER, Dylan Thomas. British council: British book news: Bibliographical series of supplements (no.90): 1957. pp.36. [25.]

Thomas, Edward.

ROBERT P. ECKERT, Edward Thomas. A biography and bibliography. 1937. pp.xxi.328. [300.]

VERNON SCANNELL, Edward Thomas. British council: British book news: Bibliographical series: 1963. pp.36. [60.]

Thompson, Francis.

TERENCE L. CONNOLLY, An account of books and manuscripts of Francis Thompson. Boston college: Chestnut Hills, Mass. [1937]. pp.xii.79. [150.]

CATALOGUE of the "Francis Thompson" collection presented to the Harris public library by mr.

J. H. Spencer . . . with supplementary list of "Thompsoniana" already in the . . . library. Preston [1950]. pp.24. [175.]

CATALOGUE of the "Francis Thompson" collection presented to the Harris public library by mr. J. H. Spencer. With supplementary list of "Thompsoniana" . . . in the . . . Harris reference library. Preston [1958]. pp.24. [185.]

FRANCIS THOMPSON centenary 1859–1959. Catalogue of manuscripts, letters and books in the Harris public library, Preston, based on the collection presented by mr. J. H. Spencer. [Preston] 1959. pp.[ii].77. [500.]*

MYRTLE PIHLMAN POPE, A critical bibliography of works by and about Francis Thompson. Public library: New York 1959. pp.37. [400.]

Thomson, Charles West.

CHARLES F[REDERICK] HEARTMAN, Bibliographical checklist of the writings of the poet Charles West Thomson. Heartman's historical series (no.60): Hattiesburg 1941. pp.15. [60.]

99 copies printed.

Thomson, Edward William.

ARTHUS S[TANLEY] BOURINOT, Edward William

Thomson (1849–1924). A bibliography with notes and some letters. Ottawa [1955]. pp.[iv].28. [50.]

150 copies privately printed.

Thomson, Samuel Harrison.

LUBOMYR R. WYNAR, S. Harrison Thomson. Bio-bibliography. University of Colorado: Libraries: Bio-bibliographical series (no.1): Boulder 1963. pp.[vi].32. [401.]

Thomson, William.

EDWARD FORD, A bibliography of William Thomson. [Sydney] 1954. ff.32. [42.]*

50 copies reproduced from typewriting.

Thoreau, Henry David.

SAMUEL ARTHUR JONES, Bibliography of Henry David Thoreau. Rowfant club: Cleveland 1894. pp.80. [240.]

90 copies printed.

FRANCIS H[ENRY] ALLEN, A bibliography of Henry David Thoreau. Boston &c. 1908. pp. xix.ff.203. [1000.]

WALTER [ROY] HARDING, A centennial check-list of the editions of Henry David Thoreau's Walden. University of Virginia: Bibliographical society: Charlottesville 1954. pp.xxxii. [132.]

Tilton, Theodore.

BIBLIOGRAPHY of Theodore Tilton, 1835–1907. Library of Congress: Washington 1922. ff.5.[68.]*

Tone, Theobald Wolfe.

M. J. MAC MANUS, A bibliography of Theobald Wolfe Tone. Dublin 1940. pp.15. [25.]
25 copies privately printed.

Tourneur, Cyril.

SAMUEL A[ARON] TANNENBAUM and DOROTHY R. TANNENBAUM, Cyril Tourneur. (A concise bibliography). Elizabethan bibliographies (no.33): New York 1946. ff.[ii].14. [186.]*

Toynbee, Arnold Joseph.

MONICA POPPER, A bibliography of the works in english of Arnold Toynbee 1910–1954. Royal institute of international affairs: 1955. ff.iii.59. [296.]*

Traherne, Thomas.

MARGARET WILLY, Three metaphysical poets. British council: British book news: Bibliographical series of supplements (no.134): 1961. pp.48. [150.]

Trollope, Anthony.

MARY LESLIE IRWIN, Anthony Trollope. A bibliography. New York 1926. pp.97. [1500.]

MICHAEL SADLEIR, Trollope. A bibliography. 1928. pp.xvi.323. [200.]

— — Addenda and corrigenda. 1934. pp.[ii].10. [4.]

HUGH SYKES DAVIES, Trollope. British council: British book news: Bibliographical series of supplements (no.118): 1960. pp.40. [125.]

Tucker, Josiah.

PAUL LEICESTER FORD, Josiah Tucker and his writings. Chicago [1894]. pp.18. [50.]

Twain, Mark [Samuel Langhorn Clemens].

[LUTHER SAMUEL LIVINGSTON], The works of Mark Twain. . . . The description of a set of first editions of his books. New York [1910]. pp.63. [450.]

75 copies printed; a catalogue of Merle Johnson's collection.

MERLE [DE VORE] JOHNSON, A bibliography of the work of Mark Twain, Samuel Langhorne

Clemens. A list of first editions in book form and of first printings in periodicals and occasional publications. New York &c. 1910. pp.[ii].xvii.204. [200.]

500 copies printed.

— — Revised and enlarged. 1935. pp.xiii.274. [300.]

WALTER BLISS, Twainiana notes.... Edited... by Frances M. Edwards. Hartford, Conn. [1930]. pp.[vii].24. [75.]

JOHN K[ELLY] POTTER, Samuel L. Clemens. First editions and values. Chicago 1932. pp.[vi].iv.82. [100.]

500 copies printed.

FLORENCE S[ELMA] HELLMAN, List of writings by Mark Twain translated into certain foreign languages. Library of Congress: [Washington] 1939. ff.14. [235.]*

SAMUEL LANGHORNE CLEMENS, 1835–1910 (Mark Twain, *pseud.*). Russian translations of his works. Library of Congress: Slavic division: [Washington 1939]. ff.4.*

AN EXHIBITION of the works of Mark Twain... including manuscripts, first editions, letters and association items. Public library: Detroit [1944]. pp.44. [200.]

[EDWIN H. CARPENTER], Mark Twain. An exhibition selected mainly from the papers belonging to the Samuel L. Clemens estate on deposit in the Huntington library. San Marina 1947. pp.35. [120.]

LUCILLE ADAMS, Huckleberry Finn. A descriptive bibliography of the Huckleberry Finn collection at the Buffalo public library. Buffalo, N.Y. 1950. pp.40. [100.]

ROGER ASSELINEAU, The literary reputation of Mark Twain from 1910 to 1950. A critical essay and a bibliography. Université de Clermont: Faculté des lettres: Paris 1954. pp.3–243. [1333.]

Tyndale, William.

FRANCIS FRY, A bibliographical description of the editions of the New testament. Tyndale's version in english. 1878. pp.viii.196. [43.]

A LIST of the material available in the Public library of the city of Gloucester concerning William Tyndale. Public library: Gloucester [1936]. pp.14. [100.]

Urwick, Lyndall Fownes.

[DAPHNE ALICE HOOK], L. Urwick. A bibliography. 1957. pp.vii.48. [200.]

Van Vechten, Carl.

SCOTT CUNNINGHAM, A bibliography of the writings of Carl Van Vechten. Centaur bibliographies [of modern american authors] (no.5): Philadelphia 1924. pp.52. [100.]
300 copies printed.

KLAUS W. JONAS, Carl Van Vechten. A bibliography. New York 1955. pp.xiv.82. [528.]
400 copies printed.

Vaughan, Charles Edwyn.

H[ENRY] B[UCKLEY] CHARLTON, A list of the writings of professor Charles Edwyn Vaughan. Aberdeen [printed] 1923. pp.13. [70.]
privately printed.

Vaughan, Henry.

E[SMOND] L[INWORTH] MARILLA, A comprehensive bibliography of Henry Vaughan. University of Alabama: Studies (no.3): Tuscaloosa [1948]. pp.44. [256.]

— — Henry Vaughan: a bibliographical supplement, 1946–1960 . . . by E. L. Marilla and James

D. Simmonds. . . . (no.16): 1963. pp.[iii].20. [127.]

MARGARET WILLY, Three metaphysical poets. British council: British book news: Bibliographical series of supplements (no.134): 1961. pp.48. [150.]

Waite, Arthur Edward.

HAROLD V[AN] B[UREN] VOORHIS, Arthur Edward Waite. A check list of his writings. Red Bank, N.J. 1932. pp.[15]. [125.]

150 copies privately printed.

Walker, William.

ROBERT MURDOCH LAWRANCE, Bibliography of the writings of the late William Walker. Aberdeen [printed] [1933]. pp.[12]. [30.]

36 copies printed.

Walpole, Horace, earl of Orford.

A CATALOGUE of books and tracts, printed at the private press of the hon. Horace Walpole . . . at Strawberry hill. . . . Together with those of his works printed by Bodoni . . . Dodsley . . . and W. Bathoe. 1813. pp.12. [Walpole: 20.]

A[LLEN] T[RACY] HAZEN, A bibliography of Horace Walpole. New Haven 1948. pp.189. [200.]

HUGH HONOUR, Horace Walpole. British book news: Bibliographical series of supplements: 1957. pp.44. [60.]

Walsh, Benjamin Dann.

SAMUEL HENSHAW, The more important writings of Benjamin Dann Walsh. Department of agriculture: Division of entomology: Bibliography of the more important contributions to american economic entomology (part i): Washington 1889. pp.49. [385.]

—— The more important joint writings of B. D. Walsh and C. V. Riley . . . (part ii): 1889. pp.50–95. [478.]

—— Index to Parts I, II and III. 1890. pp.371–454.

Walton, Izaak.

THOMAS WESTWOOD, The chronicle of the 'Compleat angler' of Izaak Walton and Charles Cotton. Being a bibliographical record of its various phases and mutations. 1864. pp.xv.64. [50.]

—— Notes and additions by Thomas Satchell. 1883. pp.xxiv.86.

CHRONOLOGICAL hand-list of various editions of The complete angler. . . . With a supplement embracing other writings of Walton and Cotton, etc. . . . exhibited at the Grolier club. [New York] 1893. pp.27. [100.]

R[OBERT] B[RIGHT] MARSTON, Walton and some earlier writers on fish and fishing. Book-lover's library: 1894. pp.xxvii.264. [50.]

ARNOLD WOOD, A bibliography of 'The complete angler' of Izaak Walton and Charles Cotton. New York 1900. pp.[ix].207. [125.]

120 copies printed.

PETER OLIVER, A new chronicle of the Compleat angler. New York &c. 1936. pp.[ii].xviii.302. [284.]

MARGARET BOTTRALL, Izaak Walton. British council: British book news: Bibliographical series of supplements (no.68): 1955. pp.40. [60.]

Ward, sir Adolphus William.

A[UGUSTUS] T[HEODORE] BARTHOLOMEW, A bibliography of sir Adolphus William Ward. Cambridge 1926. pp.xxxiv.99. [1250.]

Warner, Anna Bertlett *and* Susan.

BIBLIOGRAPHY of the works of Anna Bertlett Warner and Susan Warner. Library of Congress: Washington 1922. ff.17. [599.]*

Warton, Joseph.

WILLIAM DARNALL MAC CLINTOCK, Joseph Warton's Essay on Pope. A history of the five editions. Chapel Hill 1933. pp.xii.74. [6.]

Watson, sir William Henry.

CECIL WOOLF, Sir William Watson. 1956. pp.8. [53.]

Watt, Robert.

FRANCESCO CORDASCO, A bibliography of Robert Watt. New York 1950. pp.[vii].ii–iii.9–27.72. [35.]

250 copies printed.

Watts, Isaac.

WILBUR MACEY STONE, The divine and moral songs of Isaac Watts. An essay thereon and a tentative list of editions. The Triptych: New York 1918. pp.95. [600.]

250 copies privately printed.

BI-CENTENARY dr. Isaac Watts . . . Catalogue of exhibition. Public libraries: Stoke Newington 1948. pp.32. [100.]

Weber, Carl Jefferson.

N[IXON] ORWIN RUSH, A bibliography of the published writings of Carl J. Weber. Colby college monograph (no.10): Waterville, Me. 1944. pp.31. [200.]

495 copies printed.

Webster, John.

SAMUEL A[ARON] TANNENBAUM, John Webster. (A concise bibliography). Elizabethan bibliographies (no.19): New York 1941. pp.x.38. [650.]

Webster, Noah.

EMILY ELLSWORTH FORD SKEEL, A bibliography of the writings of Noah Webster. . . . Edited by Edwin H[ager] Carpenter. Public library: New York 1958. pp.xxxix.657. [1500.]

500 copies printed.

Weems, Mason Locke.

PAUL LEICESTER FORD, Mason Locke Weems, his works and ways. . . . Volume I. [Bibliography]. New York 1929. pp.xxi.420. [254.]

200 copies printed.

Weiss, Harry Bischoff.

PAPERS . . . by Harry B. Weiss. Trenton. N.J. 1937. pp.25. [515.]
privately printed.

Wells, Gabriel.

[CHARLES FREDERICK HEARTMAN], Bibliography of the writings and speeches of Gabriel Wells. Hattiesburg, Mo. 1939. pp.24. [200.]
'less than' 200 copies privately printed.

Wells, Herbert George.

FRED[ERICK] A. CHAPPELL, Bibliography of H. G. Wells. Chicago 1924. pp.[vii].xxi.551. [115.]

GEOFFREY H. WELLS, A bibliography of the works of H. G. Wells. 1925. pp.xv.72. [150.]

GEOFFREY H. WELLS, The works of H. G. Wells, 1887–1925. A bibliography, dictionary and subject-index. 1926. pp.xxv.274. [800.]

Wesley, Charles and John. [*see also* **Methodism.**]

RICHARD GREEN, The works of John and Charles Wesley. A bibliography. 1896. pp.292. [500.]
reissued in 1899.

— — Second edition. 1906. pp.292. [417.]

CATALOGUE of Wesleyana in the library of Queen's college, university of Melbourne. [Melbourne 1926]. pp.15. [400.]

limited to Wesley's writings.

West, Rebecca, *pseud.*

GEORGE EVELYN HUTCHINSON, A preliminary list of the writings of Rebecca West, 1912–1951. Yale university: Library: New Haven 1957. pp.102.

Westrup, Jack Allan.

[ALBERT THOMAS LUPER], A selected bibliography of the published writings of J. A. Westrup. State university of Iowa: Iowa City 1957. pp.8. [139.]*

Wharton, Edith.

LAWSON MCCLUNG MELISH, A bibliography of the collected writings of Edith Wharton. New York 1927. pp.xiii.87. [40.]

LAVINIA DAVIS, A bibliography of the writings of Edith Wharton. Portland, Maine. 1933. pp. x.64 [300.]

325 copies printed.

Wheat, Carl Irving.

GEORGE L[ABAN] HARDING, The published writings of Carl Irving Wheat. San Francisco 1960. pp.ix.23. [116.]

350 copies printed.

Wheatley, Phillis.

CHA[RLE]S FRED[ERICK] HEARTMAN, Phillis Wheatley (Phillis Peters). A critical attempt and a bibliography of her writings. Heartman's historical series (no.7): New York 1915. pp.47. [43.]

91 or 99 copies printed.

Wheeler, Henry Lord.

LIST of the more important publications of Henry Lord Wheeler. [*s.l.* 1907]. pp.4. [60.]

Whipple, Frances Harriet.

SIDNEY S. RIDER, Bibliographical memoirs of three Rhode Island authors, Joseph K. Angell, Frances H. (Whipple) McDougall, Catharine R. Williams. Rhode Island historical tracts (no.xi): Providence 1880. pp.vi.90. [75.]

White, Gilbert.

HUGH BOYD WATT, A list of bibliographies of the writings of Gilbert White. 1909. pp.4. [7.]

EDWARD A. MARTIN, A bibliography of Gilbert White. Westminster [1897]. pp.274. [58.]

— — [another edition]. 1934. pp.viii.188.[vii]. [100.]

A CATALOGUE of mss., books and periodicals devoted to Gilbert White and natural history. Ealing public libraries: Selborne society library: [Ealing] 1958. pp.34. [200.]*

White, Henry Kirke.

JOHN T[HOMAS] GODFREY, Catalogue of portraits, engravings, books, letters & manuscripts relating to Henry Kirke White, exhibited . . . in the Exchange hall. [Nottingham 1906]. pp.16. [30.]

White, William Allen.

WALTER JOHNSON and ALBERTA PANTLE, A bibliography of the published works of William Allen White. [Topeka 1947]. pp.20. [400.]

Whitehead, Alfred North.

FRANKLIN PARKER, Alfred North Whitehead, 1861–1947; a bibliography. Austin 1960. ff.13. [150.]*

Whitefield, George.

ROLAND AUSTIN, Bibliography of the works of George Whitefield. [Burnley 1916]. pp.29. [150.]

Whitman, Walt.

[G. MILLER WILLIAMSON], Catalogue of a collection of books, letters and manuscripts written by Walt Whitman, in the library of George M. Williamson. New York 1903. pp.[54]. [37.]

127 copies printed.

W. H. TRIMBLE, Catalogue of a collection of Walt Whitman literature. Compiled . . . by the owner. St. Leonards, N.Z. [1912]. pp.36. [250].

FRANK SHAY, The bibliography of Walt Whitman. New York 1920. pp.46. [68.]

500 copies printed.

CAROLYN WELLS and ALFRED F. GOLDSMITH, A concise bibliography of the works of Walt Whitman, with a supplement of fifty books about Whitman. Boston &c. 1922. pp.xiii.108. [200.]

EXPOSITION Walt Whitman. [Paris 1926]. pp.12.

ARCHIBALD SPARKE, Collection of Whitmaniana in the Reference library. Bolton 1931. pp.28. [200.]

[B. C. LANDAUER], Leaves of music by Walt Whitman from the collection of Bella C. Landauer. [*s.l.*] 1937. pp.[84]. [159.]
a bibliography of musical settings of poems by Whitman; 60 copies privately printed.

A LIST of manuscripts, books, portraits, prints broadsides, and memorabilia . . . from the Whitman collection of mrs. Frank Julian Sprague . . . exhibited at the Library of Congress. [Washington] 1939. pp.vi.71. [600.]

INDEX to early american periodical literature, 1728–1870. No.3. Walt Whitman. New York university: New York 1941. pp.20. [400.]

GAY WILSON ALLEN, Twenty-five years of Walt Whitman bibliography, 1918–1942. Bulletin of bibliography pamphlets (no.38): Boston 1943. pp.57. [800.]

[GRACE ENGLAND], An exhibition of the works of Walt Whitman. Friends of the Detroit public library: [Detroit] 1945. pp.48. [322.]

ELLEN FRANCES FREY, Catalogue of the Whitman collection in the Duke university library . . . given by dr. and mrs. Josiah C[harles] Trent. Durham 1945. pp.xvii.148. [750.]

A LIST of Whitman items gathered together by the Tulsa bibliophiles. [Tulsa 1949]. ff.[51]. [600.]*
limited to 25 copies.

WALT WHITMAN. Catalogue of an exhibition held at the American library. U.S. Information service: 1954. pp.33. [118.]

TEN notebooks and a cardboard butterfly missing from the Walt Whitman papers. Walt Whitman manuscripts in the Library of Congress. Washington 1954. pp.38.

[ARTHUR BURTON, HELEN DUDENBOSTEL JONES *and others*], Walt Whitman. A catalog based upon the collections of the Library of Congress. With notes on Whitman collections and collectors.

Library of Congress: Reference department. Washington 1955. pp.xviii.147. [1055.]

A CATALOGUE of works by and relating to Walt Whitman in the Reference library. [Bolton] 1955. pp.52. [500.]

WALT WHITMAN. A selection of the manuscripts, books, and association items gathered by Charles E. Feinberg. Catalogue of an exhibition held at the Detroit public library. Detroit [1955]. pp.xii.128. [387.]

FRANCES J[OAN] BREWER, Walt Whitman. A selection of the manuscripts, books and association items gathered by Charles E. Feinberg. Catalogue of an exhibition. Destoit 1955. pp.xiii.129. [387.]

LEWIS M[ORGRAGE] STARK and JOHN D[OZIER] GORDAN, Walt Whitman's *Leaves of grass.* A centenary exhibition from the Lion Whitman collection and the Berg collection of the New York public library. Public library: New York 1955. pp.46. [125.]

EXPOSIȚIA Walt Whitman. Institut romîn pentru relațiile culturale cu străinătatea: București 1956. pp.56. [250.]

EDWIN H[AVILAND] MILLER and ROSALIND S. MILLER, Walt Whitman's correspondence. A checklist. Public library: New York 1957. pp.x. 162. [3750.]

Whittier, John Greenleaf.

ABBY J[OHNSON] WOODMAN, Reminiscences of

John Greenleaf Whittier's life at Oak knoll. . . . With a list of the first editions, portraits, engravings, manuscripts, and personal relics . . . exhibited at the Essex institute. Essex institute: Salem, Mass. 1908. pp.52. [200.]

200 copies printed.

THOMAS FRANKLIN CURRIER, A bibliography of John Greenleaf Whittier. Cambridge, Mass. 1937. pp.xvii.693. [6000.]

Wigglesworth, Michael.

MATT B[USHNELL] JONES, Notes for a bibliography of Michael Wigglesworth's "Day of doom" and "Meat out of the eater". Worcester, Mass. 1929. pp.10. [15.]

Wilberforce, William.

WILLIAM WILBERFORCE 1759–1833. A catalogue of the books and pamphlets . . . in the reference library of Kingston upon Hull. Hull 1959. pp.36. [289.]

Wilde, Oscar Fingall O'Flahertie Wills.

STUART MASON [*pseud.* CHRISTOPHER SCLATER MILLARD], A bibliography of the poems of Oscar Wilde. 1907. pp.[xi].148. [100.]

275 copies printed.

STUART MASON [*pseud.* C. S. MILLARD], Bibliography of Oscar Wilde. Edinburgh [printed] 1908. pp.22. [250.]

11 copies privately printed.

[C. S. MILLARD], List of editions of works by Oscar Wilde which may be offered for sale in the United Kingdom. 1908. pp.[4]. [35.]

preceded by a letter headed 're Oscar Wilde deceased' and signed by Robert Ross.

STUART MASON [*pseud.* C. S. MILLARD], Bibliography of Oscar Wilde. [1914]. pp.xxxix.605. [695.]

also issued in two volumes.

ROBERT ERNEST COWAN and WILLIAM ANDREWS CLARK, The library of William Andrews Clark, jr. Wilde and Wildeiana. San Francisco 1922–1931. pp.xiv.101 + [ii].107 + iii.157 + [iii].123 + [ii].123. [750.]

50 copies printed.

JAMES LAVER, Oscar Wilde. British council: British book news: Bibliographical series of supplements (no.53): 1954. pp.36. [100.]

CATALOGUE of an exhibition of books and manuscripts in commemoration of the centenary of the birth of Oscar Wilde. Trinity college: Dublin [1954]. pp.24. [84.]

JOHN CHARLES FINZI, Oscar Wilde and his literary circle. A catalog of manuscripts and letters in the William Andrews Clark memorial library. University of California: Berkeley &c. 1957. pp.xxxiv. [242]. [2892.]*

Wilder, Thornton Niven.

J[EROME] M[ELVIN] EDELSTEIN, A bibliographical checklist of the writings of Thornton Wilder. Yale university: Library: New Haven 1959. pp. [v].62. [146.]*

Wilks, sir Samuel.

WILLIAM WALE, Bibliography of the published writings of sir Samuel Wilks, bart. [Bibliographies of Guy's men (no.1)]: 1911. pp.28. [575.]

Williams, Catharine Read Arnold.

SIDNEY S. RIDER, Bibliographical memoirs of three Rhode Island authors, Joseph K. Angell, Frances H. (Whipple) McDougall, Catharine R. Williams. Rhode Island historical tracts (no.xi): Providence 1880. pp.vi.90. [100.]

Williams, Roger.

R. A. GUILD, An account of the writings of Roger Williams. [*s.l.* 1863]. pp.11. [7.]

HOWARD M. CHAPIN, List of Roger Williams' writings. Contributions to Rhode Island bibliography (no.iv): Providence 1918. pp.7. [150.]

Williamson, Henry.

I. WAVENEY GIRVAN, A bibliography and a critical survey of the works of Henry Williamson. . . . Together with authentic bibliographical annotations by Another Hand [that is, Henry Williamson]. Chipping Campden 1931. pp.56. [35.]

Wilmot, Frank Leslie Thompson.

HUGH [MCDONALD] ANDERSON and B. M. RAMSDEN, Frank Wilmot (Furnley Maurice). A bibliography and a criticism. [Carlton, Victoria] 1955. pp.x.69. [750.]

Wilson, John Dover.

13 JULY 1961. A list of his published writings presented to John Dover Wilson on his eightieth birthday. Cambridge 1961. pp.32. [223.]

Wilson, Thomas Woodrow.

HARRY CLEMONS, An essay towards a bibliography of the published writings and addresses of Woodrow Wilson, 1875–1910. Library of Princeton university: Princeton 1913. pp.[iii]. ff.[24]. [150.]

— — 1910–1917. By George Dobbin Brown. 1917. pp.[iv].vi.52. [350.]

— — March 1917 to March 1921. By Howard Seavoy Leach. 1922. pp.[v].73. [550.]

PUBLISHED writings and addresses (supplementing bibliography by Harry Clemons). Library of Congress: Washington 1914. ff.4. [37.]*

LIST of references on president Wilson and his family. Library of Congress: Washington 1915. ff.2. [20.]*

— Additional references. 1921. ff.2. [34.]*

WOODROW WILSON: a short bibliographical list. Library of Congress: [Washington] 1927. ff.8. [75.]*

ADDRESSES of president Wilson issued as government documents. Library of Congress: Washington 1930. ff.4. [32.]*

LAURA SHEARER TURNBULL, Woodrow Wilson. A selected bibliography of his published writings, addresses and public papers. Princeton 1948. pp.vii.173. [1248.]

Winchell, Alexander.

LIST of books and papers published by prof. Alexander Winchell. [*s.l.* 1886]. pp.10. [250.]

Winthrop, Theodore.

ELBRIDGE COLBY, Bibliographical notes on Theodore Winthrop. Public library: New York 1917. pp.13. [200.]

Wise, Isaac Mayer.

ADOLPH S. OKO, A tentative bibliography of dr. Isaac M. Wise. Cincinnati 1917. pp.12. [70.]

Wise, Thomas James.

THE ASHLEY library. A list of books printed for private circulation by Thomas J. Wise. 1895. pp.18. [47.]

VARIOUS extraordinary books procured by Thomas J. Wise and now displayed on All fools day in observance of the centenary of his birth. University of Texas: Humanities research center: [Austin] 1959. pp.18. [169.]

300 copies printed.

Wolfe, Thomas.

GEORGE R[ILEY] PRESTON, Thomas Wolfe: a bibliography. New York 1943. pp.5–127. [350.]

ELMER D. JOHNSON, Of time and Thomas Wolfe. A bibliography. New York 1959. pp.226. [1623.]*

Wood, Butler.

W. H. BARRACLOUGH, Butler Wood. . . . With bibliographical references by Mabel Dawes. Bradford 1936. pp.7. [50.]

Wood, Horatio C.

BIBLIOGRAPHICAL record 1860–1900. [*s.l.* 1900]. pp.24. [268.]

the Library of Congress copy contains manuscript additions.

Woodworth, Samuel.

OSCAR WEGELIN, A bibliographical list of the literary and dramatic productions and periodicals written and compiled by Samuel Woodworth. Heartman's historical series (no.78): New Orleans 1953. pp.21. [70.]

200 copies printed.

Woolf, Virginia.

BERNARD BLACKSTONE, Virginia Woolf. British council: British book news: Bibliographical series of supplements (no.33): 1952. pp.47. [200.]

B[ROWNLEE] J[EAN] KIRKPATRICK, A bibliography of Virginia Woolf. Soho bibliographies (vol.ix): 1957. pp.xii.180. [600.]

Wordsworth, William.

W. HALE WHITE, A description of the Wordsworth & Coleridge manuscripts in the possession of mr. T. Norton Longman. 1897. pp.vi.72. [25.]

SHORT bibliographies of Wordsworth, Coleridge, Byron, Shelley, Keats. English association: Leaflet (no.23): 1912. pp.13. [250.]

THOMAS J[AMES] WISE, A bibliography of the writings in prose and verse of William Wordsworth. 1916. pp.xv.271. [190.]

100 copies privately printed.

[T. J. WISE], Two lake poets. A catalogue of printed books, manuscripts and autograph letters by William Wordsworth and Samuel Taylor Coleridge collected by Thomas James Wise. 1927. pp.xxiii.136. [250.]

30 copies privately printed.

LESLIE NATHAN BROUGHTON, The Wordsworth collection formed by Cynthia Morgan St. John and given to Cornell university by Victor Emanuel. A catalogue. Cornell university: Library: Ithaca 1931. pp.xii.124. [250.]

— — A supplement to the catalogue. 1942. pp.viii.87. [750.]

CORNELIUS HOWARD PATTON, The Amherst Wordsworth collection. A descriptive bibliography. Amherst college: [Amherst] 1936. pp. xv.134. [1000.]

AN EXHIBITION of first and other early editions of the works of William Wordsworth . . . with a few autographs and manuscripts lent from the personal library of professor John Edwin Wells. Connecticut college for women: Palmer library: New London 1938. ff.[i].8. [100.]*

JAMES VENABLE LOGAN, Wordsworthian criticism. A guide and bibliography. Ohio state university: Graduate school monographs: Contributions in languages and literature (no.12): Columbus 1947. pp.xii.304. [700.]

— — [supplement]. Elton F. Henley and David H. Stam, Wordsworthian criticism 1945–1959. An annotated bibliography. Public library: New York 1960. pp.64. [340.]

JOHN D[OZIER] GORDAN, William Wordsworth, 1770–1850. An exhibition. Public library: New York 1950. pp.31. [80.]

[R. C. BALD], The Cornell Wordsworth collection. A brief account together with a catalogue of the exhibition held in the university library. Ithaca 1950. pp.42. [62.]

HELEN DARBISHIRE, Wordsworth. British council: British book news: Bibliographical series of supplements (no.34): 1953. pp.48. [100.]

GEORGE HARRIS HEALEY, The Cornell Wordsworth collection. A catalogue of books and manuscripts presented to the university by mr Victor Emanuel. Cornell university: Library: Ithaca 1957. pp.xiii.458. [3198.]

ELTON F. HENLEY, A check list of masters' theses in the United States on William Wordsworth. University of Virginia: Bibliographical society: [Charlottesville 1962]. pp.ii.29.[xi]. [381.]*

Worthington, John.

RICHARD COPLEY CHRISTIE, A bibliography of the works written and edited by dr. John Worthington. Chetham society: Remains historical and literary connected with the palatine counties of

Lancaster and Chester (n.s. vol.xiii): Manchester 1888. pp.[iii].ix.88. [50.]

Wyatt, sir Thomas.

SERGIO BALDI, Sir Thomas Wyatt. British council: British book news: Bibliographical series of supplements (no.139): 1961. pp.42. [100.]

Wyclif, John.

WALTER WADDINGTON SHIRLEY, A catalogue of the original works of John Wyclif. Oxford 1865. pp.xx.75. [275.]

— — Shirley's catalogue of the extant latin works of John Wyclif. Revised by Johann Loserth. Wyclif society: [1924]. pp.19. [100.]

JOHN EDMANDS, Reading notes on Wycliffe. Philadelphia 1884. pp.12. [175.]

[SIR] E[DWARD] M[AUNDE] THOMPSON, Wycliffe exhibition in the King's library. British museum: 1884. pp.xix.68. [82.]

S. H. THOMSON, The order of writing of Wyclif's philosophical works. Prague 1929. pp.22. [20.]

Yeats, William Butler.

A BIBLIOGRAPHY of the writings of William Butler Yeats. Churchtown 1900.

ALLAN WADE, A bibliography of the writings of William Butler Yeats. Stratford-on-Avon 1908. pp.96. [1500.]
60 copies printed.

A[LPHONSE] J[AMES] A[LBERT] SYMONS, A bibliography of the first editions of books by William Butler Yeats. First edition club: 1924. pp.[ii]. viii.46. [46.]
500 copies printed.

WILLIAM M. ROTH, A catalogue of english and american first editions of William Butler Yeats . . . prepared for an exhibition of his works held in the Yale university library. New Haven 1939. pp.104. [650.]

ALLAN WADE, A bibliography of the writings of W. B. Yeats. Soho bibliographies (vol.i): 1951. pp.390. [850.]
— — Second edition. 1958. pp.449. [1000.]

G. S. FRASER, W. B. Yeats, British council: British book news: Bibliographical series of supplements (no.50): 1954. pp.40. [200.]

R[OBERT] O. DOUGAN, W. B. Yeats manuscripts

and printed books exhibited in the library of Trinity college. Dublin [1956]. pp.50. [154.]

GEORGE BRANDON SAUL, Prolegomena to the study of Yeats's poems. Philadelphia [1957]. pp. 3–196. [1000.]

HESTER M. BLACK, William Butler Yeats. A catalog of an exhibition from the P[atrick] S[arsfield] O'Hegarty collection in the university of Kansas library. Lawrence 1958. pp.42. [125.]

GEORGE BRANDON SAUL, Prolegomena to the study of Yeats's plays. Philadelphia [1958]. pp.106. [250.]

Young, Arthur.

LIST of works in the Library of Congress relating to Arthur Young. Library of Congress: Washington 1922. ff.7. [68.]*

Young, Edward.

JOHN LOUIS KIND, Edward Young in Germany. Historical surveys, influence upon german literature, bibliography. Columbia university: Germanic studies (vol.ii, no.III): New York 1906. pp.xv.186. [200.]

FRANCESCO CORDASCO, Edward Young: a hand-list of critical notices & studies. 18th century bibliographical pamphlets (no.11): New York 1950. pp.9. [39.]

HENRY J[EWETT] PETTIT, A bibliography of Young's Night thoughts. University of Colorado studies: Series in language and literature (no.5): Boulder 1954. pp.52. [48.]

Young, Thomas.

[T. YOUNG], A catalogue of the works and essays of the late dr. Young. (Found in his own hand-writing, to 1827). [*c*.1830]. pp.[ii].51–62. [45.]